Teachers as Researchers: Qualitative Inquiry as a Path to Empowerment

To Shirley Steinberg

Falmer Press Teachers' Library Series: 4

Teachers as Researchers: Qualitative Inquiry as a Path to Empowerment

Joe L. Kincheloe

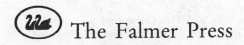 The Falmer Press

(A member of the Taylor & Francis Group)
London • New York • Philadelphia

UK   The Falmer Press, 4 John St, London WC1N 2ET
USA   The Falmer Press, Taylor & Francis Inc., 1900 Frost Road, Suite
        101, Bristol, PA 19007

First published 1991

British Library Cataloguing in Publication Data
Kincheloe, Joe L.
  Teachers as researchers: qualitative inquiry as a path to
  empowerment.–(The Falmer Press teachers' library)
  1. Education. Research
  I. Title
  370.72

  ISBN 1–85000–853–1
  ISBN 1–85000–854–X pbk

Library of Congress Cataloging in Publication Data
Kincheloe, Joe L.
    Teachers as researchers: qualitative inquiry as a path to
  empowerment/Joe L. Kincheloe.
      p.   cm. — (The Falmer Press teachers' library)
    Includes bibliographical references (p.) and index.
    ISBN 1-85000-853-1   ISBN 1-85000-854-X (pbk.)
    1. Education — Research — United States.   2. Teachers —
  United States.   I. Title.   II. Series.
  LB1028.25.U6K56   1991
  370'.7'8073 — dc20   90-25875
                                                        CIP

Jacket design by Caroline Archer

Typeset in 10.5/12pt Garamond
by Graphicraft Typesetters Ltd., Hong Kong.

Printed in Great Britain by Burgess Science Press, Basingstoke
on paper which has a specified pH value on final paper
manufacture of not less than 7.5 and is therefore 'acid free'.

Contents

Preface		vii
Chapter 1	Introduction: Teachers as Researchers, Good Work and Critical Inquiry	1
Chapter 2	Connecting Knower and Known: Constructing an Emancipating System of Meaning	26
Chapter 3	Exploring Assumptions Behind Educational Research: The Nature of Positivism	48
Chapter 4	What Constitutes Knowledge?	67
Chapter 5	Purposes of Research: The Concept of Instrumental Rationality	85
Chapter 6	The Quest for Certainty	111
Chapter 7	Verifiability	127
Chapter 8	The Value of the Qualitative Dimension	143
Chapter 9	Values, Objectivity and Ideology	162
Chapter 10	An Example: Historiographical Research for Teachers	181
Bibliography		199
Index		212

Preface

I am a teacher. I want to do good work. Having attended, worked in, and visited many schools in North America, I believe that at the end of the twentieth century teaching is not good work. As I listen to teachers talk about their jobs or watch hierarchical interactions between administrators and teachers, I sense a crisis in the teaching profession. Never sure that I am characterizing the crisis accurately, I listen intensely to the brilliant teachers who talk to me of resigning, to the brilliant teacher education students who can't get hired or who have trouble in student teaching because of their intelligence, and to the great teachers who have worked invisibly for years, rarely rewarded for their dedication.

The crisis seems to have something to do with a *general* lack of consciousness — a garbled sense of purpose, of direction. What I feel in the schools is not simply a failure of schools and school leaders, but a more general inability of Western peoples to conceptualize a system of meaning — i.e., an ethical sense on which they can build humane and evolving institutions. The only social/educational visions which have gained public attention in the last years of the twentieth century have come from people like Ronald Reagan or William Bennett who offer a misleading vision of a return to a romanticized past, a golden era when teachers enforced rules and students learned the basics. Such an authoritarian vision underlines the crisis I describe; it lays the foundation for educational reform movements that assume that if order can be re-established, if educational leaders can just lay out what it is teachers should do and teachers just do it, schools may return to their previous glory.

Such a socio-educational vision is naive and dangerous, viewing schools as if they had nothing to do with the world that surrounds them. It assumes that Western industrial organization with its bureaucratic, hierarchical structure is the only model available for constructing institutions. In this context it views teachers as blue collar workers, passive recipients of the dictates of the experts. In other words, it disregards, as does the industrial organization it unconsciously emulates, the special knowledge of those who actually do the everyday work in an organization. It assumes that teachers cannot take greater responsibility in the administration of a school and that efforts in such a direction are dangerous. On the basis of such assumptions it supports forms of teacher education which serve to deskill teachers, teaching them *not* to think in self-directed, empowered ways. The professional training which emerges is obsessed with format over substance, with teaching teachers to be 'supervisable', to be team players, to fit into organizational structures.

Teachers understand that something is not right. My conversations with them often touch raw nerves, an anger just below the surface. Such alienation finds its origins in their perception that few in the organization respect them, few value their voices, their knowledge of the educational process. Because of their sensitivity, I must be careful: I too, am perceived as an outsider, just another critic who talks at them from afar. I understand such feelings. I attempt to write this book with that understanding constantly in mind.

Without romanticizing, patronizing, or denigrating them, I attempt to engage teachers with some ideas that may be helpful in their struggle to control their own professional destinies. These ideas revolve around the notion of teachers as researchers, an old idea which when reconceptualized in conjunction with a reasonable system of meaning may provide a starting place for a democratic reorganization of the way schools work. This democratic reconceptualization of education embraces a vision which takes seriously notions of social justice, racial, gender, and class equality, and alternative ways of seeing the world borrowed from people who have traditionally been ignored. I want students of education to read this book — but most of all I want teachers to read it. My hope is that it will serve as an abrasive grain of sand which induces them to name their discontent, to act on such an articulation. To embrace hope in this era of cynicism is a revolutionary act. But as long as we can formulate visions, possibility persists.

My own sense of possibility has been inspired by some great friends and teachers. I am lucky to have been associated with Gene Rasor, Clint Allison, Jane Doyle, Joe Green, Bob Green, and William Pinar. They all provided invaluable trust, assistance, and criticism. Many thanks to Patsy Greene, Chris Peters and Randy and Kelly Hewitt. Shirley Steinberg is a superb editor. Ian, Meghann, Chaim, and Bronwyn are unmitigated joys.

Joe L. Kincheloe
Clemson University

Chapter 1

Introduction: Teachers as Researchers, Good Work, and Critical Inquiry

Many modern social scientists have observed a world marked by technicalization (and the technicalization of work in particular), a powerful mass communications industry which helps shape human interests and ideological orientations, and an increasing domination of individuals by groups with excessive power. The notion of *knowledge* has become a source of power in this society, as power is often acquired by those who via their economic position or their professional status announce just what is to be considered knowledge. Professionals in various fields determine 'healthy' child-rearing procedures, 'proper' family life, the nature of social deviance, and the form that work will take. Knowledge which must be certified by professionals results in anti-democratic tendencies as it renders individuals dependent upon experts.

Based on these observations, social scientists have become more and more attracted to visions of social research which are grounded in critical theory. These critical social inquirers are interested in questioning the dominant assumptions in modern industrialized societies, rejecting earlier constructions of meaning and value structures, and embarking on a quest for new meanings and practices (Popkewitz, 1981a:14–15). Ever concerned with the centrality of the individual and the powerfulness of individual endeavor, critical researchers refuse to see the individual as a puppet of wider forces. We must protect the creative, active, meaning-seeking aspects of humans; social scientists in particular must see men and women as potentially free and marked by the capacity to set and achieve their own goals. Thus, the forces which preclude this human agency must be exposed and changed. A social science, for example, which deifies the social scientist as expert and purveyor of truth must be confronted (Gibson, 1986:10).

Personal authority has been undermined by the authority of professional experts who gain unquestioned knowledge through rigorous (methodologically exacting) social scientific research. The family, for example, is subject to state determination of its competence. Parents have little authority over those experts in the legitimized institutions who make pronouncements about normal child-rearing. The family's dependence on the professional is representative of a larger pattern of dependence in modern industrialized, bureaucratized societies. Individuals depend on organizations, citizens depend on the state, workers depend on managers, and, of course, parents depend on the 'helping professions'. A professional oligarchy of doctors, psychiatrists, welfare workers, civil servants, and social science researchers exert significant influence on the governance of the state and on the 'knowledge industry'.

The professional assault on the autonomy of the family and its members as well as on other institutions and individuals must be viewed in light of its historical moment. The advent of industrialization and its companion, monopoly or corporate capitalism, set the stage for the rise of the expert. As the family was being assaulted by the expert, the advertising industry was persuading people that store-bought goods were superior to home-made items. The growth of scientific management of industry and the expansion of the expert both represent new forms of control within an industrialized, corporate state. The struggle against the destruction of personal authority necessitates a struggle against the general authoritarian trends of the modern industrialized, corporate state. Individuals cannot protect their personal autonomy unless they regain their voice in the workplace and (very important to this work) demand a role in the production of the knowledge on which the modern state and its experts ground their authority. In this context, critical social researchers call for individuals to take the solution of their problems into their own hands. The goal of arresting the erosion of competence will be accomplished, they argue, by ordinary citizens who create their own 'communities of competence'. Thus, teachers, students, and parents must participate in the research act in education. They must help determine what is designated educational knowledge (Lasch, 1979:394–7).

In order to create their own knowledge individuals must understand that such an endeavor is both important and possible. Certain critical theoretical ideas allow for such an understanding. A critical social science is concerned with uncovering the ways ideology shapes social relations — relations, for example, in the workplace, in schools, between classes, races, and genders, as well as relations between experts and ordinary citizens. Critical social science is also concerned with extending a human's consciousness of himself or herself as a social being. An individual who had gained such a consciousness would understand how, why, his or her political opinions, religious beliefs, gender role, or racial perspectives had been shaped by dominant perspectives.

Critical social science thus promotes self-reflection which results in attitudinal changes. The basis of these changes rests on insights into causalities in the past. Individuals, as Habermas argues, thus come to know themselves by bringing to consciousness the process by which their perspectives were formed. Action which is to be taken by individuals to correct social and thus individual pathologies can be *negotiated* once self-reflection has taken place. Prudent action which proceeds only while asking questions of ethics, morality, and politics does not take the form of rules and precise regulations. Critical theory provides a framework of principles around which action can be discussed rather than a set of procedures. Teachers who engage in critical research are never certain of the exact path of action they will take as a result of their inquiry (Popkewitz, 1981a:15–16).

Thus, critical social science is concerned with the notion of the practical. This implies that it is interested in the relationship of scientific research to society, of theory to practice. Because of this practical concern, critical social science must always examine social relations and social processes historically. Such an examination reminds the inquirer that our traditions, ceremonies, institutions, and belief systems are constructed by human beings. This human construction is often obscured from our sight as we go about the mundane rituals of teaching, administrating, interacting, and relaxing. Thus, the dynamics of social change are lost, the forces which have shaped modern educational institutions are forgotten. History dies as we come to celebrate and attend only to that which exists; indeed, that 'which is' seems as if it could have been no other way. Critical social science moves us to uncover the genesis of those assumptions that shape our lives and institutions and to ask how they can be altered (Lather, 1986:268; Popkewitz, 1981a:16).

The notion that teachers as well as research professors and other 'experts' should engage in critically-grounded social inquiry rests on a democratic social theory which assumes that social research is not the province of a small élite minority. John Dewey argued in 1908 and 1932 that though the theoretical knowledge of the sciences is confined to specialists, it affects all persons. Its human effect, he continued, is not so much beneficent as it is exploitive, for those who possess the knowledge of the sciences often use it to take advantage of others. Considerations of private profit limit the social usefulness of scientifically-based research.

The limitations, Dewey maintained, of the hierarchical workplace prevent the non-élite from gaining access to the methods of social inquiry. Thus, they have little chance to develop their capacities. Aware of the worker-control strategies of his contemporary, Frederick Taylor, and his scientific management strategies, Dewey charged that workers, who in the industrial era were becoming merely operators of machines, found their creative and participatory sensibilities deadened. 'The maldistribution of material goods,' he wrote, 'is reflected in an even greater maldistribution of cultural goods.' The greatest form of moral loss which comes from industrialism's worker control, he argued, is related to the effect of this policy 'upon participation in the higher values of friendship, science, art, taking an active part in public life, in all the variety of forms which these things are capable of assuming'. The democratic ideal is based on the premise that there is an ethical basis on which social institutions are constructed. This conception, as old as Plato, requires that every human counts, regardless of social position. Moreover, whether in the workplace of the factory or the school, leaders must make sure that the wide variety of abilities and interests among individuals must be considered so that the unique potentialities and the contributions of each one may be realized (Dewey, 1908:408).

On these premises rest the concept of good work. If the schools are to become democratic and offer challenges to the anti-democratic tendencies of the industrial era, they must pursue the concept of good work for teachers and individuals in the society as a whole. Many labor and educational theorists have pondered the key characteristics of democratic work. The notion of teachers/workers as researchers certainly fits into any notion of democratic work. Characteristics of good work might include:

1 *The principle of self-direction.* Workers/teachers are ultimately their own bosses. Except in unusual circumstances, the worker/teacher should be free from supervisory direction. Teachers operating under this principle would not be subjected to the humiliation of supervision which requires them to submit stylized lesson plans where format takes precedence over purpose. Teachers would be free of control by supervisory forms which use the tyranny of pre-packaged materials, and curriculum guides and supervisors who demand coverage of specific information at specific times, e.g., 'I want you on page 30 at 1:30'. Teachers freed from such constraints would need research skills to conceptualize and carry out the goals of their classrooms.

2 *The principle of the job as a place of learning.* Workers/teachers who are encouraged to set their own goals by necessity must view the workplace as a laboratory. Workers are equal partners in research and development, as their 'shop-level' experiences are valued as unique insights to the production process. In schools, teachers with their 'child-level' experiences are viewed similarly. Thus, teachers are encouraged to contribute to our knowledge about the educational act, while at the same time they are challenged (by administrators and one another) to push their knowledge to new levels via new questions involving topics which transcend mere teaching technique. Understandings of psychological theory, socio-economic context, and political outcomes of learning are pursued. The central role of research is apparent.

3 *The principle of work variety.* Workers in industrial contexts are plagued by repetitive, boring tasks. In the democratic workplace, workers struggle to provide opportunities for variations of routine

which preclude boredom. Teachers who are learners and thus who are involved with the difficulties of research and conceptualization are rarely bored. A school organization which would allow teachers periodically to perform effectively in these varied roles would be grounded by a research facility.

4 *The principle of workmate cooperation.* Industrialization has unfortunately produced conditions where it is not in one person's interest to help another; indeed, one person's gain is often another's loss. Teachers are not unaffected by such impulses, as they hoard materials away from one another and rarely exchange ideas about successful practices. The idea of sitting down together and seriously discussing educational purpose and how it might be achieved is not typically found in the teachers' lounge. The democratic workplace transcends this fractured set of relations. Teachers who are researchers share their findings with one another, discuss interpretations of the findings, and work together to implement strategies based on new understandings which emerge.

5 *The principle of individual work as a contribution to social welfare.* When workers/teachers employ this principle, they reconceptualize their work so that it serves the social good. If work is not socially ameliorative then it must be made so. Workers in a factory who produce items that are ecologically harmful contribute to the redesign of the product. Teachers who are faced with school policies which serve to limit children's potential and/or reproduce socio-economic inequality change the policies. Teachers who are researchers are much more likely to recognize the socially deleterious effect of certain educational strategies than non-researching teachers (Emery and Thorsrud, 1976:159).

6 *The principle that play is a virtue which must be incorporated into work.* Herbert Marcuse argued that labor in the industrial era has been determined by objectives and functions that are not controlled by individual human beings. The value of protecting the free play of human abilities and human desires is not expected in the rationality which directs the workplace. Individuality in a work context is not a value or end in itself. Play, Marcuse maintained, is basic to human civilization. When such a premise is accepted, labor must be grounded on a commitment to the protection of the free evolution of human potentiality (Marcuse, 1955:195). Once we overcome our adult-centered bias against play as one of the highest expressions of human endeavor, we may incorporate its principles into our work lives. Play principles which may be utilized as means of democratizing work would include: (a) rules of play are not constructed to repress freedom,

but to constrain authoritarianism and thus to promote fairness; (b) the structure of play is dynamic in its relation to the inter- action of the players — by necessity this interaction is grounded on the equality of the players; (c) the activity is always viewed as an autonomous expression of self, as care is taken not to subordinate imagination to predetermined outcomes. Thus, in play exhaustion is not deadening since the activity refreshes the senses and cele- brates the person. Research can be viewed as a form of play when the teacher is guided by the play principles (Aronowitz, 1973:61–2).

Thus, good work progresses from the pursuit of these democratic principles. The delineation of the democratic principles of good work confronts us with the reality that much of the time in the late twentieth century work is not good — it is not in line with these principles. Based on his reading of Freud, Herbert Marcuse set the stage for our under- standing of 'bad work' with his notions of surplus repression and the performance principle. Surplus repression involves the additional controls over and above those necessary for civilized human association and species perpetuation. The performance principle is the prevailing historical form of the reality principle. The reality principle is one of the value systems human beings use to govern themselves in order to perpetuate the species. It embraces delayed gratification, the restraint of pleasure, work, and productiveness. The victory of the performance principle and its accom- panying surplus repression in the modern industrialized world has ushered in a period where instrumental rationality (the separation of means from ends and the preference for ends; the disconnection of fact and value and the preference for fact; and the removal of human feeling and human concern from disinterested intellect and the preference for intellect) defines our view of work. In a context shaped by the idea of instrumental rationality the argument that work should be guided by the concept of play would appear silly and outrageous (Marcuse, 1955:12, 35, 37).

If we are to avoid the continuation of the exclusion of teachers from participation in research grounded in the critical social sciences we must expose and defeat bad work. Teachers must be capable of identifying that instrumental rationality which not only shapes bad work but also in- fluences a form of teacher education which promotes an obsessive concern with means (technique of instruction) over ends (critical examination of educational purpose). Leo Tolstoy anticipated a similar manifestation of instrumental rationality in *Anna Karenina*, as he wrote of the artist, Mihailov. Some art patrons are discussing an artist's work in which Christ is a main figure.

> 'Yes — there's a wonderful mastery!' said Vronsky.... 'There you have technique.'... The sentence about technique sent a pang

through Mihailov's heart, and looking angrily at Vronsky he suddenly scowled. He had often heard this word technique, and was utterly unable to understand ... a mechanical facility for painting or drawing, entirely apart from its subject (Tolstoy, 1981:62).

This concern with means/technique crushes critical attempts to assess the nature of an education which promotes self-direction while blinding us to forms of labor which fall into the categories of bad work.

The concept of 'bad work' in the modern period is based upon a specific set of ideological assumptions:

1 *Social Darwinism.* Every human is out for himself or herself. The strongest and the most resourceful will gain the rewards and privileges; the weakest will fall by the wayside into demeaning situations. The position is inherently naive as it fails to question the forces which privilege certain groups and impede others. Success, thus, is founded not simply on one's resourcefulness but on one's initial acquaintance (often attained through socio-economic background) with the forms of knowledge, the attitudes, and the skills required for success, often called 'cultural capital'. Therefore, undemocratic hierarchical work arrangements are viewed not as anti-humanistic but as natural and just.

2 *Nature as enemy.* Ever-increasing material growth requires that nature be viewed as a collection of objects to be acted upon and exploited (Wirth, 1983:10–11). Nature is viewed as an object that is to be used, worked upon, and controlled. It is not intrinsically valuable: to hold significance, it must serve the ends of human beings. Scientific research is the human creation which allows for this — the laws of nature can be known and thus manipulated and controlled. Human beings as products of nature can be known in a similar way and, as a result, be manipulated and controlled. Like the ancients with their myths designed to control nature, scientific man attempts a similar goal. The control of men and women in the workplace is simply a natural extension of the 'control impulse' (Held, 1980:151–6).

3 *Science as 'fact' provider.* Scientific research provides humans with indisputable knowledge. Values are subjective opinions which have little role in the world of research and work. Operating from this assumption, scientific managers have objectified the workplace, focusing on measurable factors related to the bottom lines of productivity and profit. The examination of human values as represented by Dewey's assertion that good work must be pursued as an ethical imperative does not fit into a view of work based on such a notion of science.

4 *Efficiency as maximum productivity.* The productivity of humans and their machines can be measured only one way — quantitatively. Only in a social context where human beings and nature could be viewed in anyway other than intrinsically valuable could this assumption exist. The notion of efficiency becomes deified in bad work. Worshipping this false god, school supervisors in the school workplace encourage modes of teaching which answer to the goal of efficiency rather than goal of human nurturing. Methods of evaluation are developed on the basis of efficiency rather than on an appreciation of the attempt to learn about the learner, the forces which move him or her, and the possible pathways which might be taken to help them realize their potential. The subtle emotional forces which move teachers and other workers to pursue excellence are crushed by the search for efficiency.

5 *The supremacy of systems-efficiency and cost-benefit analysis models.* Such models assume that work goals are already agreed upon by all parties involved. 'Isn't the omnipresent goal of the workplace to increase profits?', the systems analysts ask. 'Isn't the ultimate goal of schooling to increase test scores?', educational systems analysts ask. The systems researchers view the goal of scientific inquiry as the identification of so-called production functions. These entities refer to the effectiveness of certain inputs in the attempt to reach pre-specified objectives. Effectiveness in this context involves the cost-benefit of the production function, as it is examined in terms of its economic efficiency. Thus, the effectiveness of educational methods could be compared in terms of test score results. When researchers combine this measure of effectiveness with an analysis of cost-benefit factors, decisions could then be made on which educational methods to require teachers to use. All teachers, regardless of context, would thus be expected to teach in the same 'efficient' way. Questions about non-measurable outcomes such as the dignity of the laborer in the workplace or student happiness in the educational workplace are irrelevant in systems analysis. Questions concerning the tacit professional knowledge of teachers and the subtle actions they take to connect learning to life, to ground learning in humane and ethical concerns, or to make students feel secure, are suppressed by the research model. Questions about teacher happiness, control of the conceptualization of their work, and their dignity as professionals are deemed trivial and unscientific. Teaching becomes bad work (House, 1978:394, 401; Wirth, 1983:110, 113–14).

6 *The purpose of work as the promotion of at least short-term personal welfare and at most short-term national welfare.* Bad work holds no vision of work as an activity which concerns itself

with the long-term welfare of other human beings or of subsequent generations. Little effort is made in the workplace to cultivate the notion of the community of human beings past, present, and future. Such a concept would negate tendencies such as dynamic obsolescence which serves as a symbol of bad work's alienation from human need. Educational researchers too often fail to consider the social and futuristic consequences of educational policy as they examine short-term skill acquisition. The inclusion of concerns with the long-term welfare of the human community into research design is often viewed as frivolous and unscientific. In the rush to conform to the norms of the scientific peer group it is neglected. Labor and teaching and research into them are ethically fragmented; laborers and teachers see little connection between their work lives and the needs and concerns of the human community. Work is further separated from life.

7 *The contingency of human happiness on the acquisition of better consumer items.* Industrial progress is viewed as the result of more centralized, more mechanized work. In a well-administered world better consumer items will result from efficiently managed industries and institutions. Education becomes an arm of the ideology which promotes this view of work. Schools are designed to turn out individuals who fit comfortably into the bad workplace. Students are taught (by a variety of teachers who are found far beyond the classroom, e.g., television advertising) to embrace an important commandment. In a sense consumption becomes a ritual of salvation for the modern worker as he or she attempts to regain psychic peace after a forty-hour week of mechanized bad work. It is not unusual that 'Born to Shop' bumper stickers have achieved so much popularity in recent times, as shopping becomes a *raison d'être*. Social and educational researchers concern themselves with studies of how better consumer goods can be produced, how humans can be convinced that their happiness and self-worth depend on the acquisition of these goods, and how schools can contribute to the production of the labor pool needed to produce these items and even these attitudes (Wirth, 1983:10).

No one has to remind us of the psychic, social, economic, and educational effects of bad work — we are confronted with them every day. Bad work produces waste, shoddy products, apathy, hostility, alcohol and drug abuse, nihilism, reliance on 'experts,' and depression. Opinion polls conducted periodically indicate that Americans are alarmed by the poor quality of goods produced in the American workplace. A study published in the *Harvard Business Review* indicates that 20 per cent of all consumer purchases lead to some form of purchaser dissatisfaction — this does not include dissatisfaction based on price. Automobile recalls are legendary. Obviously, technological advance by itself does not ensure quality of workmanship. Indeed, we honor the label 'hand-made' as an indication of high quality. It implies a sociological relationship missing in modern industries which operate on the principles of bad work. Products which have been hand-made historically emerged from cultures where producers and consumers were the same individuals or close kin. Men made their own spears; women wove their own baskets. Even when technology advanced, material culture grew more complex, and specialization developed, the relationship between consumer and producer remained intact.

Since World War II mergers in American industry have rendered manufacturing corporations more unwieldy than ever before. Even though products grew shoddier and shoddier, horizontal industrial organization allowed large companies to stay in business. Bureaucratization of labor unions and the contracts which resulted from negotiations in the 1950s and 1960s protected incompetent workers from dismissal. Thus, workers who were understandably alienated, bored, and careless understood their immunity from management threats of dismissal. Management's lack of concern about the quality problems which result from the mega-corporation's workplace is well-illustrated by the virtual absence of life-cycle data on consumer products. Life-cycle studies follow products from birth to death under actual conditions of use to learn how an item breaks down, the type of repairs it needs, and how long a consumer can use it. There was no need for such data in industries which profited from planned obsolescence. Add to these factors the fact that the conglomerates which emerged from the mergers are not primarily in the business of producing goods — they are interested in buying and selling companies. Most executives in the United States have never been involved with the manufacturing process. Profit-mad MBAs (holders of Masters of Business Administration degrees) are often primarily interested in building empires and good 'quarterly numbers'. The company's reputation for quality is not the concern of these money managers and marketing specialists — they are interested in immediate profits during their short stays with individual companies.

We have been conditioned in the last few years to believe that work is improving both in terms of job satisfaction for workers and product quality for consumers. Management is aware of bad work, we argue, and things are getting better. The service and information-based economy, we are told, with its computerization, is producing more white collar workers who are less deskilled and more professionalized. Such claims do not meet the test of scrutiny. First of all, service and information jobs are primarily low-paying positions. Contrary to popular opinion, even goods-producing jobs demand higher pay than service and information jobs. Secondly, women hold over half of the service and information jobs, and females have traditionally received less money and less decision-making power in the workplace than males. The feminization of service and information jobs does not bode well for the possibility of improving work unless a dramatic change occurs in the way women are treated in the workplace. Good work demands respect for the dignity of women in the workplace (Harris, 1981:18–44).

In response to labor's and the general public's sense that something should be done about bad work and its resulting problems, managers have initiated Quality of Working Life (QWL) programs. The worker-as-decision-maker rhetoric of the programs has found its way into the educational workplace, as principals and supervisors speak of teacher as partner, teacher as decision maker and participant. Such programs are particularly dangerous because they have given the public the impression that workers are full participants in management decision making. In his book, *Empty Promises: Quality of Working Life Programs and the Labor Movement*, Donald M. Wells exposes the true interests of QWL programs. Given the threat from emerging industrial giants such as Japan, American industry must find new ways to remain competitive. Management realizes that such a goal demands massive investment. In order to protect their profit margins (and their substantial salaries) managers must squeeze their workers harder than ever. Thus, companies are desperate to increase labor productivity. To accomplish such an objective, managers have concluded that they need more power over job conceptualization. It is not enough to *make* workers obey — management through QWL programs hopes to induce workers to *want* to obey (Lynd, 1987:xii).

Engaged in programs which ostensibly grant them more decision-making power in the workplace, workers come to trust the pronouncements of management. Through QWL, managers hope to produce enthusiastic workers who will unleash their creative capacities which managerial control has traditionally squashed. Granted more autonomy to make microcosmic decisions on the shop floors, workers (managers believe) will be less inclined to demand more voice in the larger decisions of production. Workers imbued with a sense of self-direction will be less likely to press collective bargaining demands. In the early 1980s, executives at General Motors circulated a confidential memo encouraging plant managers to use QWL programs to convince workers that their demands were dangerous to the health of the company. Workers must be aware of the way that democratic, participatory rhetoric can be used to secure undemocratic, non-participatory ends. If worker alienation is to be seriously addressed, employees must have genuine input into the control of the workplace. Workers must be true partners in the formulation of policies of personnel selection and training, product design, the use of new technologies, and the scheduling of production (Wells, 1987:119). The possibility of good work for educators rests on similar concerns as teachers attempt to control the educational workplace.

In the quest for enhanced educational productivity, teachers' work has become increasingly controlled from above. Public perception of teacher incompetence, like public perception of worker incompetence, has provided justification for an increasing teacher-deskilling process by educational managers. Teacher education has often neglected those traditional teacher skills based on a knowledge of academic subject matter, an understanding of a variety of child development theories, an appreciation of the social context in which education takes place, an acquaintance with the relationship between educational purpose and the needs of a democratic society, and an overview of the social goals which education has historically been expected to accomplish. Colleges of education have often emphasized the technique of teaching, focusing on the inculcation of the 'best' method to deliver a body of predetermined facts and the familiarization of teachers with the 'proper' format for lesson plans which enhances supervision efficiency and thus allows for stricter accountability.

Just as the technicalization of the workplace deskilled workers by making them an appendage to their machines, teacher deskilling has proceeded by tying teachers to pre-packaged curricular materials. In many of these pre-packaged programs, even the exact words of the teacher are specified. Traditional teaching skills are deemed unnecessary in this situation, for all the conception and planning goes on far away from the school and the unique students it houses. Thus, teachers relinquish control of the teaching act — teaching is rendered bad work.

In a strange sense, the world of teaching and its workplace might possibly be characterized as a Third World culture with hierarchical power structures, scarce resources, traditional values, and teachers as disenfranchised peasants (Oldroyd, 1985:113, 117). If we accept such a metaphor, the work of Paulo Freire becomes quite relevant to our attempt to make teaching good work. Like their Third World counterparts, teachers are preoccupied with daily survival — time for reflection and analysis seems remote and even quite fatuous given the crisis management atmosphere and the immediate attention survival necessitates. In such a climate those who would suggest that more time and resources be delegated to reflective and growth-inducing pursuits are viewed as impractical visionaries devoid of common sense. Thus, the status quo is perpetuated, the endless cycle of underdevelopment rolls on with its peasant culture of low morale and teachers as 'reactors' to daily emergencies. I see the modern teacher as the plate juggler on the old Ed Sullivan Show, frantically running from plate to plate, keeping each one spinning atop each stick, unable to pause long enough to reflect on the purpose of the enterprise. Time to reflect might be dangerous — why juggle the plates in the first place? Academic research seems to avoid such basic questions, researchers prepare their research for other researchers, the teacher is viewed as the aborigine to be studied objectively.

Indeed, the status of teachers is quite low; can the 'natives' truly be expected to conduct their own research? Even though the practitioner may be in the school every day, engaged in an intensely personal relationship with students, he or she is simply incapable of conducting research in the situation. Research and theory building are the domains of the academic expert — teachers should stick to the execution of their tasks. Such élitism precludes teacher-directed research and the democratization of the workplace; it reinforces authoritarian hierarchical distinctions which disempower teachers and ultimately their students (Altrichter and Posch, 1989:25). Teachers are 'studied down' in the sense that those who control the research use their inquiry to inform themselves about their subordinates (mere practitioners), later using their information to manipulate and control them. Because of the asymmetrical power relationships teachers are excluded from inquiring into how those who employ, supervise, judge, and administrate them make their policies (Tripp, 1988:3). Research loses a liberatory function as it is coopted as a mechanism of domination, as a manifestation of the low esteem in which teachers are held. A vicious circle, a tornado of bad work thus develops: because of their low status teachers are excluded from research; researchers 'study down' the teachers; not informed by the valuable insights of teachers, the resulting research is abstracted from the lived world of school; outside reforms of education emerge from an ungrounded knowledge base; and as such reforms are imposed teachers are further disenfranchised and alienated.

At the same time, ironically, that calls to increase the autonomy and self-direction of teachers are becoming common, state boards and even local districts have been imposing policy after restrictive policy. Protected from public concern with centralized control of education because they emanate from state and local agencies, such reform measures specify what is to be taught, how it is to be taught, and what constitutes student and teacher competence. As a result of such specification, the task of teaching becomes more technical and less autonomous, i.e., more deskilled. Such hierarchical domination can occur only when teachers are viewed as low status executors, members of a craft culture, not a profession. The logic of such reforms posits that the unvenerated intuitive knowledge of these 'teachers as craftspeople' must be replaced with research-based algorithmic teaching strategies (Porter, 1988:508; Elliot, 1989a:9, 18). One of the many flaws in the logic of such hierarchical reform involves the genesis of the so-called research base. Such knowledge is often verified by a snapshot of the complex, highly contextualized classroom. Professional researchers observe for brief moments and administer problem-riddled tests to measure student progress. The focus is far too simple, much too narrow, the observation much too short and devoid of context to understand the dynamics of the classroom, not to mention, prescribing generalizable procedures for effective teaching.

Thus, schools and teachers fall prey to the bad work syndrome of over-management. School leaders fail to see educational problems as teachers see them, resulting in policies far removed from the daily world of teaching and learning. Such policies are notoriously insensitive to the reasons that teachers under-achieve, why they withdraw from engagement with students. Typical of such a situation is the implementation of time-on-task research in schools in the United States. Empirical research showed, not surprisingly, that when student time spent on a particular subject increases, student standardized test scores increase. Accordingly, principals and supervisors in some systems have sought to control teacher work-time to insure that they teach directly to specific objectives. Teachers were not included in the process of negotiating the policy implications, the meaning of such research. Teacher perspectives on the loss of classroom autonomy, the loss of a practitioner's freedom to assess the level of student understanding and to adjust the pace of instruction accordingly were not relevant in policy making. Policy and the lived world of the classroom were bifurcated by over-management (McCutcheon, 1981:188–90).

The concept of teacher as researcher in a democratic, critical context is incompatible with such a form of institutional management (neo-Taylorism) (Wallace, 1987:98). Thus, teacher research, much like the Quality of Working Life programs in industry, is vulnerable to cooption by uncritical educational managers. John Elliott argues that teacher research has already been hijacked by the leaders of technocratic educational reform. Teachers are being trained to view action research in schools as a form of inquiry into the best techniques to produce pre-specified curriculum objectives or increases in standardized test scores. The socio-political and ethical dimension of teaching and learning is not a part of the teacher research envisioned by these educational managers. It is only a matter of time, Elliott concludes, before action research will be promoted as the newest strategy to help teachers improve pupil achievement in order to meet national curriculum targets (Elliot, 1989a:6).

But those of us committed to democratic education, and democratic workplaces for teachers can take heart. Hope rises from the ruins of mandated change imposed from above — reform coming from outside the school doesn't work. The school is a unique socio-cultural system marked by complexities rarely recognized by external agents. The teacher-as-researcher movement, especially the critical democratic conception of it, is gaining in popularity because of the recognition of the failure of technocratic, teacher-proof reform. The plethora of small changes made by critical teacher researchers around the world in individual classrooms may bring about far more authentic educational reform than the grandiose policies formulated in state or national capitals (Oldroyd and Tiller, 1987:14; McKernan, 1988:179; Chattin-McNichols and Loeffler, 1989:27). But our optimism must be tempered; merely granting teachers more power will not, at this historical juncture, make education democratic and teaching good work.

The teaching corps is large and heterogeneous. As Michel Foucault repeatedly pointed out, knowledge is power; and though it may be difficult for many of the proponents of action research to admit, part of the reason why teachers don't appropriate more authority involves the fact that they are insufficiently educated to take this step. Teachers with weak academic and pedagogical backgrounds must, out of necessity, defer to the judgments of their administrators, the certified experts (Porter, 1988:508; Maeroff, 1988:508). Theoretical understandings are necessary to the teacher's appropriation of authority — to his or her empowerment. The culture of teacher education, however, has tacitly instructed teachers across the generations to undervalue the domain of theory while avoiding basic questions of the ideological, psychological and pedagogical assumptions underlying their practice (Tripp, 1988:19).

Even when teachers have taken research courses, which are often offered at the graduate level, few ever recognize the relationship between their research experience and their lives as teachers (most of the research courses taken involved a survey of quantitative, statistical techniques of data analysis). Neither the on-the-job socializing forces of schooling nor in-service education is committed to the cultivation of the teacher's role as researcher. Evidence seems to indicate that if students are not introduced to the power of practitioner research during initial teacher training, chances are they will never be involved in it. Too much teacher education focuses student attention on short-term survival skills that do not offer the prospective teachers frames for examining their own teaching or subjecting their own and their school's practices to questions of educational purpose or social vision (Chattin-McNichols and Loeffler, 1989:23; Ruddick, 1989:7–8).

Teacher education has failed to connect teacher education coursework with the teaching workplace in any more than an obvious, technical way. Devoid of theoretical and analytical frames, young teachers fall easy prey to an unceremonialized initiation into the alienation and disillusionment of the bad teaching workplace. Donald Schon argues that if teacher education is to produce reflective, ethical practitioners who are equipped to resist the demoralization of bad work, colleges of education must connect teachers' ways-of-knowing to social and educational theory. One of the most important aspects of teacher education might involve the study of the processes by which teachers acquire the practical knowledge, the artistry that makes them more or less effective as professionals. When such inquiry is pushed into a critical dimension teacher educators would address the process of how professional consciousness is formed, how ideology contributes to the teacher's definition of self. Without such inquiry and analysis teachers remain technicians, and teaching remains bad work (Noblit, 1984:98; Schon, 1987:312; Oldroyd and Tiller, 1987:14).

Teaching can be good work. To make it so teachers and teachers' organizations must be aware of the nature of good work and the forces which serve to preclude it. Teachers who understand the guiding democratic social theory of Dewey, the purposes of a critical social science, and the issues which confront all social researchers as they attempt to produce 'knowledge' will be better prepared to avoid the bad work of teaching. If teachers are to control their work lives, they must control the conceptualization of the teaching act. To control their teaching they must not allow 'educational experts' to control knowledge production. To insure good work teachers must become researchers. It is important to explore what exactly it means for teachers to become researchers.

The very basis of teacher research involves the cultivation of restless, curious attitudes that lead to more systematic inquiries. Such attitudes preclude unreflective orientations which fail to subject school practices and life in general to criticism. All educational acts become problematic to the teacher as researcher. This critical consciousness sees all educational activity as historically located. The perspective cannot view the educational act separately from a social vision, i.e., a view of a desirable future. Educational acts, the researcher comes to understand, imply certain purposes, political positions, teaching strategies (recitation, simulation, dialogue, rote-based exercise, etc.), forms of knowledge (subject matter content, skills, competencies, conceptualization, tacit understanding, etc.), and relationships between participants, e.g., students and teachers.

John Dewey well understood the relationship between teaching as democratic work and the teacher as researcher. In *The Sources of a Science of Education* (1929) he argued that one of the most important roles of a teacher was to investigate pedagogical problems through inquiry. Writing of the 'teacher as investigator', Dewey saw teachers as the most important inquirers into the successes and failures of the school — he did not see how viable educational research could be produced in any other way. Not only did Dewey's teacher investigations lead to knowledge about the school, but they led to good teaching (Dewey, 1929, pp. 46–48). Indeed, the ultimate benefit of teacher research over sixty years later continues to be good teaching, defined not simply as effective ways of getting facts across but as understanding the significance of ideas and their effect on humans (McCutcheon, 1981:186; Duckworth, 1987:139).

Certainly, one of the quickest ways to apply teacher research to the pursuit of good teaching involves, simply, teachers listening to students. This 'research on students' is a cardinal tenet of good teaching, as the teacher details his or her observations of the student as well as his or her reaction to the learner. These observations must be contextualized by an examination of the social context in which student *and teacher* consciousness is formed and education takes place. As teachers come to understand how they themselves and their students construct understandings of the educational process, they can move themselves and in turn their students into unknown territory, new frontiers of thinking. In this way teacher research revolutionizes traditional conceptions of staff development, making it a democratic, teacher-directed activity rather than a manifestation of the hierarchicalized imposition of the bad workplace. It promotes good work by assuming that teachers are knowledgeable and entitled to make decisions about their profession (Wood, 1988:148–9).

In many ways this conception of teacher research is little more than a common sense explanation of what good teachers already do; but by making teacher research a central point of the conversation about good teaching we can extend the value of the concept. When Patricia Wood began her work with teacher research, like many of us, her impression was that she already incorporated the basic elements of the action research model: planning, acting, observing, and reflecting. By focusing her attention on the process she sharpened her observation skills and began to reflect in a more textured, conscious manner (Wood, 1988:146). A more textured reflection on one's teaching involves a teacher's self-understanding of his or her practices, especially the ambiguities, contradictions, and tensions implicit in them. When the teacher as researcher connects with other teachers as researchers and with college of education faculty interested in these ambiguities, contradictions, and tensions, a dynamic process ensues. This is the basis of educational change, of critical pedagogy, of a democratic workplace (Elliot, 1989b:50; Torney-Purta, 1985:73).

Teacher education which neglects these aspects of teacher research misses the point — it misses the distinct demands of the teaching workplace, the implications of democracy for educational theory, the ambiguity of practitioner ways of knowing. Piaget argued that teacher educators must acquaint teachers with the nature of research as quickly as possible (Piaget, 1973:37). The notion of teacher research cannot be separated from any single component of teacher education. Research is an act which engages teachers in the dynamics of the educational process, as it brings to consciousness the creative tension between social and educational theory and classroom practice. What exactly does this creative tension mean? Although many readings are possible it involves a form of thinking which moves into a 'post-formal' realm of *problem discovering* — it has transcended the Piagetian formal stage of *problem solving*. In this context the teacher travels into a realm of analysis which forces him or her to confront the relationship between social vision and its concern with the nature of justice (social theory), educational purpose and its concern with the effects of the way we define education (educational theory), and how we as educational leaders and teachers conduct our daily professional lives. A teacher education which confronts this three-dimensional relationship cannot be simplistically technocratic, it cannot help but connect theory and practice, by necessity it must view teachers as self-directed agents, sophisticated thinkers, active researchers in a never-static, ambiguous context. Here, teachers are encouraged to construct their own views of their practice; they do not implement the constructs of others or act in response to the officially certified knowledge base. They discover the asymmetries and contradictions created by the pursuit of harmony between critical conceptions of justice and the untidy world of learners and schools.

A recurrent theme here is teacher education's history of ineffective incorporation of research into professional education programs. Teachers involved in on-site action research projects often have difficulty adapting their teacher education-inculcated notion of research in education into the context created by the teacher research proponents. Even after their involvement in educational action research teachers are reluctant to say that they really did research; even if they admit to having done research they maintain that it was unscholarly or of low quality (Ross, 1984:114). Their college of education-generated definition of research as a positivistic, controlled experimental design, replete with systematic statistical analysis, seems to undermine their ability to reconceptualize what form research might take or how it might be connected to their lives as practitioners.

It seems apparent that teacher education has to do more than *train* teachers in quantitative research methods. When critical teacher research is incorporated into teacher education, research methodology cannot be separated from conceptual analysis. Teachers as researchers in a democratic workplace are capable of meta-theoretical thinking. The assumption perpetuated in many graduate research courses that the analysis of pre-theoretical assumptions has little to do with the research act will have to be challenged (Van Hesteren, 1986:217–18). Transformation of the educational workplace is impossible without a concurrent transformation of teacher education.

Thus, in the good workplace of the democratic school educational improvement occurs when the practitioner learns to think more precisely and conceptually. In educational or workplace reforms in bad work situations the idea of improving practitioner thinking and self-direction simply does not appear — the external imposition of rules on the practitioner brings about the desired change. Thus, the primary purpose of critical research activity for teachers is teacher empowerment. This empowerment involves teachers providing themselves with the skills and resources that enable them to reflect on educational practice. The purpose of educational research, therefore, is not merely to turn out better theories about education or more effective practices. Democratic educational research performed by teachers renders teaching practice more theoretical in that it is supported by reflection and grounded in socio-historical context. Teachers as researchers gain the skill to interrogate their own practices, question their own assumptions, and to understand contextually their own situations (Carr and Kemmis, 1986:39, 56, 123).

Some scholars have termed this research by participants (or practitioners) action research. Researchers in the 1940s (Lewin, 1946:34–6) called for such forms of research, and such approaches have been discussed in Britain and Australia in particular for several years. Drawing upon several traditions mid-century, action research was praised as an important innovation in social inquiry. Kurt Lewin in social psychology probably did the most to popularize the term, but the method was utilized in a variety of contexts from industry to American Indian affairs. During the post-World War II era Stephen Corey at Teachers College led the action research movement in education. Corey argued that action research could reform curriculum practice, as teachers applied the results of their own inquiry. There was considerable enthusiasm for the movement in the post-war period, but by the late 1950s action research became the target of serious criticism and started to decline. Analysts have posited that the decline was precipitated by the bifurcation of science and practice which resulted from the growth of the cult of the expert. As policy makers came to rely more and more on expert educational research and developmental laboratories, the development of curriculum and pedagogical practices was dictated from the top down. Thus, the production of research was separated from the world of the practitioner (McKernan, 1988:174–9).

By the 1970s action research was rediscovered and by the 1980s had aligned itself with the attempt to redefine teacher professionalism. Many teacher educators have expressed concerns over the foundations of much of what passes for action research. Theorists interested in democratic conceptions of education and the teaching workplace have raised ideological questions about neo-action research. Reflecting John Elliott's fear of the technocratic cooption of action research, Patti Lather warns teachers that much which has been called action research has not been critically grounded. Much of it is ahistorical and apolitical and thus lends itself to subversion by educational leaders who are tempted to employ the technical form of action research as a means of engineering practitioner 'improvements.' To avoid such appropriation of action research it must be carefully conceptualized and defined (Lather, 1986:263). Critically grounded action researchers must promote a self-reflective form of analysis which improves the rationality and justice of their own practices.

For action research or any type of research to be considered 'critical' it must meet five requirements.

1 It must reject positivistic perspectives of rationality, objectivity, and truth. Critical research will reject the positivistic notion that all educational issues are technical and not political or ethical in character.

2 It must be aware of the interpretations of educational practices held by those who perform educational acts. The self-understandings of educational practitioners who are reflective will lead them to be conscious of their own value-commitments, the value-commitments of others, and the values promoted by the dominant culture. Such consciousness will dramatically affect the way the practitioner interprets his or her professional activities.

Teachers who become critical researchers will hold this consciousness of the relationship between personal values and practice as a
goal of inquiry.

3   Critical research must attempt to distinguish between ideologically distorted interpretations and those which transcend ideological
distortion. When practitioners seek to become aware of the interpretations they place on their practice, they always face a danger.
Their interpretations, their consciousness of their own values and
other values in the society may be distorted by illusory beliefs
which sustain contradictions in the life of the society. Critical
research, therefore, attempts to unveil this false consciousness
while providing methods for overcoming its effects.

4   Critical research must reveal those aspects of the dominant social
order which block our attempt to pursue rational goals. Often the
goals that teachers work toward are not the result of their personal choice but are dictated by the social structure and the educational bureaucracy which it creates.

5   Critical research is always guided by an awareness of how it
relates to practice. Its purpose is to help guide the work lives of
teachers by discovering possible actions they might take if they
are to overcome the obstacles social structures place in their way
(Carr and Kemmis, 1986:129–30, 162).

Critical research is praxis. Praxis involves the inseparability of theory
and practice — i.e., informed practice. We must understand theoretical
notions in terms of their relationship to the lived world, not simply as
objects of abstract contemplation. Thus, truth of research must be proved
in practice. Approaching truth, Max Horkheimer argued, is an active
process where human beings apply it and 'bring it to power'. Verification
of ideas, he continued, does not consist in mere laboratory experiments or
the search for historical documents, but in historical struggle. Truth,
Horkheimer concluded, is found in and is a moment of correct practice.
Viewing research as praxis, we use our research to help participants
(ourselves included) understand and change their situations (Held,
1980:191).

It is important to note that teachers are not the only educational
actors who engage in research. If we are serious about Dewey's notion of
a democratic community where all parties have a voice in the formulation
of policy, then parents and community members must be participants in
the public conversation about education. These people will also be empowered by an understanding of critical research. One of the most democratic roles a public educator might play involves sharing critical research
skills with the public, especially the disempowered public. This is a radical
action on a number of levels. First, it negates the cult of the expert. It
helps destroy the myth that men and women should seek guidance from

those blessed with society's credentials to direct them. In this way it celebrates human self-direction. Second, it expands the role of the teacher. The teacher moves from classroom technician to active political agent, as he or she views education as a vehicle to build an egalitarian community. And third, it sees the school as an agent of democracy which is dedicated to an ethic of inclusion and negotiation. As a democratic agent, the school seeks to uncover those forces which thwart participation.

Critical research, of course, involves the production of new knowledge. Paulo Freire and Ira Shor write of a critical theory of knowing, arguing that there are two moments of knowing: 1) the production of new knowledge; and 2) when one knows the existing knowledge. What typically happens is that we separate these two moments. Critical research insists that they be brought together. Knowledge is produced far from the teacher and the students. Knowing is thus reduced to taking existing knowledge and transferring it. The teacher is not an inquirer who researches existing knowledge; he or she is merely a specialist in knowledge transference.

Teachers in this situation lose the indispensable qualities that are mandated by knowledge production: critical reflection, a desire to act, discomfort, uncertainty, restless inquiry, etc. When such qualities disappear from teachers, schools become places where knowledge which supports dominant interests is stored and delivered. Knowledge is produced by official researchers, scholars, textbook writers, and sanctioned curriculum committees — it is not created and re-created by teachers and their students in the daily life of the school. Teaching and researching, the official story goes, are separate entities. Critical teaching is not viewed as a form of inquiry. The symbiotic ties between teaching and research are not seen (Shor and Freire, 1987:8).

There are countless examples of the way teachers act on their research abilities. They develop curricula for their schools, they research problems and share their findings with other teachers during in-service education meetings, they devise methods grounded on their research to bring dignity and intelligence to self-evaluation procedures. Stephen Kemmis describes the critical research of a group of junior high school teachers on ways of improving remedial reading in their school. They began by exploring various strategies which had been used by remedial reading teachers around the world and by examining a variety of problems associated with remedial reading. Different teachers examined different reading strategies and used the information to improve the remedial reading teaching. Based on their work they implemented programs which involved more teachers in the attempt to help children with reading problems, altered the school day to devote more time to the development of reading, and formed teams of classroom teachers and specialist remedial teachers to tie remediation into the regular classroom.

Teachers involved in this project gained sophisticated understandings of remedial reading based on their own research, not the research and pronouncements of 'experts'. They learned how some techniques for teaching remedial reading worked to separate reading skills from the learning situations which necessitated them. Some of the methods utilized often served to perpetuate the status of students labeled remedial rather than allowing them to break away from the stigma. Other strategies resulted in student deskilling by removing remedial students from the learning context of the classroom, with the result that their poor classroom performance was maintained. Several techniques created situations where teachers found it hard to work together to develop reading skills in various curricular contexts. Teachers were becoming conceptualizers, not mere executors of someone else's plans (Carr and Kemmis, 1986:168–9). Examples of teachers as researchers are numerous and can be found in a variety of recent publications (Kemmis, *et al.*, 1982).

One of the most important examples of the liberating possibilities offered by teachers as researchers is presented by Paulo Freire and Ira Shor. Teachers, they argue, must research their own students. It is a research which focuses on the spoken and written words of students in order that the teacher may understand what they know, their goals, and the texture of their lived worlds. I can teach effectively, Ira Shor asserts, only if I have researched my students' levels of thought, their skills, and their feelings. I conduct this research in the classroom, he continues. Success is possible only if the teacher creates a situation where students feel comfortable to open up and express what they are authentically feeling. To accomplish such openness teachers must exercise restraint. They must avoid monopolization of classroom conversation in order to encourage student talk — talk which reveals their idiom and their consciousness. The words of students are the ore of teacher research. From this ore the teacher as researcher extracts valuable insights into the student's cognitive levels, their pedagogical intuitions, their political predispositions, and the themes they consider urgent.

Freire and Shor are desperately concerned that the teacher understand student experience. They read what their students read, watch TV, listen to the radio, and go to popular movies in order to stay in touch with student reality. I may not prefer Motley Crue. But if I am to understand my students, part of my research activity as teacher may involve listening to their heavy metal act enough to understand the basis of their appeal. Critical teachers might juxtapose an understanding of the popular culture which forms the terrain on which student values are often negotiated with the dominant school script. The interaction between the two worlds and the enculturation process which accompanies them may provide important insights into student *and teacher* behaviors in school settings.

Freire and Shor advise teachers as researchers not to be submissive to school texts. Fight with the text, re-write it as a form of research. Resist the demand of the official curriculum for deference to the texts — a demand predicated on the dominant culture's requirement to condition students to the industrial world's need for submission to authority, to reliance on the expert (Shor and Freire, 1987:8–9, 145, 184). One of the first research acts I undertake in my role as teacher is the effort to expose the assumptions of the texts. 'What is not said here?', I ask myself and my students. What does the tacit message tell us about the beliefs and goals of the textbook writer? Do these goals conflict with the overt goals of our school? If so, why does the conflict exist? How does this conflict affect your role as student, citizen or potential worker? or my role as a teacher?

Indeed, the outcomes of teacher research can be dramatic. Critical research by teachers is not a technique for bringing about democracy; it is an embodiment of democratic principles as it allows teachers to help determine the conditions of their own work. It leads to group decision making, a basic principle of democracy. Critical action research allows teachers to organize themselves as communities of researchers dedicated to the achievement of their own and ultimately their students' enlightenment. As we see so clearly with Freire and Shor, critical research improves educational practice, curriculum, and school organization. When teachers and parents come together in research activities no single activity better serves to improve school and community relations (Carr and Kemmis, 1986:221). Teachers, parents, and members of the community when engaged in such a process come to ask serious questions about what is taught, how it is taught, and what should constitute the larger goals of education (Giroux and Aronowitz, 1985:81).

As long as teacher work is bad work such activities are unthinkable. In a context where labor is divided to the point that teachers have little influence in shaping the conditions of their work, such visions of the possibilities of the role of teacher may be disregarded with ridicule of the visionary. To become critical researchers teachers face a political struggle. As in any political struggle, organization is a key. Teachers must organize groups to investigate school policy, government education policies, the terms of employment of teachers, and strategies to educate the community (Carr and Kemmis, 1986:222–3).

In other words, critical teachers as researchers cannot avoid the political role of promoting critical self-reflection in the society. Undoubtedly, there will be critics who will argue that such a role politicizes the school. The school should remain neutral, they will argue. Such a position reflects a common *naïveté* which fails to recognize dominant definitions of neutrality as problematic. The role of teacher as transmitter of pre-arranged and often isolated fact bits, is not understood as a politicized role. The question of 'what could be' is submerged to the 'what is', as the status quo is rendered natural. The implicit message of such teaching is that knowledge is already known, the information worthy of being known has already been discovered, and that the student role is ultimately a passive role. If schools are to be places which promote self and social empowerment, teacher work will have to be redefined. Teachers will find it necessary to develop knowledge and skills that allow them to connect educational practice with larger social visions. When they inevitably pass such knowledge and skills along to students and community members, they will be providing the tools which will allow them to become leaders rather than simply managers or civil servants.

In their political role as critical researchers, teachers must form alliances with social groups which share their concerns and social visions. An essential aspect of these alliances will involve research networks which connect teachers with laborers, theologians, social workers, lawyers, doctors, politicians, environmental activists, etc. Not only will such alliances further the goals of democratic empowerment, but they will help bring about the conditions which allow teaching to become good work and teachers to become scholars. Society does not at present view elementary, junior high, and high school teachers as scholars. The public does not hold an image of teachers which is characterized by individuals engaged in reflection, research, sharing their work with others, constructing their workplace, producing curriculum materials, and publishing their research for other teachers and community members in general. To destroy dominant images teachers will have to confront engrained values of competition, individualism, and patriarchy which inhibit most attempts at change (Giroux and Aronowitz, 1985:32, 42–3).

Change is a fundamental goal of the teacher as critical researcher. Henry Giroux develops this idea with the conception of what he calls the transformative intellectual. Transformative intellectuals treat students as active agents, render knowledge problematic, utilize dialogical methods of teaching, and seek to make learning a process where self-understanding and emancipation is possible. Giroux interprets this to mean that transformative teachers 'give students the opportunity to become agents of civic courage, and therefore citizens who have the knowledge and courage to take seriously the need to make despair unconvincing and hope practical (Giroux and Aronowitz, 1985:37).

Such teachers hold a vision and act through their research to achieve that vision. These critical researchers come to understand and then transform the bureaucratization which wipes out our memory of what educational institutions might be. With their memory of educational possibility intact, transformative teachers work to relate student experience, popular culture, and the effects of dominant modes of thinking in the attempt to help students and community members make sense of their relationship to the world which surrounds them. When such concerns are informed by the academic perspectives of disciplines such as history, literature, sociology, anthropology, political science, philosophy, and others, the possibility of critical thinking and self-direction is enhanced. The cultivation of teaching as good work leads to creative, research-grounded, motivated teachers. Research ability provides the vehicle by which teachers reach the emancipatory goal of learning to teach oneself. Our purpose now is to explore in more detail the nature of this critical research and the debate it elicits about the nature of educational research in general.

Chapter 2

Connecting Knower and Known: Constructing an Emancipating System of Meaning

To begin our exploration of the debate about educational research in the late twentieth century, let us briefly examine a few basic premises of the philosophy of science. We will explore the relationship of the knower to the known (i.e., the researcher to their research) and from this understanding begin an attempt to construct a system of meaning, a foundation on which to ground an ethical, democratic orientation toward the research act. Using the principles of good work in conjunction with our system of meaning, we will theorize a research/pedagogical orientation called critical constructivism.

A critical constructivist position assumes that there is no knowledge without a knower. Before we say anything else, the knower is a living human being. As a living human, a perceiving instrument, the perspective of the researcher must be granted the same seriousness of attention as is typically accorded the research design, the research methods in traditional forms of inquiry (Lowe, 1982:163; Gordon, Miller and Rollock, 1990:17). Like knowledge, the knower also belongs to a particular, ever-changing historical world. The human being as a part of history is a reflexive subject, i.e., an entity who is conscious of the constant interaction between humans and their world. This reflexivity recognizes that all knowledge is a fusion of subject and object. In other words, the knower personally participates in all acts of understanding. Moreover, the world in general, the social and educational world in particular, is not an objective structure, but a constructed, dynamic interaction of men and women organized and shaped by their race, class and gender. Thus, it is impossible from the critical constructivist perspective to conceive knowledge without thinking of the knower (Reinharz, 1979:245; Lowe, 1982:163).

But the constructivist notion of knower-known inseparability has not been the dominant position in educational research. Teacher researchers need to understand that the Myth of Archimedes, the belief in an objective body of knowledge unconnected to the mind of the knower, has helped formulate how educators have conceptualized the research act. Such an assumption tacitly constructs not only what counts as research but, via the shaping of educational research, it formulates what we 'know' about education. The myth assumes that the human perceiver occupies no space in the known world; operating outside of history, the knower knows the world of education and its students, teachers, and leaders objectively. This separation of the knower and the known is a cardinal tenet of the Cartesian-Newtonian paradigm. The impact of this 'way of seeing' on the theory and practice of Western science has been profound. René Descartes' analytical method of reasoning, often termed reductionism, has formed the foundation of modern scientific research. Cartesian reductionism asserts that all aspects of complex phenomena can be best appreciated by reducing them to their constituent parts and then piecing these elements together according to causal laws (Mahoney and Lyddon, 1988:192).

All of this took place within Descartes' bifurcation of the mind and matter/body. Known as Cartesian dualism, human experience was divided into two different realms: 1) an internal world of sensation; and 2) an objective world composed of natural phenomena. Drawing on this dualism, scientists asserted that the laws of physical and social systems could be uncovered objectively; the systems operated apart from human perception, with no connection to the act of perceiving. Descartes theorized that the internal world and the natural world were forever separate and one could never be shown to be a form of the other. Constructivism rejects such a dualism and posits an alternative to the Western traditions of realism and rationalism (Lavine, 1984:124; Lowe, 1982:163; Mahoney and Lyddon, 1988:192–3). Briefly, realism presumes a singular, stable, external reality that can be perceived by one's senses; rationalism argues that thought is superior to sense and is most important in shaping experience. Our notion of constructivism contends that reality, contrary to the arguments made by proponents of realism, is not external and unchanging. In contrast to rationalism, constructivism maintains that human thought cannot be meaningfully separated from human feeling and action. Knowledge, constructivists assert, is constrained by the structure and function of the mind and can thus be known only indirectly. The knower and the known are Siamese twins connected at the point of perception.

Constructivism draws upon an anti-Cartesian tradition emerging from the New Science of Giambattista Vico in the early 1700s and extending to the phenomenology, critical theory, and women's epistemology of the twentieth century. Vico insisted to the consternation of the Cartesians that a different conceptual apparatus was necessary for the analysis of social and cultural phenomena from that which might be used to study the structure of the physical world. The tradition that Vico established insisted that human beings were more than objects; when conceived as such, the uniqueness of men and women is lost — they are reduced to things, to 'its'. When people are seen as objects serious ethical questions arise. For example: is manipulation acceptable?; is self-determination a basic human right?; is the purpose of research the improvement of the human condition?; should democracy be considered in the conceptualization of the research act?

The point is clear: the objectivism, the separation of the knower and the known implicit in the Cartesian tradition denies the spatio-temporal location of the knower in the world and thus results in the estrangement of human beings from the rhythms of life, the natural world (Lowe, 1982:164; Mahoney and Lyddon, 1988:199–201; White, 1978:197). Alvin Gouldner extends the anti-Cartesian critique, arguing that the social sciences promote a form of inquiry suitable for an alienated age and an alienated people. The dominant expressions of the social sciences serve to accommodate researchers to socio-cultural alienation rather than working to overcome it (Reinharz, 1979:240–1). Descartes argued that knowledge should be empirical, mathematical, and certain, and the orientation toward research which emerged worked to exploit the forces of nature in a way which mutated the landscape of the Earth. As a result of this objectivist epistemology and the positivism which emerged from it, we now inhabit a human-made, artificial environment. Emerging from the tradition was a behavioral science which set out to manipulate people and an educational system which utilized the behavioral sciences to mold students and their consciousness in a way which would foster efficiency and economic productivity, often at the expense of creativity, social justice, and good work.

The anti-Cartesian recognition of such alienation sets the stage for our attempt to develop an emancipatory system of meaning to ground ourselves as teacher researchers. If knowledge is the prerequisite for social action, and if social action transforms knowledge, then knowledge cannot be conceived as static and certain — the foundation is laid for the social construction of reality. Donald Lowe theorizes that there are first- and second-degree constructs of social reality: first-degree constructs involve knowledge in the world, direct experiences and the understanding derived from them which helps shape the behavior of men and women; second-degree constructs involve the social scientific interpretations of first-degree constructs — i.e., outsider constructs of the insider, first-degree constructs made by the actors on the social scene. The central concern of educational research, it would follow, is the relationship between first-degree construction of the lived world of education and the second-degree explanation of that reality by the educational researcher. Does the second-degree explanation expand our consciousness and appreciation or reduce and simplify our understanding of the meaning of first-degree reality? Critical constructivism argues that the traditional methods of educational science have often reduced our understanding of educational reality. Thus, it attempts to develop new ways for educational researchers, teacher researchers in particular, to approach the study of first-order educational reality (Lowe, 1982:165).

The first step in such a process, as you might guess, is to understand the relationship between researchers and what they are researching. Where do we start such a process? I would argue that an awareness of self and the forces which shape the self is a prerequisite for the formulation of more effective methods of research. Knowledge of self allows researchers to understand how social forces and research conventions shape their definitions of knowledge, of inquiry, of effective educational practice. Knowledge of the self allows them consciousness to choose between research traditions which depersonalize the process of knowing in hopes of gaining certainty, pure objective knowledge and research orientations which assert that since the mind of the observer is always involved, it should be utilized as a valuable tool. Humans possess a tacit knowledge which can be drawn upon to make sense of social and educational situations. Such tacit, intuitive knowledge guides researchers as they conduct interviews, observations, document analyses, etc. A primary purpose of the critical constructivist approach to teacher research is to connect teachers to the nature and formation of such a form of knowledge and, in turn, learn how to employ it for maximum benefit. Let us examine some of the dimensions of this tacit knowledge which makes humans the most valuable of all research instruments.

To begin with humans are sensitive to subtle, hard to categorize dimensions of social life. Because of such sensitivity the human inquirer can interact with a situation in such a way that the unspoken, the hidden can be made explicit. The empirical research instruments which are capable of assessing particular factors are inappropriate for assessing other factors. Such is not the case with human instruments — they are almost unlimited in their adaptability. Researchers as agents freed from reliance on particular instruments of inquiry are capable of simultaneously collecting information about a variety of factors at a variety of levels. Humans, unlike research instruments, can perceive holistically. In the maelstrom of confusion which constitutes the socio-educational world, only humans can see connections between the disparate parts; only humans can grasp and perceive dominant themes in the ostensibly unrelated remnants of the socio-educational fabric. Human inquirers can extend knowing to a higher level through their capacity to grasp the realm of the felt, the emotional, the unconscious. Those unexamined usages, those unintended meanings which reveal insights that open windows into the significance of experience, are the type of understandings that only humans are capable of grasping. These are the insights that allow us to comprehend the actual educational and ideological effects of schools and other institutions.

Unlike empirical instruments, humans can synthesize information, generate interpretations, and revise and sophisticate those interpretations at the site the inquiry takes place. In the process the human as research instrument can explore the unusual, the idiosyncratic situation — the traditional empirical research instrument may have no use for the atypical situation because it does not fit the categories delineated. Such idiosyncrasy may serve as the path to a new level of understanding of the effect of a curriculum on a student or a community. While such dimensions of research are quite valuable and very sophisticated, we can look at them merely as extensions of everyday human activities: listening, watching, speaking, reading, etc. The cult of the expert will undoubtedly be uncomfortable with such research populism, but our understanding of social and educational life will be enhanced in the application of such a perspective (Lincoln and Guba, 1985:187–99). Teacher researchers can revolutionize professional practice by viewing themselves as potentially the most sophisticated research instruments available.

In order to sophisticate as teachers our abilities as researchers we need to appreciate the value of comprehending the relationship between the knower and the known. To accomplish such a task teacher researchers must understand more fully the insidious ways that traditional research orientations have worked to restrict our understanding of that relationship. Feminist theory provides an excellent analytical tradition from which to begin such an exploration. Feminist scholars start with the anti-Cartesian assumption that researchers and the researched are always historically situated and assert that researchers should take this as a given and build it into their methodological and theoretical strategies. Thus, the claim of traditional researchers that objective knowledge exists independent of the researcher's historical location is false (Smith, 1974:11). Thus, feminist theory or women's ways of knowing radically transforms traditional research, forcing us to conceptualize new relationships between the knower and the known. Research must be considered from a new perspective that attacks the traditional deference to authority, to science as a form of power. The androcentric principle of a neutral, hierarchical, non-reciprocal interaction between researcher and researched is transcended via feminist theory, as feminist researchers attempt to reconnect the knower with the known (Fee, 1982:383; Mies, 1982:120–1).

No longer can emancipatory-oriented researchers allow science to blind the knower intentionally, thus restricting what science can 'see' in the world of education. By revealing what can be learned from the every-day, the mundane, feminist scholars have opened a whole new area of inquiry and insight. They have uncovered the existence of silences and absences where traditional scholars had seen only 'what was there'. Women scholars were able to uncover such absences by applying their own lived experience to the research process, thus connecting knower and known (Belenky, Clinchy, Goldberger, and Tarule, 1986:19, 134). Traditional researchers had weeded out the self, denied their intuitions and inner voices, in the process producing restricted and object-like interpretations of socio-educational events. Using the traditional definitions, these object-like interpretations were certain and scientific; feminist self-grounded inquirers were inferior, merely impressionistic, and journalistic (Reinharz, 1979:242).

Feminist theorists realized that the objective science of the Western tradition was released from any social or ethical responsibility. Objectivity in this sense became a signifier for ideological passivity and an acceptance of a privileged socio-economic position. Thus, scientific objectivity came to demand separation of thought and feeling, the devaluation of any perspective maintained with emotional conviction. Feeling is designated as an inferior form of human consciousness — those who rely on thought or logic operating within this framework can justify their repression of those associated with emotion or feeling. Feminist theorists have pointed out that the thought–feeling hierarchy is one of the structures historically used by men to oppress women. In intimate heterosexual relationships if a man is able to present his position in an argument as the rational viewpoint and the woman's position as an emotional perspective, then he has won the argument — his is the voice worth hearing.

The power dynamics of this relationship are projected onto a larger scale in the domain of educational research: the research experts occupy a male role, while the researched, and even the consumers of the research, occupy a female role. Thus, on a variety of levels research is not a value-free, non-ideological activity. Traditional science reproduces particular power relations which lead to the production of specific forms of knowledge. In this context certain questions are asked, while others are deemed irrelevant. Presuppositions, try as traditional scientific researchers might, cannot be eliminated. They can be brought to consciousness, confronted, and transformed over time, but they cannot be discarded (Fee, 1982:384–5, 388; Reinharz, 1979:242). Thus, the methodologies of scientific research emerge from these dominant presuppositions. Revered as sacred, traditional methodologies are rarely questioned even when they separate research technique from research purpose. To initiate inquiry with a question of method rather than with a question of purpose, feminist researchers alert us, is irrational. It is irrational in the sense that it bifurcates the way we obtain knowledge and make judgments. Flannery O'Connor argues that 'judgment is implicit in seeing', that is constructing judgments is not an isolated process and when it is it is so diluted that the insights derived are bland and trivial (Westkott, 1982:211, 217).

Thus, our notion of critical constructivist teacher research maintains that inquirers connect knower and known, purpose and technique by utilizing the human as instrument. From this perspective inquiry begins with researchers drawing upon their own experience. Since the educational researcher is a human being studying other human beings he or she is privy to the inner world of experience. Utilizing his or her own empathetic understandings, the observer can watch educational phenomena from within — i.e., they can know directly, they can watch and experience. The gap between experience and traditional scientific description begins to close. On a variety of levels the private is made public. Not only do we get closer to the private experience of our students, other teachers, and administrators and the effect of these experiences on the public domain; but we also gain access to the private experience of the researcher and the effect of that experience on the public descriptions he or she presents of the phenomena observed. In our situation as teacher researchers, of course, *we* are the researchers, and it is our private experience and its relation to our public descriptions (and our public actions as teachers) that is being analyzed. Thus not only do we learn about the educational world which surrounds us, but we gain new insights into the private world within us — the world of our constructed consciousness (Reinharz, 1979:253; Reinharz, 1982:166–7).

These ideas do not have to remain in the isolated world of academia, the subject of discussions between educational researchers in academic journals or educational conferences. They are important understandings for teachers who are contemplating ways of improving their everyday professional practice. Not only does feminist theory help us formulate the purpose of research in general but it also provides a model for how action research can be implemented in various contexts — action research which is grounded on an anti-Cartesian fusion of knower and known. Maria Mies theorized a women-as-researchers project which set out to empower women to make their own history, to take control of the social changes to which they had been subjected. To accomplish this task Mies and her researchers set four goals.

First, the women set out to document their life histories. Such a project allowed the action researchers to achieve a critical distance from their own subjective biographies. As a result, they were paroled from the incarceration of their own pasts, using the knowledge of their imprisonment to liberate their futures. Secondly, the researchers wrote their biographies and in the process gained a form of objective documentation that enabled them to recognize their lives. Thirdly, the women analyzed their biographies in a historical and sociological manner which took into account not only their individual stories but explored the relationship between their stories and larger historical forces of race, class, and gender. Individual lives were viewed as intrinsically important but also as manifestations of the social contradictions and fissures of late twentieth century life. Fourthly, the women used their biographical and ideological knowledge to formulate strategies of individual and collective political action. The purpose of such action was to create a collective critical consciousness among women which would move them to fight oppression in their own lives and social contexts. The women staged plays and made videos, showed them to women's groups, and initiated discussions of the productions. In the discussions they began to move beyond their isolated lived experiences as they realized that women as a group have a collective social destiny. Teacher researchers, both female and male, have much to learn from such a process. Like the women action researchers, teachers can also come to understand the forces which constrict them and the ways they become victimized by historical constructions of what constitutes an effective, efficient workplace. Through such understandings teachers can formulate strategies of resistance — political action which helps them take charge of their professional lives (Mies, 1982:127–35).

Renate Duelli Klein extends our notion of feminist-based action research by elaborating on the connection between the researcher and the researched, the knower and the known. She describes a research project involving battered women. The researched, the battered women, were never looked upon as research objects but as subjects who were sisters, mirrors of self. Researchers approached the project with the assumptions that the battered women were co-researchers; as such the researchers and the researched compared their own experiences as women and negotiated the findings of the project in a way where the experience of each group was extended by interaction with the other. Our notion of critical teacher research is informed by such experiences (Klein, 1982:94–5). As the researcher and the researched interact — in our case teachers and students, teachers and teachers, teachers and administrators, teachers and community members — experiences can be compared, insight can be gained through interaction, democratic perspectives toward the teaching act can be fostered.

Before we continue our discussion of critical action research, we need to establish clearly the system of meaning, the way of seeing which underpins our approach to research. Throughout the book we will expand our system, but at this point we need to delineate the assumptions which guide our notions of the role of teacher and the purpose of education, and how action research fits into such visions. Henry Giroux is extremely helpful in our attempt to develop an emancipatory system of meaning. In *Schooling and the Struggle for Public Life* Giroux theorized a reconceptualization of the meaning of a democratic education which we will use as a starting point in our attempt to empower teachers via action research. The most innovative aspect of Giroux's book involved his attempt to integrate his understanding of critical theory, semiological/textual analysis, feminist theory, Deweyan educational philosophy, and liberation theology into a critical educational/curriculum theory. Giroux's educational perspective views teaching as an act of deconstructing knowledge for the purpose of understanding more critically oneself and one's relation to the larger culture. Instead of fitting the marginalized into the dominant culture, e.g., to train workers for jobs that require 'functional' reading and writing, Giroux's view of schooling emphasizes the importance of naming and changing social situations which thwart the development of a democratic community. Informed by Paulo Freire, Giroux theorizes that critical literacy involves the development of the capacity for self-criticism of the historically constituted nature of one's consciousness. Giroux's pedagogy never detaches context, or history from the teaching act; on the contrary, teaching and culture are binary stars revolving around one another in a reflexive relationship that includes community, difference, remembrance, and historical consciousness as orbiting planets in their solar system. Without this capacity for historical consciousness and self-criticism, Giroux fears that teachers are in danger of assuming the role of passive followers of administrative directives — regardless of the ethical issues at stake.

Extending Giroux's work into the realm of action research, we can argue that teachers are obligated to become researchers of themselves, revealing the interests implicit in their own teaching. Our emancipatory system of meaning will alert teachers to the need to cultivate and listen to the voices of students, understanding from the beginning that student voices encompass complex and contradictory relationships between students and the world. Teachers operating on the basis of an emancipatory system of meaning will find the need to incorporate a variety of qualitative research strategies into their teaching repertoire. Making use of such strategies, teachers can uncover those often concealed social constructions that shape particular curriculum structures, curriculum materials, and eventually the consciousness of students, teachers, administrators, and community members.

Thus, teachers as researchers become active producers of meanings — not simply consumers. Conservative leaders tell teachers and the public that the basis of the crisis in modern education revolves around the loss of authority in the modern socio-educational world. Rejecting the conservative attempt to reconstruct an undemocratic, patriarchal, obedience-based theory of authority, Giroux argues that authority must be redefined in a democratic context. In Giroux's attempt to define a progressive, democratic inclusive notion of authority, we find an important base to begin our construction of an emancipatory system of meaning. This system of meaning must be grounded on our notion of good work, an inclusive community, citizen-to-citizen solidarity and hope. Applied to the context of education, this critical system of meaning helps us to visualize schools as places where students learn and work together to establish the socio-economic conditions that make possible individual freedom and social empowerment (Giroux, 1988). Such a theoretical orientation requires that teachers critique those right-wing notions of authority that establish hierarchical divisions of labor that serve to disempower both students and teachers. Our emancipatory system of meaning rests on a rejection of social relations and serves to ground a view of teacher professionalism which uses action research as a vehicle for empowerment via a more sophisticated appreciation of the often tacit outcomes of schooling, the inner world of students, the ideological effects of the structure of schools and school reform, and the forces which shape teacher self-image. Let us now extend these basic principles and explore in more detail the ideas which form the foundation of an emancipatory form of action research in education.

No emancipatory system of meaning can be contemplated outside of the Frankfurt School's formulation of critical theory, in particular, their attempt to explore how consciousness is tied to history. A critical democratic approach to teacher research would always be mindful of the relationship between teachers', students', and administrators' consciousness and the socio-historical contexts in which they operate. In this way the critical theory of feminism helps us open the door to the analysis of the personal — how our private selves have been shaped by historical forces. Guided by feminism in our action research, we expose those buried parts of ourselves which we hold in common with our brothers and sisters — such solidarity allows us to overcome impediments to self-direction together. To study the links between women's history and modern women's education, for example, is to open the possibility for discovering how one's lived experiences are connected to those of other women or, for that matter, other men. Thus, the bonds between consciousness and history reveal a new form of knowledge to the teacher inquirer: the self-understanding and possible empowerment which comes from the uncovering of the ways that one's psyche has been constructed by historical gender roles (Westkott, 1982:211–12).

Guided by such concerns, teacher researchers inspired by critical theory seek to expose what constitutes reality for themselves and for the participants in educational situations. How do these participants, critical teachers as researchers ask, come to construct their views of educational reality? Critical constructivist action researchers see a socially-constructed world and ask what are the forces which construct the consciousness, the ways of seeing of the actors who live in it. Uncritical action researchers attempt to provide accurate portrayals of educational reality, but they stop short of analyzing the origins of the forces which construct actor consciousness. Without such information, critical constructivist teacher researchers maintain, emancipatory action is impossible. Descriptions of educational reality outside the boundaries of the socio-economic cultural context hold little meaning for educators concerned with social justice and ethical action. Why are some constructions of educational reality embraced and officially legitimized by the dominant culture while others are repressed? (McLaren, 1989:169; Lincoln and Guba, 1985:78). This is the type of question that critical action researchers seek to answer. Indeed, the essence of critical constructivism concerns the attempt to move beyond the formal style of thinking which emerged from empiricism and rationalism, a form of cognition which solves problems framed by the dominant paradigm, the conventional way of seeing. Like Einstein's physics, critical constructivist action researchers attempt to use their understanding of the social construction of reality to rethink and reconceptualize the types of questions we ask about the educational enterprise (Yeakey, 1987:30; Noblit, 1984:98).

A central theme of these reconceptualized questions involves the inquiry into whose constructions of reality prevail and whose ought to prevail. Michael Young argues that the dominant definitions, the official ways of seeing in schools, are constructed realities which benefit some groups and not others. The ways that schools distinguish bright from stupid, good citizenship from bad, model behavior from disruptions, good work from bad work, are constructions which emanate from those in a position to induce less privileged actors to grant their consent to the dominant definitions. Much of the inquiry into education commences without an attempt to construct a system of meaning on which to ground analysis of the questions it pursues — it merely accepts the unproblematized assumptions of mainstream research. Even when we do attempt to construct a system of meaning to ground our inquiry, it may be intellectually immature if we neglect an analysis of the hidden ideological forces which define our methodology, shape our logic, anesthetize our ethical sense, and select our questions. Without attention to such concerns our inquiries lapse into an irrelevancy and a myopia which constrain the educational possibilities offered by empowered, insightful teachers (Young, 1971:2; Yeakey, 1987:30).

Thus, teacher researchers informed by critical theory seek a system of meaning which grants a new angle, a unique insight into the social consequences of different ways of knowing, different forms of knowledge, and different approaches to research. Inquiry and the knowledge it produces is never neutral but constructed in specific ways that privilege particular logics and voices while silencing others. Why do science and math curricula in the United States, for example, receive more attention and prestige in public schools than liberal arts? Critical researchers searching for the way power helps shape individual and social consciousness uncover links between the need of large corporations to enhance worker productivity and the goals of educational reform movements of the 1980s and 1990s to re-establish 'excellent' schools. They discover relationships between the interest of business and the exclusion of the study of labor history in Western schools. They expose the connections between the patriarchal, Euro-centrism of educational leadership and definitions of classics which exclude the contributions of women, minorities, and non-Westerners to the literature, art, and music curricula.

Power regulates discourses; discursive practices are defined as a set of tacit rules that regulate what can and cannot be said, who can speak with the blessing of authority and who must listen, whose socio-educational constructions are scientific and valid and whose are unlearned and unimportant. In the everyday world of teachers, legitimized discourses insidiously tell teachers what books may be read by students, what instructional methods may be utilized (Madeleine Hunter, etc.), and what belief systems, definitions of citizenship, and views of success may be taught. Schools may identify, often unconsciously, conceptions of what it means to be educated with upper-middle class white culture; expressions of working class or non-white culture may be viewed as uneducated and inferior. In this context teachers are expected to sever student identification with their minority group or working class backgrounds, as a result alienating such students through the disconfirmation of their culture. Thus, the culture of schooling privileges particular practices and certain methods of discerning truth. Foucault argues that truth is not relative (i.e., all world views embraced by different researchers, cultures, and individuals are of equal worth), but is relational (constructions considered true are contingent upon the power relations and historical context in which they are formulated and acted upon). The question which grounds our attempt to formulate a system of meaning on which to base our action research asks: If what we designate as truth is relational and not certain, then what set of assumptions can we use to guide our activities as professionals, to inform our questions as teacher researchers? (McLaren, 1989:167–82).

This is why our system of emancipatory meaning is so important. This is why liberation theology is so important to our attempt to develop an emancipatory system of meaning. Liberation theology, with its roots deep in the Latin American struggle against poverty and colonialism, morally situates our attempt to formulate an explicit set of assumptions, an ethical starting line from which to begin our formulation of educational questions. Liberation theology makes no apology for its identification with the perspective of those who are excluded and subjugated. Proclaiming their solidarity with the marginalized, liberation theologians work alongside them in their attempt to expose the existing social order as oppressive and unethical. All aspects of our emancipatory system of meaning and teacher research which grows out of it rest on this notion of identification with the perspective of the oppressed. Accordingly, one of the main goals of critical teacher research is to reveal the ways that dominant schooling serves to perpetuate the hopelessness of the subjugated (Welch, 1985:31). On the basis of this knowledge, of their 'dangerous memory', strategies for overcoming such oppression can be built.

There is no doubt that our emancipatory system of meaning and the action research which it fosters will elicit changes of educational politicization, of tainted, unobjective research with predetermined outcomes. Critical constructivism asserts that such forms of pious pseudo-objectivity must be confronted. If critical educators cave in to such objectivist critics, the possibility of taking a moral stand in education, of seeing education as something more than a technical act, will be destroyed. As they argue that we must keep politics out of education and avoid emancipatory action research, they misrepresent the basic tenets of emancipatory action research and critical pedagogy in general. Critics miss the point that research is never neutral — alas, when we attempt to remain neutral, like Pilate, we support the prevailing power structure. Thus, a recognition of the ideological nature of research implies that researchers by necessity must take a position and make it explicit to their readers and to those they are researching. They do not impose their positions or their interpretations as the truth — of course, readers, co-workers, and the researched have the right to reject everything asserted.

Along with other advocates of critical pedagogy and critical research, I would maintain that non-critical, mainstream researchers are every bit as guilty of value-laden research as any critical inquirer. To assume a position which refuses to seek the structural sources of human suffering and exploitation is to support oppression and the power relations which sustain it. The arguments of traditional objectivist researchers that any inquiry grounded on explicit value assumptions is subjective to the point of worthlessness is similar to the nineteenth-century ruling class idea that engaging in social criticism violated a 'gentlemanly' code of civility. It is similar to a twentieth-century notion of positive thinking (cf. Dale Carnegie) which views overt oppositional behavior as a form of negativity which is not only politically incorrect but distasteful as well. Indeed, the difference between critical constructivist research and objective traditional educational research rests on the willingness of critical constructivist researchers to reveal their allegiances, to admit their solidarities, their value structures and the ways such orientations affect their inquiries.

Revealing their solidarities, critical teacher researchers operate on the anti-Cartesian assumption that knower and known are inseparable. Learning from the liberation theologian, critical researchers embrace subjugated knowledges, in the process disallowing an objectivist subject-object dualism. When researchers respect subjugated knowledge and the unique perspective of the oppressed, they, as a matter of course, begin to subvert the relationship of domination that permeates traditional objectivist research. It is a relationship of domination which allows for both the manipulation of natural processes to serve the logic of capital (the needs of profit-making) and the manipulation of human beings as the passive objects of social engineering. This separation of knower and known, this epistemological distancing, produces a tacit logic of domination between researcher-researched and knower and known; not content to occupy only the terrain of inquiry, this logic trespasses into the domain of race, class, and gender relations (Fee, 1982:386). Indeed, it is the logic of hierarchy and authoritarianism, not democracy — it is the logic of bad work.

Operating within this domain of Cartesian logic, educational research has often served the interests of power élites. Critical constructivist action research, with its commitment to the perspective of the oppressed, seeks to confront such consequences. The view from above of the traditional paradigm gives way to views from below. Emerging from an understanding and respect for subjugated knowledge, such an epistemological position (or at least a way of knowing) not only boasts of ethical assets but holds scientific benefits as well. The scientific dimension revolves around the hierarchical relationship of researcher and researched; much of the information gathered by traditional methods is irrelevant because the subordinate researched, realizing their inferior position, often develop a profound distrust of the researchers interrogating them. Oppressed groups interviewed by researchers from a higher social stratum often provide expected information rather than authentic data. Respect for subjugated knowledge helps construct a research situation where the experience of the marginalized is viewed as an important way of seeing the socio-educational whole, not simply as a curiosity to be reported. Such a research perspective is counter-hegemonic (i.e., a threat to entrenched power), and radically democratic as it uses the voice of the subjugated to formulate a reconstruction of the dominant educational structure. It is a radical reconstruction in the sense that it attempts to empower those who are presently powerless (Mies, 1982:123; Connell, 1989:125).

With this reconstructive imperative in mind, one of the central tasks of a critical constructivist researcher is to formulate questions which expose the conditions which promote social and educational advantage and disadvantage. For example, it is obvious to many that when the methods of evaluation of advocates of the competitive, basics curriculum are employed, non-white and working class students do not generally do well — their performance is interpreted as a manifestation of slowness, of inferior ability. Researchers devise tests to evaluate school, student, and teacher performance, forgetting throughout the process that evaluation is based on uncritically grounded definitions of intelligence and performance. The definitions of intelligence and performance employed are not generated by the marginalized. When liberals attempt, for example, to develop curricula or initiate research based on a recognition of the existence of marginalized experiences, they miss the lessons provided by an understanding of subjugated knowledge. A common liberal reform involves the inclusion of women or blacks in a history curriculum which has traditionally emphasized the contributions of famous (especially military) men. In a traditional curricular framework this simply adds a few new facts to be committed to memory: it is a tokenism which perpetuates the power relations of the status quo. Another such reform might involve making sure that respondents to a survey include a percentage of women and minorities (Connell, 1989:125–6).

The advantage of subjugated perspectives, the view from below, involves what has been termed the 'double consciousness' of the oppressed. If they are to survive, subjugated groups develop an understanding of those who control them (e.g., slaves' insight into the manners, eccentricities and fears of their masters); at the same time they are cognizant of the everyday mechanisms of oppression and the way such technologies shape their consciousness, their lived realities. Because of their class, race, and gender positions, many educational researchers are insulated from the benefits of the double consciousness of the subjugated and are estranged from a visceral appreciation of suffering. Contemporary social organization, thus, is viewed through a lens which portrays it as acceptable. Why would such researchers challenge research methods, modes of interpretation which justify the prevailing system of education? What lived experience would create an ethical dissonance within the minds of such researchers that would make them uncomfortable with the status quo? The oppressed — while often manipulated by mechanisms of power to accept injustice and to deny their own oppression — often use their pain as a motivation to find out what is not right and to discover alternative ways of constructing social and educational reality (Mies, 1982:121; Jaggar, 1983:370). Women's ways of knowing as a subjugated form of knowledge have initiated a virtual revolution in our conception of what we know and how we come to know it. Serious consideration of such subjugated ways of knowing transforms forever our conceptions of the relation of the knower to the known and the conceptualization and execution of the research act — our system of meaning is intimately tied to these different ways of knowing.

By the 1990s we have come to recognize and accept that there is a connection between gender and ways of knowing. Machismo inquiry as reflected in Cartesian science is characterized as cold, hard, rational, and certain; feminine inquiry is characterized as humane, deep tactile, and concerned with the world of consciousness. Rational 'man' is a gender-specific concept in that it refers to the style of knowing and discovering characteristic of traditional males. The rational man is rational as opposed to emotional; he is objective as opposed to subjective; immersed in the public realm instead of the private. Rational men love truth, women beauty; rational men are active, women passive. Rational man is the maker of history, while woman maintains a closeness with nature, i.e., the body, sexuality, passion, and human interaction. The way of knowing ascribed to rational man defines abstraction as the highest level of thought — symbolic logic, mathematics, signifiers far removed from their organic function. Women's modes of inquiring and knowing are grounded in an identification with organic life and its preservation. Rational man contends that emotions are dangerous as they exert a disorganizing effect on the progress of science (Reinharz, 1979:7; Fee, 1982:379–80). Informed by feminist perspectives, critical constructivist teacher researchers admit that, indeed, emotions do exert a disorganizing effect on traditional logocentric (reason-centered) ways of knowing and inquiring. But such disorganization is a positive step in the attempt to accommodate and integrate (in a

Piagetian sense) our perceptions of ourselves and the world around us. Emotions thus become powerful knowing mechanisms that extend our ability to make sense of the universe (Mahoney and Lyddon, 1988:216–17.

Madeleine Grumet extends our understanding of the feminist attempt to transcend logocentrism by connecting the language of the body, of feeling, with inquiry. Social science, she argues, whether guided by right-wing or left-wing impulses, has been enmeshed in a male-dominated snare of abstraction. Grumet has sought new methods of inquiry which were capable of drawing the body and feeling into the public conversation about education. Making use of qualitative methodologies such as history, theater, autobiography, and phenomenology, she confronts androcentric abstraction with the uncertainty, specificity, and contradiction of the private, the corporeal, the feminine (Grumet, 1988:3–15). From the perspective of the guardians of the Cartesian tradition such epistemological confrontations constitute overt subversion. After exposure to such theorizing, inquiry can no longer be viewed as a cold, rational process. As feeling, empathy, the body, are injected into the research process, as the distinction between knower and known is blurred, as truth is viewed as a *process* of construction in which knowers play an active role, passion is injected into inquiry. Critical constructivist teacher researchers see themselves as passionate scholars who connect themselves emotionally to that which they are seeking to know and understand.

Several decades ago Michael Polanyi wrote about personal knowledge — that is, a way of knowing which involves the passionate participation of the knower in the act of knowing. Guided by such notions, critical constructivist action researchers embrace a passionate scholarship, a reconceptualized science which is grounded upon and motivated by our values and solidarities (Belecky, Clinchy, Goldberger, and Tarule, 1986:140–1). Passionate knowers use the self as an instrument of understanding, searching, as Madeleine Grumet has, for new methods to sophisticate the way the self is used in research. Soren Kierkegaard anticipated this notion of feminist passion, arguing in the first half of the nineteenth century that there *is* an intimate connection between commitment and knowing. Subjectivity, he maintained, is not simply arbitrary — instead, it reflects the most profound connection between an individual thinker and the world. As inquirers grow passionate about what they know, they develop a deeper relationship with themselves. Such a relationship produces a self-knowledge that initiates a synergistic cycle — a cycle which grants them more insight into the issue being investigated. Soon, Kierkegaard argued, a form of personal knowledge is developed which orients the mind to see social life as more than a set of fixed laws. Social life is better characterized as a process of being, a dialectic where the knower's personal participation in events and the emotional insight gained from such participation moves us to a new dimension of knowing. Not only did

Kierkegaard anticipate feminist theory's concept of passionate knowing and Polanyi's personal knowledge, but he also foreshadowed a post-Piagetian, post-formal mode of thinking which forms a central tenet of our notion of critical constructivism (Reinharz, 1979:242–3).

Another precursor of the feminist notion of passionate scholarship which shapes our system of meaning (and which should serve to humble Euro-centric academicians) concerns the ways that indigenous peoples have defined knowing. Note the similarities of Afro-centric and American Indian ways of knowing with the anti-Cartesian perspectives of Kierkegaard, Polanyi, and modern feminists. To such peoples reality has never been dichotomized into spiritual and material segments. Self-knowledge lays the foundation for all knowledge in the African and Native American epistemologies. Great importance has traditionally been placed on inter-personal relationships (solidarity), and diunital logic has moved these traditions to appreciate the continuum of spirit and matter, individual and world. Indeed, indigenous ways of knowing and the European Cartesian tradition come into direct conflict over the epistemological issues of mind and body, individuals and nature, self and other, spirit and matter, and knower and known — a conflict which has generated serious historical consequences. It is only in the last thirty years that some Euro-centric people have come to recognize the epistemological sophistication of the indigenous paradigm which recognizes a unity in all things and a connected spiritual energy embedded in both human and natural elements. Thus, that deemed primitive by traditional Western scholars becomes, from the perspective of critical constructivist researchers, a valuable source of insight into our attempt to reconceptualize an emancipatory system of meaning (Myers, 1987:73–5; Nyang and Vandi, 1980:245).

Antonio Gramsci well understood some of these epistemological concepts as he wrote from Mussolini's prisons in the late 1920s and 1930s. The intellectual's error, he wrote, consists of believing that one can know without 'feeling and being impassioned' (Gramsci, 1988:349). The role of intellectuals and researchers from Gramsci's perspective revolved around their attempt to connect logic and emotion in order for them to 'feel' the elementary passions of the people. Such an emotional connection would allow the inquirer to facilitate the struggle of men and women to locate their lived worlds in history. Finding themselves in history, they would be empowered by a consciousness constructed by a critically distanced view of the ways that the structural forces of history shape lives. One cannot make history without this passion, without this connection of feeling and knowing since without it the relationship between the people and intellectuals is reduced to a hierarchical formality. The logic of bureaucracy prevails, as intellectuals move to the higher rungs of the organizational ladder, assuming the privileges of a superior caste, a modern Egyptian priesthood (Gramsci, 1988:349). The essence of action research rests on an appreciation of Gramsci's exposure of the power relations between intellectuals and non-intellectuals.

Peter McLaren grounds this analysis of passionate knowing educationally with an insightful analysis of the difference between the ways of knowing in the street-corner world of Toronto's Jane-Finch Corridor and the world of classroom knowledge. In the streets students gained a 'felt' knowledge which made use of the body, organic symbols, and intuition. Classroom knowledge was abstracted from the lived world, objectified, and corrupted by a Cartesian rationalism. To the students the abstracted knowledge of the classroom was light years away from their everyday experience. Students resisted what seemed to them to be useless ways of knowing in a variety of creative and often disconcerting ways. They struggled for creative control of knowledge production, viewing experience as open to question rather than something simply to be taken for granted. In other words, McLaren argues that street-corner epistemology challenged the school's tendency to present knowledge as unproblematic, not open to emotional negotiation. Students from such subjugated cultures questioned the school view of them as passive recipients of concrete facts. Teachers themselves have assumed the same passive position in relation to expert educational researchers. Teachers are the passive recipients of the objectified, abstracted knowledge handed down to them. Even though they formulate their own understanding of classroom life and teaching on both an emotional and logical base, they are induced to sophisticate their understandings of the educational process by consuming and incorporating the scientific knowledge of the experts into their professional labors (McLaren, 1989:214–15).

Thus, by synthesizing feminist notions of passionate knowing, indigenous people's epistemology, subjugated knowledges, and liberation-theological ethics, we are constructing a critical system of meaning. From this base we are able to critique the existing knowledge base of education and to formulate methods and questions for our own work as teacher researchers. In essence, we are moving ourselves into another socio-educational dimension, a land of uncertainty where the traditional rules of knowing no longer apply. We are beginning an exploration of a new universe — a world where the distortions of the Cartesian dualism are exposed, where multiple ways of knowing are sought and valued. Of course, what we are doing is taking a step into the uncharted world of postmodernism, a land where the rational voice is no longer a universal one (Poster, 1989:30).

Postmodern analysis, though diverse in the ways it is conceptualized, has consistently laid bare the assumptions of Cartesian logic by illustrating the ways that the structure of traditional science constructs imaginary worlds. Like a novel, science is 'written'; both the novel and science operate according to the arbitrary rules of a language game. Such postmodern understandings confront us with a dramatic socio-educational dilemma: how do we function in the midst of such uncertainty? Constructivism offers us aid in our dilemma — not salvation, just help. Using our system of emancipatory meaning, tempering it with a dose of postmodern self-analysis and epistemological (or maybe post-epistemological) humility, let us now take our notion of critical constructivism one more step — employing our emancipatory system of meaning as a basis for conceptualizing a democratic form of action research which leads to a new way of seeing, a post-formal way of perceiving the educational world.

What are the limits of human ways of knowing? Where might we go from here? Such questions have both research and pedagogical implications — as do our emancipatory system of meaning and our notion of critical constructivism. Drawing upon our system of meaning, we cannot help but anticipate ways of knowing and levels of cognition which move beyond Piagetian formalism. Adults do not reach a final cognitive equilibrium beyond which no new levels of thought can emerge; there have to be modes of thinking which transcend the formal operational ability to formulate abstract conclusions, understand cause-effect relationships, and employ the traditional scientific method to explain reality. We know too much to define formality as the zenith of human cognitive ability (Arlin, 1975:602–3).

Formalism implies an acceptance of a Cartesian-Newtonian mechanistic world view which is trapped within a cause-effect, hypothetico-deductive system of reasoning. The formal operational thinker/researcher employs a science which breaks a social or educational system down into its basic parts in order to understand the way it works. Emphasizing certainty and prediction, formal operational thinking/researching organizes verified facts into a theory. The facts which do not fit into the theory are eliminated, and the theory developed is the one best suited to eliminate contradictions in knowledge. Thus, formal operational thought and its attendant mode of inquiry operates on the assumption that contradiction resolution is an important objective (Kramer, 1983:95–9). Schools and standardized test-makers, assuming that formal operational thought represents the highest level of human cognition, focus their efforts on its cultivation and measurement (though sometimes they fail to get too far beyond concrete forms of thinking). Students who have moved beyond formality are rarely rewarded and sometimes even punished in educational contexts. Researchers who transcend formality have been severely criticized for their lack of rigor, their subjectivism (Sternberg, 1985:63, 282–90).

Post-formal thinkers/researchers are comfortable with the uncertain, tentative nature of knowledge emerging from critical constructivist research. They are tolerant of contradiction and value the attempt to integrate ostensibly dissimilar phenomena into new, revealing syntheses. In other words, post-formal thinkers/researchers escape the confines of

Cartesian-Newtonian modernity and venture into the postmodern realm. Post-formalism underpins a form of inquiry suitable for a postmodern world: only a post-formal thinker is cognitively and conceptually equipped to handle the uncertainty of postmodernism. Where the formal operational orientation functions on the basis of the Cartesian assumptions of linear causality and determinism, the post-formal perspective assumes reciprocity and holism (the complex, non-linear interconnection of events) (Van Hesteran, 1986:214; Kramer, 1983:92–4).

Thus, simple, privileged vantage points from which to view socio-educational phenomena are rejected by post-formal thinkers, as they come to realize that there are many ways of approaching an event. Researchers will see multiple depictions of the phenomenon depending both on the context from which it emanates and the system of meaning they employ to help formulate their questions and research strategies — i.e., do they adopt a view from above or a view from below? Traditional Marxism argued in its own deterministic way that humans see only what their conceptual lenses allowed them to see, and that they understood what the context for understanding permitted. In the spirit of hope, possibility, and anti-determinism critical constructivist researchers seek to liberate themselves from such determinism by taking control of our perceptual abilities, by transcending what the context permits. In this way we emancipate ourselves from the constraints of the Cartesian dualism and the structural forces which limit our ability to see the world from outside our restricted vantage point. In its logocentrism modernity discounted the terrain of private inner reality. What good was such a landscape in the process of industrialization, material progress, and the conquest of nature? As post-modernity rediscovers the sensuous, post-formal modes of thinking incorporate such notions into new ways of exploring and perceiving the social, educational, and even physical world (Gordon, Miller, and Rollock, 1990:15–16; Kramer, 1983:95; Slaughter, 1989:262).

Such new modes of thinking and researching incorporate sensual knowledge and self-knowledge in interesting ways. Researchers who do not understand themselves tend to misconstrue the pronouncements and feelings of others. The complexity and multiple readings characteristic of postmodern analysis are remote to formal thinkers, as they seek comfort in the prescribed methods, the objectivity, the depersonalization of traditional social scientific, educational research (Van Hesteran, 1986:223). In a sense, the Cartesian objectivist tradition provides a shelter in which the self can hide from the deeply personal issues which permeate all socio-educational phenomena — personal issues, which, if it were not for the depersonalization of traditional inquiry, would force an uncomfortable element of researcher self-revelation. Post-formal thinkers/inquirers seek insight into how their own assumptions (as well as those of the individuals they research) came to be constructed. They transcend formalism's concern with problem solving by seeking to determine the etiology of the problem — in other words, they seek to learn to think about their own thinking.

In his effort to explore post-Piagetian thinking Robert Kegan theorizes that an essential characteristic of post-formality involves the individual's attempt to disengage himself or herself from socio-interpersonal norms and ideological expectations. This post-formal concern with questions of meaning, emancipation via ideological disembedding, and attention to the process of self-production rises above the formal operational level of thought/inquiry and its devotion to proper procedure. Post-formalism grapples with purpose, devoting attention to issues of human dignity, freedom, authority, and social responsibility (Kegan, 1982:42). Many conceptions of post-formalism contend that an appreciation of multiple perspectives necessitates an ethical relativism which paralyzes social action. Our conception of post-formal perceiving and inquiring is tied to the construction a system of meaning which is used to guide the research/cognitive act. Never content with what they have constructed, never certain of the system's appropriateness, always concerned with the expansion of self-awareness and consciousness, the post-formal thinker/researcher engages in a running meta-dialogue, a constant conversation with self, a perpetual reconceptualization of his or her system of meaning.

Such a dialogue focuses the post-formal thinker/researcher's attention on the process of question formulation, as opposed to formalism's concern with question answering or problem solving. This question-formulating, problem-posing stage, Einstein argued, is more important than the answer to the question or the solution to the problem. Critical constructivist teacher researchers are post-formal question formulators, problem posers. When teacher researchers set up a problem, they select and name those things they will notice. Thus, problem posing is a form of world making — how we select the problems and construct our worlds is based on the system of meaning we employ. Without a system of meaning teachers and administrators learn how to construct schools but not how to determine what types of schools to construct. In other words, teachers, school leaders, and teacher educators need to realize that school and classroom problems are not generic or innate. They are constructed and uncovered by insightful educators who possess the ability to ask questions never before asked, questions that lead to innovations that promote student insight, sophisticated thinking, and social justice (Schon, 1987:4; Ponizo, 1985:41). If the genius of, say, an Einstein revolved around his ability to see problems in the physical universe which no one else had ever seen, then the genius of a teacher researcher revolves around his or her ability to see educational problems that no one else has ever seen. The application of such skills by action researchers moves inquiry to a level unimagined by researchers trapped within the Cartesian tradition. Not only is such a research orientation grounded on a democratic conception of teacher empowerment, but it serves to expose previously hidden forces which shape the consequences of the educational process. It is a testimony to what can happen, what can be revealed, when researchers transcend the limitations of traditional definitions of research and explore the relationships between the knower and the known. Let us now turn our attention to the prevalent ways educational research has been conducted in the Western world and the unfortunate effects it has engendered; we will begin our analysis with an examination of positivism.

Chapter 3

Exploring Assumptions Behind Educational Research: The Nature of Positivism

Equipped with an understanding of the Cartesian tradition, we are prepared to understand its epistemological extension — positivism. Few epistemological orientations have exerted so much influence or have been so little understood. An historical overview is in order to begin our exploration of positivism. The Enlightenment of the seventeenth and eighteenth centuries realized its rational self-fulfillment with the advent of modern science. True reality, the Enlightenment thinkers posited, was founded upon scientific understanding — the world could only be comprehended via science and scientific methodology. This form of science was universal in the sense that it applied to all subjects of study and was based on mathematics. With the realization of this type of scientific enterprise during the Enlightenment, Western thought was prepared for the advent of what many have called 'the era of positivism' (Held, 1980).

The label, positivism, was popularized by Auguste Comte, the nineteenth-century French philosopher, who argued that human thought had progressed through three stages: the theological stage, the metaphysical stage, and the scientific or positivistic stage. One could only designate scientific findings as certain in the scientific stage. Comte sought to discredit the legitimacy of thinking which did not take sense experience into account, i.e., *a priori* modes of thought. Advocating such a position, Comte extended the scientific orientation of the Enlightenment (Kneller, 1984:137; Smith, 1983:6).

Comte did not see a distinction between the methods used for research in the physical and the human sciences. Thus, from Comte's perspective, sociology was a reflection of biology. Society came to be viewed as a body of neutral facts governed by immutable laws. These facts and laws could be researched in the same manner as any physical object could be researched. Like nature, society is governed by natural necessity. It therefore followed that social movements would proceed with law-like predictability (Held, 1980:160–1).

The Vienna Circle of the 1920s extended the work of Comte. Coming from a variety of specific backgrounds, the members of the Vienna Circle (or the logical positivists) enumerated several positivistic axioms:

1 *The separation of science from metaphysics.* It was certainly true that European metaphysics in the 1920s was marked by an intellectual pomposity and inbreeding which had choked the life out of philosophy. As they expunged metaphysics from philosophy, the logical positivists attempted to remove it from science as well. Thus, metaphysical questions, with the discomforting uncertainty which surrounded them, were not appropriate for *scientific* inquiry.

2 *The importance of the verifiability principle of meaning.* The verifiability principle implied that something is meaningful only if it can be supported empirically (observation via the senses) or is a tautology (an expression whose truth is known merely by understanding the meaning of the statement, e.g., 'today is tomorrow's yesterday') of mathematics or logic.

3 *The significance of observation statements.* As the logical positivists promoted the verifiability principle, they had to confront the questions: 'What is the proper process for the verification of scientific statements?'; and 'What will count as verification?'. The positivists responded to such queries by referring to what they called the necessity of 'observation statements'. Verifiability, they contended, had to take place in terms of simple and direct descriptions of sense experience. We proceed from these observation statements, the most epistemologically primary form of knowledge (i.e., the given). These statements form the basic elements of our constructional system of scientific knowledge. The universe, thus, is reduced to a set of observation statements that are forged into the smallest possible number of axioms. That which fell outside these observation statements was suspect. To the Vienna Circle, the idea that thought might encompass knowing more about the universe than that which could be expressed in observation statements was not a viable possibility (Philips, 1983:5; Giroux, 1983:13–15).

Many educational researchers emphasize the point that Comte's positivism and the Vienna Circle's logical positivism died long ago. Indeed, one of the leading proponents of logical positivism, A.J. Ayer, proclaimed before his death that the biggest problem with logical positivism was that it was fundamentally wrong. Why then do we speak of the great debate over positivism in educational research? The answer to that question is quite simple. While the formal systems of positivism died in the 1950s,

1960s, and 1970s, some of the main themes of the tradition lived on. For convenience, let us call this new form of positivism, neo-positivism. It is this neo-positivism which often sets the parameters of the modern debate over educational research (Shweder and Fiske, 1986:16). It is neo-positivism which continues to inform a good portion of the work conducted in educational research and is reflected in the training of young researchers in teacher education. Fred Kerlinger (whose textbook, *Foundations of Behavioral Research*, has been a leading seller in colleges of education for decades) provides numerous examples of neo-positivistic thinking in educational research.

Kerlinger argues in the first chapter of his 'bible' for students of educational research that educational scientists, as they attempt to explain relations between the phenomena they have observed, must exclude 'metaphysical explanations'. He defines a metaphysical explanation as a 'proposition that cannot be tested'. Science is not concerned with questions of value, Kerlinger continues, for they are not publicly observable or testable. If questions cannot be publicly observed or tested, he concludes, 'they are not scientific questions' (Kerlinger, 1973:5).

Positivism has never been a neat, easily categorized system. During the heyday of logical positivism in the 1920s and 1930s, it was marked by ambiguity and argument among its principal proponents. In the attempt for clarity, I will try to delineate the main themes of what is referred to as neo-positivism in contemporary social science parlance (Frankel, 1986). Such a delineation, I believe, will help lay the foundation for our understanding of the complex web of ideas associated with modern research on human beings, particularly the research on the education of these humans. The four main themes of neo-positivism would include: scientism, the positivist conception of science, the doctrine of scientific politics, and value freedom.

1   *Scientism*. This positivistic doctrine insists that only science should be regarded as an authentic form of human knowledge. Science here is not merely one form of knowledge; knowledge must be identified with science. Non-science is thus held in disdain, as ways of knowing such as religion, metaphysics, and ideological issues, are dismissed as unverifiable nonsense. The second positivistic doctrine clarifies scientism by specifying the nature of scientific knowledge.

2   *The positivist conception of science*. Here positivists maintain that science should be concerned with the explanation and prediction of observable events. The ability to predict is founded upon the fact that observable phenomena are micro-expressions of universal laws that are appropriate in all contexts. The positivistic conception of science must be protected from the intrusion of meta-

physics. The elimination of the unobservable from the scientific reality serves to exclude metaphysics from the exclusive fraternity of scientific knowledge.

3 *The doctrine of scientific politics.* The knowledge of the social sciences, positivistic advocates argue, should provide the basis for political decision making. Arguments in politics should be settled in the same way that arguments in engineering or medicine are resolved. Engineering and medical arguments are settled not on the basis of personal values, nor on the basis of the status of the proponents and opponents, nor as a result of the oratorical prowess of a disputant; indeed, the positivists argue, they are settled on the basis of objective aspects of the subject in question. The issues are objective because they are measurable and empirically testable, and as such the subjective, emotional, and conjectural ingredients which characterize political discussions would disappear once approached scientifically. Scientifically-based political arguments would allow for testable conclusions and, as a result, fulfill the promise of a correct solution to a specific problem. Unsubstantiated opinion would be eliminated from the political sphere and scientifically-grounded, 'rational' solutions would ameliorate the social world.

4 *Value freedom.* Positivists contend that values should not play a role in scientific investigation. Research has focused not on the ends that it serves but the means of achievement. The knowledge which emerges from inquiry should be value free. Indeed, values are the nemesis of facts and are viewed as potentially irrational responses. Scientific knowledge, the positivists conclude, should be objective. Methodological choice should proceed outside the realm of values, and the researcher should aspire to value-free inquiry. Values in positivistic research are discomforting because they do not lend themselves to true or false judgments, i.e., verifiability (Keat, 1981:16–18; Giroux, 1981:37–44).

These positivistic doctrines evoke great emotion from many different analysts for many different reasons. Henry Giroux attacks neo-positivism in the spirit of the critical theorists from the Frankfurt School. Drawing upon the earlier critiques of positivism presented by Max Horkheimer, Theodor Adorno, and Herbert Marcuse, Giroux accuses positivistic thought of crushing the traditional desire of scholarship to improve the human condition, substituting in its place an inclination to pursue only that perceived to be technically possible. This characteristic commits positivism to specific political positions and thus uncovers new dimensions of complexity in the debate over educational research. To say the least, Giroux and the critical theorists are unimpressed by the positivistic claims to value freedom and political neutrality; on the contrary, they argue, positivism has become an important prop for the dominant ideology.

Denis Phillips strongly disagrees with Giroux and the critical theorists, arguing that they use the word, positivism, as a blanket to cover any position contrary to their ideology, regardless of whether or not the position is positivistic or not (Phillips, 1983:4, 8). Indeed, Giroux's critical use of the term, positivism, does transcend strict philosophical definitions of the position. But, Giroux argues, this transcendence is precisely his point — positivism has taken on a life of its own. To illustrate this point Giroux employs the phrase, 'the culture of positivism'. In this culture the traditional epistemological position known as positivism affects not only inquiry but moves into the realm of ideology and social practice. As a result, it supports a frame of mind which views the world without the benefit of an understanding of the social-political context which gives reality its meaning. Let us examine the critical perspective on positivism in more detail.

Giroux argues that since the assumptions of positivism are drawn from the logic and methods of investigation associated with the natural sciences, the hermeneutical principles of interpretation hold little status. What is important in the culture of positivism involves explanation, prediction, and technical control. How we decide what constitutes a desirable state of affairs is of little consequence, he contends. This is a retreat from the Western humanistic tradition, for the Greeks viewed scholarship as a means of freeing oneself from uninformed opinion in order better to pursue ethical action. Theory and research, from the classical perspective, played the role of extending ethics and contributing to the search for truth and justice. Prevailing positivist consciousness, Giroux maintains, has forgotten this valuable role.

Knowledge to the positivist, Giroux continues, is worthwhile to the extent that it describes objectified data. Questions concerning the social construction of knowledge (this would involve the codes, media, ideologies, and socio-economic structures which shape facts (Scholes, 1982) and the political interests which direct the selection and evaluation of data) are irrelevant when knowledge is assumed to be objective and value free. The information which is gleaned from the subjective realm of intuition, insight, philosophy, and non-scientific theoretical frameworks is not considered important.

This objectivity, this value freedom comes at a great cost to those of us interested in the pursuit of truth, Giroux claims. To most people the pursuit of value-free knowledge through objective research is a worthwhile goal. The quest hides more than it uncovers, however. Those who challenge the goals of value freedom and objectivity are often perceived to be advocating bias and unfairness in research. The point that what is designated as objective research is socially agreed upon by communities of scholars — and thus not 'objective' in any real sense — is missed by many scholars and by the public at large. Value-free research is an impossible goal, Giroux tells us, and the attempt to separate value from social research is tantamount to an attempt to draw a map that portrays every detail of a specific part of the earth. Such an attempt is a value-laden activity, as the mapmaker uses his or her judgment and values to decide what to include and what not to include on the map.

Since the hidden values of knowledge are unexamined by the positivistic tradition, Giroux argues that this cult of objectivity suppresses political discussion in the public sphere. Since the knowledge has supposedly been arrived upon in a value-free manner, it is immune from political interrogation. Thus, the culture of positivism is silent about its own ideology, as it is incapable of gaining insight into how oppression hides in the language and lived experience of everyday life. Since it is incapable of reflecting on its own assumptions, it ultimately offers uncritical support for the status quo.

Positivism glorifies the present, Giroux continues, and in the process rejects the future. By focusing on 'what is' rather than 'what should be', positivism ignores ethics as a category of research. This process promotes the idea that society has a life of its own, and no matter what human beings might do they cannot interfere with this social determinism. If human beings cannot see beyond the 'what is', they are incapable of formulating an alternative vision to the status quo. Research in the positivistic model merely examines the details of the status quo, maintaining a calculated disinterest in a questioning of the power interests and assumptions which support it.

Positivistic culture, Giroux asserts, presents a view of research, knowledge, and ethics that has no use for a world where humans decide their own meaning, order their own experiences, or fight against the social forces which crush their efforts to do so. By downgrading the importance of such efforts at self-direction, the culture of positivism ignores how humans ought to live with one another and tacitly supports forms of domination, hierarchy, and control.

Knowledge which is collected by positivistic researchers is often treated as an external body of information, independent of human beings. This objectified information is temporally and spatially independent, existing outside of an historical context. Since it is expressed in a language that is technical it is supposedly value free and context free (Giroux, 1981:41–53). This means that it is separated from the political and cultural traditions that provide its meaning. Knowledge becomes a body of isolated facts to be committed to memory by overwhelmed and baffled students. Stanley Aronowitz argues that the factual memorization characteristic of schooling is so pervasive that students have enormous difficulties when they are asked to undertake conceptual learning (Aronowitz, 1973).

The 'facts' of the curriculum appear to be value free, devoid of any underlying set of assumptions; after all, they are 'just the facts' as Sergeant Joe Friday once put it. For the positivists research appears to be liberated from any theoretical pre-assumptions. This appearance of theory freedom renders positivism the great deceiver, wrapping itself in the cloak of objectivity while often unconsciously promoting specific values, world views, and assumptions about what constitutes an educated person. Thus, any teacher who wants to engage in research or familiarize himself or herself with the work which exists might want to analyze how hypotheses are generated. Such an exercise might be especially valuable when a practitioner wanted to examine the origins of the research which produced the knowledge base on which modern educational reforms are based. What, for example, were the assumptions behind Madeleine Hunter's research on lesson organization? (Astman, 1984:305; Yeakey, 1987:25).

To engage in empirical research without understanding the need for philosophical analysis of the assumptions behind it, John Goodlad argues, is to guarantee its irrelevance. In the positivistic research which has dominated education, empirical inquiry has preceded our conceptual/ philosophical analysis. Without such analysis we fail to understand that positivistic science only examines portions of the world — to the positivist the world is only what science says it is (McNay, 1988:354; Yeakey, 1987:25). Conceptual analysis helps us deconstruct the values implicit in such a world view and such a view of research. Positivistic research, we discover, can only operate on the basis of the researcher's prior theory, interest, and insight — it is tainted with subjectivity from the beginning. Beginning with a question that is of interest to them, educational researchers formulate a hypothesis and a research question which are derived from a theoretical construct. The inquiry is then conducted in a prescribed manner which stays carefully within the boundaries of the established research tradition (Lincoln and Guba, 1985:80–81).

The tradition dictates that the hypotheses and the research procedure must not be altered even if the field experiences encountered suggest such a strategy. All in the name of objective procedure, the results of the empirical research are examined in light of the original theory which generated the hypothesis; the research is confirmed or falsified on the basis of its congruence with the hypothesis. This hypothetico-deductive research procedure, as it is called, posits a discrete sequence of steps with each step influencing the following one — e.g., formulation of hypothesis, data collection, data analysis, etc. Since the procedure does not allow for the adaptation of research procedures to the circumstances encountered in the observation, the inquirer must not look at anything not explicitly anticipated in the original design of the research (Altrichter and Posch, 1989:22–3). For the positivistic researcher to attend to the 'extraneous noise' of the research site is to risk turning into a pillar of salt, that is, to risk the invalidation of the entire project. Of course, the noise of the research consistently turns out to be the source of the clues which grant insight into the mystery, the data which yield the subtle insight into the significance of an educational situation.

Shulamit Reinharz writes of her research experience in a study of teachers in Washington, D.C. It is impossible to know, she contends, which questions will facilitate understanding a situation until data has been obtained from other questions. The positivistic project of which she was a part was flawed, she concluded, because the researchers had no philosophical, conceptual basis from which to formulate their research questions — with no grounding relevance could not be judged. Reinharz reports that without grounding, without on-site time to rethink and fine tune the project in light of deeper understandings, the inquiry came to reflect stereotypical thinking. On these stereotypes their eventual analysis was constructed and, accordingly, was well within the regime of truth, the prevailing conception of 'what is' in the public schools — the status quo was thus reified through the project, as no alternative way of viewing the teachers' realities was uncovered.

Reinharz's experience is not uncommon. Without the researchers even knowing it, their work is mechanized, their findings are predestined given the research design. Without a familiarity with a conceptual critique of positivism, researchers fail to think about their own thinking, research their own research. Reinharz's co-researchers accepted everything at face value, never examined their own motivations, and never posed meaningful questions. They never asked the Washington teachers to help them re-formulate their questions, they never made use of the teachers' knowledge of their own situations. Teachers, Reinharz reflects, were not human beings but objects of our project. As a result, those leaders who had commissioned the research found out what they already knew and used the information to 'stay the course'. Teachers saw the project for what it was — an expensive waste of time (Reinharz, 1979:69–71). The 'facts' of the project were not simply facts — they were facts that assumed a variety of notions about research and values relating to how we regard human beings.

Isolated contextually, educational research reproduces the fun-damental assumptions of the positivist paradigm. Researchers who fail to question the assumptions of educational institutions accept definitions of school reality provided by school professionals in leadership positions. Unexamined definitions of, say, intelligence are accepted without subject-ing them to political and cultural interrogation. Definitions which reflect very specific political orientations or cultural backgrounds are allowed to pass as objective descriptions. Consumers of the research which emerges from this situation are unaware of the spate of assumptions on which it rests. This is another example of the insidiousness of the culture of positivism, Giroux concludes (Giroux, 1981:56–7).

How can the culture of positivism continue to exert such a profound effect on the nature of educational research? If teachers are to be researchers they need to understand from a critical perspective the assumptions the culture makes about the nature of the world and its inhabitants, i.e., the ontology of positivism. Only then will teachers understand positivistic research and be empowered to act in opposition to the policy implications which come from it. One of the first characteristics of positivism which teachers as researchers need to grasp is its simplistic view of human behavior. Positivism assumes that the personal histories of individuals and the social histories of their contexts are not germane to an appreciation of an educational setting and its significance. Such contextual information is invariably ambiguous and thus complicates the reductionism, the attempt to simplify the cause and effect relationships so important to a positivistic study (Astman, 1984:304). But the rub is that human activities like education are rarely free of ambiguity, and to miss their complexity is to miss the point.

When positivist researchers examine the social and educational world using the methods of the physical sciences, they adopt a dehumanizing view of such a world; they look at education as if it were a concrete structure. As they manipulate (think of the use of this term in a human context) data via multivariate statistical analysis, such researchers are trying to freeze the world as if it were made of concrete and were structurally immobile (Bogdan and Biklen, 1982:215). Humans are thus reduced to mere pawns trapped in the immobilized structure, ever subject to the influence of the predetermined forces emanating from it.

Thus, the researchers assume that the objects they study will remain constant. Our experience as teachers tells us, however, that such is not the case — students do not remain stable, they change as we teach and/or study them. The researchers from a positivist background fancy that the environment of the objects they study will stay constant. We know as teachers that the learning environment of children is constantly changing. To attempt a study of educational influence of a particular learning environment is quite an ambitious task, for the situation changes from day to day in a multitude of ways. A laboratory situation in chemistry is very different from a laboratory school — to try to study both in the same way constitutes a basic conceptual mistake. Indeed, a physical scientist knows at what temperature water freezes, but an educational researcher cannot measure at what temperature a child's imagination freezes. The questions are very different and involve different conceptual and analytical strategies. In the same vein physical scientists assume that any quartz crystal they study will be identical, different crystals will behave the same. Obviously, this is not the case in education, for no two children are identical and cannot be expected to behave the same. Thus, the positivistic educational research that examines categories of children as if they were categories of crystals is inherently flawed (Besag, 1986b:20). Even though two children may both be Hispanic, female, upper middle class, and visually handicapped they will not 'crystalize' at the same time.

It seems safe to argue that human and educational research differs from research in the physical sciences in some basic ways. Human contexts are so contingency-laden that the attempt to generalize cause-effect and make predictions is unrealistic. Non-positivistic educational research is less ambitious than its positivistic counterpart — it seeks understanding and interpretation of these human contexts. Educational contexts involve moral considerations at practically every level of action. While physical science-oriented positivistic research may certainly involve moral elements such as what questions to ask about the physical world or how to make use of the knowledge produced, the moral dimension of a question involving the temperature at which oxygen freezes is quite different from an inquiry into what constitutes a socially just way of providing equal educational opportunity to the children of the poor. Teachers, administrators, and educational policy makers must make daily moral decisions about the 'right' thing to do. Positivistic research is of little help to such practitioners because it assumes that research exists only to describe and help make predictions and, of course, has no value dimensions. It is unequipped to evaluate educational purposes or to assess various strategies for improving schooling (Culbertson, 1981:41–2). Educational knowledge obtained through the use of physical science methods, then, is not simply unhelpful to practitioners, but potentially very misleading because of its attempt to erase the moral dimension of human life. When the morality of an educational act is removed as a research consideration the data produced inevitably reproduces the inequity of the status quo, for it has no mechanism to question and to visualize what might be a just situation.

Positivistic process-product researchers, for example, have shown that most teachers react to student responses, whether correct or incorrect, in very much the same way. Researchers have counted and categorized teacher responses to student answers in class; one study reported that in over three out of four incorrect student responses teachers made positive comments. Researchers labeled such statistics as irrational and bizarre and indicative of teacher inconsistency and weakness. When one abandons the physical scientific, positivistic interest in counting long enough to examine contextual and ethical factors, a very different picture of this teacher behavior emerges. The multi-dimensionality of classroom life demands particular forms of coping strategies from teachers. Teacher communication with students has to do with many more factors than simply supplying praise for correct answers and corrective responses for incorrect answers. The teacher has to juggle a myriad of concerns simultaneously, ranging from factual consistency on the part of students, to interpersonal sensitivity, to teacher accountability in regard to bureaucratic demands, to maintenance of a viable learning environment. Upon deeper analysis the so-called inconsistency of providing positive responses to incorrect answers is not so bizarre after all (Doyle, 1977:178).

Feminist educational researchers are painfully aware of the 'quick and dirty' nature of physical science-oriented, positivistic research and its simplistic view of human behavior and education. The most illustrative examples involve studies which ignore gender differences or look at gender as simply a causal factor not taking into account the existence of other variables in the situation. When positivistic research ignores the wider context and the multitude of other variables which attend it, the conclusions drawn from such studies typically suggest innate differences (often hierarchical) between the sexes. Studies, for instance, that look only at gender differences in math achievement might discover (accurately) that boys do better than girls on particular standardized math tests. By not examining the results contextually, not pursuing explanatory factors, positivistic researchers fail to consider the panoply of reasons for the different scores. Appealing to the accuracy of their statistics as authority, researchers fail to confront the quick and dirty simplicity of their research design. Thus, 'what is' appears to be only what has to be; the public is provided with further 'proof' that boys are naturally better than girls in math (Jayaratne, 1982:152–3).

Non-positivistic, critical, qualitative educational researchers might describe their approach to inquiry as methodological humility. As opposed to the quick and dirty positivist who seeks concrete structures and validated data which can be used to make predictions, the humble researcher practices a form of inquiry which is humble in the sense that it respects the complexity of the socio-educational world. Humility in this context is not self-depreciating nor does it involve the silencing of one's voice; humility implies a sense of the unpredictability of the educational microcosm and the capriciousness of the consequences of one's inquiry. Methodological humility is an inescapable characteristic of a postmodern world marked by a loss of faith in scientific salvation and the possibility of a single frame of reference, a common vantage point from which we might all view the world. Methodological humility eschews the positivistic impulse to dominate the world through a knowledge of it. Though it was on the *lam* for a long time, positivistic science can no longer escape the creeping skepticism that dominates our postmodern conversations about almost everything else (Ruddick, 1980:351; Aronowitz, 1983:60).

Schulamit Reinharz is always helpful in analyzing the failure of positivism in educational research. The use of questionnaires, she contends, which force a 'yes', 'no', or 'no opinion' is an example of the positivistic distortion of the socio-educational lived world. Using such instruments positivistic researchers substitute a controlled reality, a social situation with its own conventions and rules for the ambiguity of the world of schools. They make a serious conceptual error when they correlate respondents' answers to questionnaires (responses peculiar to the controlled situation of being questioned about their attitudes) to their attitudes in another, completely different social situation, the lived world of their workplace, their teaching situation. Reinharz appreciated the limitations of such questionnaires when she tried to answer the questions herself. She could not answer the questions seriously for her feelings and thoughts were not capable of being translated into simple, codable responses. Like the educational lived world, her attitudes were subtle, often ill-defined and were capable of being discovered and articulated only in dialogue with friends or during silent introspection (Reinharz, 1979:73–4).

Positivistic research, then, is inappropriate in a practitioner field such as education — it simply does not produce insights relevant to the professional life of the teacher. Positivistic educational research is limited in the sense that its language, the language of propositions, does not speak to the practitioner. Propositional language is concerned with the specification of the criteria by which statements about the world can be verified or refuted. The needs of a teacher transcend the language of propositions, for they revolve around the particularity of certain entities: the creativity of *one* child, the 'feel' of a child's anger or affection, the ambiance of a classroom full of students captivated by a lesson. This is the stuff of teacher knowledge; and this is precisely the type of thing that positivistic propositional language cannot address. It is irrelevant in such contexts for it cannot capture the subtleties of interpersonal emotion — these subtleties which expose the essence of the teaching act (Eisner, 1984:451–2). Simply put, positivistic measurements or frequency studies cannot convey a nuanced understanding or feeling for the individuals and social contexts under observation. In its quest for propositional generalization positivistic research misses an essential point: for the practitioner it is often the infrequent behaviors, the deviations from the general tendency that are most important to pedagogy (Mies, 1982:146; Doyle, 1977:168–9).

Positivistic research is also inappropriate in educational contexts since teachers do not 'own' such inquiry. The positivistic impulse renders research inaccessible to teachers in that it prevents teachers from conducting their own research. The practicalities of school life preclude teachers from collecting the number of samples that the method requires, not to mention the time it takes to process the copious data demanded. Only trained professional researchers have the time or interest to engage in such research. Because of their status-superiority relative to the practitioner, the professional researcher sets the research agenda, formulating questions primarily of interest to him or her. Thus, the practitioner is excluded; the professional researcher is the real proprietor of the inquiry — indeed, the professional researcher becomes both producer and consumer of the knowledge gleaned. Practitioners are the passive objects that are acted upon; they are invalidated as reflective teachers (Van den Berg and Nicholson, 1989:12–13; Tripp, 1988:2). This is one of the many obvious reasons that the concept of teachers as researchers is so valuable.

Not only is the teacher excluded from ownership of research in a positivistic context, but such an orientation dictates our idea of what constitutes a professional in education. We are left with a notion of the professional teacher as technician — the hard-to-qualify concept of professional wisdom or artistry does not fit into the schema. Thus, teacher education programs retreat into a vicious circle of technical rationality focusing on a 'how-to' curriculum which promotes general methods of teaching. Practicing teachers are judged along the lines of technical criteria — a procedure which tends to erode their professional autonomy as they scramble in the name of accountability to meet their superiors' expectations of competence. In such a context the idea of a self-regulating professional who conducts research into his or her own practice is quite out of place. Why should teachers engage in such activities, the positivists ask, when educational science has produced a knowledge base and researchers know which procedures work? (Schon, 1987:314–16). But the positivists are wrong. Qualitative research in education over the last decade has challenged the efficacy of research designed to uncover the generic features of effective classrooms. What works in one classroom may not be effective in another (Strickland, 1988:757). The development of particular learning skills is situation specific — the entire effort of positivism to develop verified, generalizable knowledge about educational practice may be inappropriate.

When positivists argue that nothing which is not practically demonstrable can be regarded as truth, we are forced to assume that a truth's practical demonstrability revolves around the ability to generalize it. Any particular human behavior is motivated by a panoply of unobservable factors (Odi, 1981:53, 57). If the positivists' goal is to make generic statements about what constitutes an effective educational practice, then even within their own microcosm of logic such an attempt is misguided. There is no way in human situations to control the unobservable factors. If such factors are uncontrollable then generalization is impossible. The implications here are frightening. If positivistic generalization in human situations is impossible, then what forces shape the generalizations that are made by positivistic educational researchers? This is where the Frankfurt School of critical theory has had so much to offer educational researchers. It is the Frankfurt School's notion of ideology which informs our understanding of the political interests of positivism — ideology involving world views unknown to even the researchers themselves which shape the assumptions they bring to the inquiry (Habermas, 1970:81–122; Grady and Wells, 1985–1986:34–5). Werner Heisenberg had a similar idea when he maintained that 'what we observe is not nature itself, but nature exposed to our method of questioning' (Lincoln and Guba, 1985:98). The questions emerge from the ideological preconceptions of the researcher. When researchers are unaware of the very presence of ideology, then they cannot be aware of the ways it shapes their research.

The last decade has witnessed valuable work by critical theorists in education who have argued that the attempt to dispense with values, historical circumstance, and political considerations in educational research is misguided. Our understanding of an educational situation depends on the context within which we encountered it and the theoretical frames which the researcher brought to the observation. These ideological frames are the glasses through which we see the world — they are not subject to empirical verification. Positivism tells us that as researchers we must be non-partisan, we must serve no particular cause; but we have come to realize that every historical period produces particular rules that dictate what counts as a scientific fact. Different rules privilege different causes — facts are generated, they are not just 'out there' waiting to be discovered (Aronowitz, 1983:60; Elliott, 1989a:214). Thus, the implicit rules which guide our generation of facts about education are formed by particular world views, values, political perspectives, conceptions of race, class, and gender relations, definitions of intelligence — i.e., ideology. Research, then, can never be non-partisan for we must choose the rules which guide us as researchers; critical theory's disclosure of the hidden ideological assumptions within social research marked the end of our innocence.

Thus, positivistic research in the name of rigorous method and a hard realism about the nature of the world fails to recognize the forces which work to shape research. Not only is the researcher isolated from the forces that shape him or her but that being researched is isolated from the conditions that grant it meaning. So-called scientific controls help achieve a more perfect isolation of the educational setting being studied. In this controlled context attention to circumstances surrounding the object of the study must be temporarily suspended. This suspension of attention is based on the interesting assumption that these extraneous circumstances will remain static long enough to allow the study to be validated; these extraneous circumstances, of course, never remain static. Research isolated in this way from its context can never be validated (Longstreet, 1982:136).

Yet research of this type continues to dominate the field of education. Most attempts by educational researchers, even here at the end of the twentieth century, to study something as contextually contingent as, say, the growth of human understanding have been made outside of natural settings, such as classrooms. Researchers have followed the rules of research laid down by positivism and opted for controlled settings, e.g., laboratories, clinics, or research institutes. It seems obvious that such settings could not allow for a textured picture of the growth of human understanding. Any research strategy that locks the subject of the study within the confines of the laboratory, or is satisfied with partial photographs of isolated events at a particular point in time, insults the subject by denying its complexity, its multi-dimensionality. The laboratory upsets the educational environment so dramatically that the outcomes observed in a controlled setting may have meaning only in the confines of another laboratory. Are we to be suprised when the results of such studies are so often replicated in one laboratory setting after another? Thus, in the positivistic isolation of the laboratory researchers learn about situations that are short-lived and would rarely appear in a natural educational setting (Armstrong, 1981:15; Lincoln and Guba, 1985:179, 190–1). What exactly have we learned? Not much about education as it occurs in the lived world, I'm afraid. Couldn't teachers have told us this about research a long time ago?

But we must remember the origins of positivism to explain the absurdity of its application in education. Comte and the founders of positivism believed that through the process of reductionism general laws could be reduced to propositions that could then be verified through empirical research. The goal of such knowledge was to predict and control both natural and human phenomena. In education positivism has attempted to predict the relationship between educational objects (students) and educational events (teaching). Invariably, particular rules of the research act will focus our attention on certain aspects of education and away from others — in the case of positivism our attention is focused on education as a technical act. When we measure certain portions of education to determine how well school systems, or particular schools, or particular teachers are doing, we cannot separate this question from the political issue of what schools should be doing. Therefore, if positivist researchers can establish the criteria via their research instruments that measure how well we are doing in education, they have also established what schools *should* be doing. Positivism thus becomes a political instrument of social control while its adherents are all the while proclaiming their neutrality, their disinterestedness, their disdain of mixing politics and education. And they are telling the truth — they do not even know that they are positivists! When teachers are unequipped to see beneath the surface of these claims of neutrality, they are rendered powerless. They are encouraged by the positivists in the name of professionalism to deskill themselves. They are not encouraged to acquire the wisdom to evaluate their own teaching in terms of its relationship to larger visions of educational purpose or social justice. Instead, they are expected to implement scientifically validated, and thus uncontestable, criteria of educational quality. In their and their pupils' conformity to such criteria, positivism accomplishes its insidious social control.

Any scientific orientation which seeks to control human beings cannot view humans as sacred, as very different from other, non-living objects of scientific research. Thus, the human is viewed as an entity to be tailored to fit the proper social order. People are subordinated to a controlled environment where values are seen as non-rational, as outside the realm of science. In schools this ideology of social control, this minimization of the human, is seen in practices such as labelling, homogeneous grouping, tracking, positive reinforcement, behavioral management systems, etc. (Dobson, Dobson, and Koetting, 1987:6; Noblit and Eaker, 1987:7; Porter, 1988:504; Van den Berg and Nicholson, 1989:12–13). In all of these practices complex human processes are reduced to a technical calculation of means and ends — human intentions are virtually unimportant. Humans do not simply respond to the social world. Human beings actively contribute to the creation of the world, they construct it (Lincoln and Guba, 1985:179). They base their constructions on their experiences, but positivism devalues the experience of both the subjects and objects of research. By definition, when human experience is devalued social alienation sets in. In other words, educational and social scientists have fashioned their own alienation from the world and from themselves (Yeakey, 1987:25; Reinharz, 1979:72, 78). As they devalue the role of the human, positivist researchers become educational voyeurs, peering at the school through binoculars, never experiencing the situation themselves, never knowing what it really feels like.

But these voyeurs are the experts. Our happy model of teachers doing research on their practices and the world of the school does not fit into the positivistic microcosm of authoritarianism and hierarchy. The culture of positivism fosters the notion of the researcher as expert — an expert anointed by the holiness of science. The cult of the expert succeeds because it is blessed by the 'scientific neo-divinity'. With such blessing the positivist researcher enters the school with little need for interpersonal skills. Indeed, such skills may be an impediment; interpersonal distance is important in the pursuit of objectivity. The researcher has been brought to the school by the school administration and uses that relationship to define his or her interaction with the teachers. Thus, the social relations between outside researcher and teachers at the research site are well-defined in terms of a patron-client framework. The researcher is the client of the patron sponsor (the administrative staff). He or she must show deference and fidelity to the administrators during the contract negotiations in order to gain access to the schools and to maintain power and credibility during the final processes of conclusions and recommendations (Noblit and Eaker, 1987:7; Van den Berg and Nicholson, 1989:12).

The framework represents the 'top-down' approaches to educational change and to workplace reform that have characterized positivistic scientific management strategies of the twentieth century. In this framework teachers are seen as the targets of research and often as the research problem to be solved. Such a set-up inevitably results in exploitive relations between the researcher and the teachers. Teachers are often coached by administrators before the researcher comes on how to answer questions. Teacher guilt is tapped by administrative announcements that the data derived from the study will be used to improve the school. The conception of school improvement utilized in this context is disturbing in its paternalism: if something needs improvement we do not draw upon the strengths of our own staff for the solution, we hire an outside researcher to question the participants and make recommendations. Change will thus be imposed; it will not be based on the experiences of those who actually teach the children. As a result, teachers are delegated a secondary position, reduced to the role of respondents to a researcher's questionnaire. Peering in from their voyeuristic perspective, the researchers use their 'instruments' to collect data that will be employed to change the workplace for teachers (Jayaratne, 1982:146; Reinharz, 1979:72, 78).

Such exploitive relationships between researchers and teachers are possible only in a social context where science has enjoyed the status of the sacred. The more obscure its propositional, mathematical language becomes to the layperson, the more it is seen as something holy, something authoritative. We are shocked when we stop and examine how much scientific authority shapes our daily lives. Late industrial culture teaches us to revere science and the scientific method unscientifically. The authoritative voice of positivist science silences our natural language — the way *we* talk about schools and our professional lives as teachers. The worth of such language is undermined by a view of science which regards it as soft, effeminate, impressionistic, and non-scientific. Cowed by the authority of positivistic science, we accede to its demands and humbly allow it to define our role as mere practitioner (Aronowitz, 1983:60; Koller, 1981:108; Eisner, 1984:452).

The salient point here is that empowered teachers as researchers need to understand that research is not simply a way of gathering data. A society's or a profession's orientation toward research makes more of a cultural impact than we might at one time have imagined (Aronowitz, 1983:60). There is a direct connection between the shape of our professional lives as teachers, our schools, and how we consider the research act. Such a connection pushes the topic of research to the center of our discourse about a democratic transformation of schooling. This is the importance of positivism to our exploration of the teacher as researcher — its centrality, invisible though it may be, to making schools what they are at the end of the twentieth century. Look at the schools in the 1990s — even though much progress had been made in universities around the world in theorizing alternatives to positivist research, schools are still directed by positivist assumptions.

Teachers are subjected to positivist empirical expectations. Student scores on competitive tests are used to measure the performances of teachers. The number of graduate courses amassed determine teacher pay. I.Q.'s and grades categorize students. Student knowledge is based on the notion of replication rather than interpretation, as students are deemed 'to know' only when they can display a fragment of data at a teacher's bidding. Schools reflect positivist assumptions when they affirm that the most significant aspects of school can be measured. In their positivist tunnel-vision objective tests deny students a chance to transcend the reductionism of measurability, they cannot in this context respond creatively, develop a relationship between their lived experience and the information, or learn intrapersonally by establishing a personal position on the issue. Such an approach encourages a stimulus-response reflex, erasing the totality of the person from the learning process. In the positivistically defined school, student subjectivity is viewed with suspicion if not hostility. Students seeking self-definition and clarification of their identity are injected into a context that is externally oriented, rewarding efficiency and economic expedience (McMahon, 1970:515–17). The process of self-discovery, emancipation, creative consciousness can no more be measured than can a child's curiosity. The teacher who understands the learning process, the field being taught, the students involved, the social context in which learning takes place and acts as a self-directed, reflective professional is often in danger of administrative rebuke.

One finds little challenge to the authority of the culture of positivism in the schools of the 1990s. The traditional conservative-liberal dichotomy in political analysis does not help (it actually impedes) our attempt to analyze and address the power of positivism in education. Both conservatives and liberals have been uncritical of the culture of positivism. The failure of late twentieth century liberalism is directly connected to its inability to understand the underside of scientific hyper-rationality (Giroux, 1988:53–60). Indeed, the cult of the expert has grown in a liberal soil. Social engineering finds some of its most important historical roots in university departments of sociology with their liberal visions of the good life (Bourricaud, 1979:14–16). In the last thirty years this liberal vision has fallen into disrepute around the world. The brief challenge to professional authority of the late 1960s was as much anti-liberal as it was anti-conservative. One of the keys to understanding the success of right-wing movements of the 1970s and 1980s was the right-wing cooption of the anti-authority rhetoric of the 1960s counterculture, translating it into the anti-government rhetoric of Reagan, Bush and Thatcher and the anti-educational expert rhetoric of William Bennett. They were able to portray the domain of the expert as a liberal domain. If we are to be successful in our attempt to critique positivism and those positivists who hide behind anti-positivist labels, we will have to move beyond liberalism with its blindness to the various ways that the poor, the non-white, and women are dominated and its concurrent blindness to the underside of western science.

The critically-grounded teacher-as-researcher movement is designed to provide teachers with the analytical tools to overcome such conservative and liberal blindnesses. Researching teachers would possess the ability to challenge the culture of positivism, exposing the origins of many of the constraints which obstruct their ability to implement educational strategies that respond to the experiences and lived worlds of students from all backgrounds. But even the action research projects which have been established are not free from the blindnesses of modern conservatism and modern liberalism and the culture of positivism. Many of the conceptions of teachers as researchers are informed by a form of liberalism which supposes that teachers can bring about change without recognition of the historical, social, and epistemological dimensions of educational change (Van den Berg and Nicholson, 1989:18; Tripp, 1988:15). Critical theory's critique of power relations and modernity's conception of science is an invaluable tool in formulating our view of teacher empowerment through teacher research. In subsequent portions of this work we will explore in greater detail the implications of the critical perspective on research. The challenge of critical analysis is extremely valuable to practicing educational researchers. The critical theorists dare us to look beyond common sense, to challenge accepted definitions, to uncover manifestations of hidden power, to break the tacit codes of human meaning, and to search for new and more appropriate methods of researching the lived world of education.

Chapter 4

What Constitutes Knowledge?

What we refer to as knowledge is problematic. Human knowledge, knowledge about humans, and knowledge derived from research about human education is constituted by a variety of forces. In this section let us contemplate the nature of this complex notion in light of its effect on educational research. We might start with the idea that any research strategy presupposes an epistemological stance. It is our charge to interrogate that stance.

One task of epistemology is to provide theories of the nature of knowledge, of its genesis and its justification. Traditionally, scholars have assumed that once we were conversant with theories of knowledge we would be better prepared to proceed with our research. These diverse theories of knowledge, of course, conflict with one another over the definition of true knowledge; indeed, some epistemologies deny even the possibility of true knowledge. Nevertheless, different epistemologies promote different forms of knowledge along with different methodologies and ways of knowing. Thus, we accept religious knowledge and ways of knowing, ethical knowledge and ways of knowing, and linguistic knowledge and ways of knowing.

In the social sciences and in educational studies scholars in the last two decades have been confronted with an epistemological crisis. The crisis has produced some difficult questions for researchers: What is the proper method of pursuing social and educational knowledge?; and, What constitutes knowledge in these domains? There is great dissatisfaction among social scientists and educational researchers with the positivistic definitions of knowledge — though the discomfort is not by any means universal. Among the uncomfortable, no consensus has been reached on a new definition of social knowledge.

As students of metatheory in social science have in the last couple of decades become more and more aware of the social construction of what we call knowledge, they have begun to realize that research findings are largely specific to the method or methods utilized. The uniqueness of the data obtained from each method of inquiry has led to the existence of separate bodies of knowledge in the social sciences. Even when the same event is studied via a variety of methods, the information obtained often has little covariation. In other words, researchers using different methodologies share so little common ground that they have no way to relate their disparate findings.

When a particular intelligence test, for example, is examined by a critical sociologist and an educational statistician divergent analyses emerge. To the critical sociologist the test reflects an unexamined set of socio-economic assumptions about the nature of intelligence. To the statistician the test may suffer from internal inconsistency, i.e., its rank order of individuals relative to their intelligence differs from other intelligence tests. Thus, it is a flawed instrument. The point, of course, is that depending on the paradigm and the purpose of the researcher what constitutes our 'knowledge' about this test may vary widely. The possibility for covariation or the recognition of interrelation by the scholars operating from the diverse paradigms is, unfortunately, limited.

Metatheorists argue that social science will continue to develop many diverse bodies of knowledge in the future. It thus becomes the task of the educational researcher to understand both the various ways this knowledge is produced and the specific forces which contribute to its production. The *Zeitgeist* influences knowledge production as it directs our attention to certain problems and potentialities — e.g., the questions of equity emerging from the civil rights movement, of the nature of fundamentalism coming from the rise of the New Right, or of gender bias growing out of the women's movement.

As the *Zeitgeist* changes, some bodies of knowledge go out of fashion and are forgotten for the time being. Other bodies of knowledge are shelved because they seem to be tied to one particular methodology and/or are not amenable to extension into different contexts. Of course, other bodies of knowledge persist, transcending the concerns of a particular *Zeitgeist* as they influence educational analysis in some way or another, generation after generation. Thus, social knowledge is vulnerable to the ebb and flow of time with the changing concerns and emotional swings of the eras. This vulnerability to the temporal will probably continue, for social science shows no sign of developing consistent universal strategies for evaluating the validity of these various forms of knowledge. Indeed, such a unified strategy would probably be positivistic in scope (Fiske, 1986:68–71).

To put the point simply, what we designate as knowledge is fickle, subject to change given our context and interest. The best illustration of this concept was presented by Jürgen Habermas in his theory of cognitive interests (or knowledge-constitutive interests). The premise on which the theory rests involves the idea that knowledge cannot be separated from human interests. Knowledge, he argued, in the nineteenth and twentieth centuries has become a product of an empirical-analytic methodology — the positivistic tradition. 'Where did this methodology arise?', he asks. Did it just emerge from trial and error? Habermas bases his theory on the answer to these questions.

There are three forms of knowledge, Habermas maintains, and all three exist as a result of specific historical circumstances. As humans struggle to survive and confront the problems which challenge them, they develop particular concerns (interests) which determine their definition of knowledge. The three forms of knowledge are based on: 1) the technical interest — data which increases the human power of technical control; 2) the practical interest — information which allows for people to be understood symbolically; and 3) the emancipatory interest — information which helps bring about human autonomy by the analysis of distorted communication activities (critical knowledge) (Keat, 1981:4–6; MacDonald, 1975:286–7). Let us examine these interests in a little more detail. The understanding of the implicit interests which help humans define the nature of what is called knowledge is an important step in making sense of *how* research is conducted in education and *what* it tells us.

1 *The technical interest.* This interest is based on an understanding of the human's role as a tool-making animal who survives via his or her use of the natural world. Thus, humans have a need for knowledge which contributes to the control of natural processes — technically useful knowledge. In this empirical-analytic mode of knowing, particular phenomena are classified under general categories. When one examines phenomena with these categories in mind, knowledge is produced which enables researchers to duplicate conditions and to reproduce results. Thus, the technical interest is served as empirical-analytic knowledge is used to predict patterns of events. Such predictability allows for a measure of control. Thus, positivism is a child of the technical interest. It is not inappropriate, Habermas concludes, to study phenomena (even social phenomena) in this manner. The point is that researchers who are tied *exclusively* to this procedure are incapable of comprehending the social world.

2 *The practical interest.* This interest is based on an understanding of humans as language-using beings. Human beings need a form of knowledge which would allow them to communicate with their fellows through the employment of mutually-understood symbols. Such communication allows for the development of common traditions and the practical action which would emerge from such commonality. Thus, the hermeneutical sciences are an outgrowth of the practical interest. Habermas argues that the hermeneutical study of language fails at times to comprehend the ways that language hides the conditions of social life. Indeed, he argues that

language sometimes serves as a force for domination and as a means of legitimizing power interests. The attempt to expose such ideological characteristics of language is not a concern of the practical interest.

3   *The emancipatory interest.* This interest goes beyond the technical interest of controlling objects in the environment and the practical interest of fostering intersubjective understanding. The emancipatory interest, Habermas argues, is concerned with a form of knowledge which leads to freedom from dominant forces and distorted communication. Assuming that history is marked by domination and repression, Habermas tells us that emancipation and self-knowledge are restricted by often unrecognized conditions. If humans are to unleash their rational capacities, a special form of knowledge is necessitated to abolish these hidden impediments. The emancipatory interest promotes a relationship between knowledge and interest that is quite different from the ones promoted by the technical and practical. Unlike the other two interests, the emancipatory interest connects the act of knowing with the immediate utilization of knowledge. The act of knowing is a form of self-reflection that allows an individual to gain an awareness of the connection between knowledge and interest. Habermas contends that if we are to understand research we must pursue the emancipatory nature of critical theory which dissolves the dominant forces which separate humans from an understanding of their own histories and contexts — not to mention the forces which limit the self-understanding and social awareness of those who conduct research (Held, 1980:254–5, 297–317).

How has this technical interest (the form of knowledge which lays the basis for Giroux's culture of positivism) come to exert such an important influence on the ways we define knowledge and the ways we conduct social and educational research? Habermas attempts to answer the question by outlining what he calls the dissolution of epistemology. Post-Enlightenment thought, with its emphasis on the technical interest of knowledge, turned away from the examination of the conditions which inform our definitions of knowledge. Epistemology dissolved into a restricted examination of questions about the technique of research. The scientific idealist concern with the role of the knower (often called the epistemic subject) in the process faded away. Epistemology could not question the meaning or social role of science because there was no recognized form of knowledge independent of science which could be used to analyze and criticize scientific endeavor. Habermas hopes that his theory of the interests which determine the forms of knowledge will help re-establish the critical dimension of epistemology.

What would Habermas's reassertion of critical epistemology imply for the ways we define knowledge and conduct educational research? Hopefully, the attempt of this present work to examine the relationship between teachers and research in education is an extension of Habermas's hope for epistemological introspection. Teachers as researchers who are familiar with the philosophical, historical, and political context in which inquiry takes place, will, I believe be better able to understand their roles as producers of knowledge. Hopefully, consumers of educational research who understand this context will be better equipped to evaluate the various assumptions which underlie the research they read. In addition both producers and consumers of research will be more familiar with the impact exerted on the lives of teachers, students, and the public when the 'knowledge' derived from research seeps into our world view and our practice. Further discussion may help illustrate the value of Habermas's conception of epistemological self-analysis on the part of the researcher.

A research orientation which Habermas might argue results from the absence of epistemological reflection is sometimes called methodological unitarianism. Advocates of such a stance would argue that all research calling itself scientific must utilize the classical method of the natural sciences. Knowledge here is scientific knowledge. Many students of research epistemology would argue that such a position is marked by a philosophical flaw. The flaw would result from the fact that in social research utilizing an empirical physical science methodology the unobservable and mental are eliminated from consideration. Moreover, it is argued that this unobservable and mental dimension (the non-empirical) is possibly the most important aspect of social and educational research (Frankel, 1986:353–4; Howe, 1985:14; Held, 1980:254, 259; Eisner, 1983:23).

This methodological unitarianism has resulted in positivism in theory and practice as social and educational researchers have emulated the methods of physical science research. When researchers fail to reflect on the interests and assumptions behind knowledge, inquiry becomes a means of acquiring information that can be used for social engineering. The capacity of researchers to think beyond the technical interest is severely impaired. Problems are reduced to the cause-effect rationality of empirical science. As this takes place social knowledge is viewed as a tool to control not nature but people themselves. Thus, humans might be understood, used, and controlled just like any other *thing*.

The objects of social research, humans, possess a special complexity which sets them apart from other objects of study. This complexity precludes the possibility of research neatness desired by physical scientists. The variables with which the social researcher is forced to contend dispel any illusions of methodological simplicity of outcome and applicability (Eisner, 1983:23; Soltis, 1984:6; Baldwin, 1987:17; Popkewitz, 1981b:310). To the positivist this lack of a precise, simple outcome is not precipitated by the special nature of the subjects of social research but is caused by a deficiency or a lack of rigor in particular social science research methods. When educational research is marked by ambiguity and disagreement, the positivists blame the research strategy. To the positivist the untidiness of social knowledge is a fatal flaw (Shweder and Fiske, 1986:13).

If social researchers are blind in their application of physical scientific methods to complex social phenomena, they stand to miss the essence of the meaning of the social world. These epistemologically unreflective researchers will fail to recognize that in the natural sciences observations are imposed on the objects being observed. Natural scientists do not have to consider the thoughts of their objects of study or their history and socio-cultural context. Such a situation requires a research methodology which differs from the classical method of the physical sciences. Critical social researchers will choose strategies of inquiry which recognize the ambiguity of the human condition, the nature of knowledge, the importance of context, the fact that the outcomes of the inquiry may not be quantifiable or replicable, and that the method chosen may produce knowledge which profoundly promotes specific conceptions of man and certain value orientations.

Science and scientific methodology are cultural artifacts. Though most people fail to understand it, the techniques of science affect most institutions, especially education, in some way or another. The techniques seep into our thinking process, covertly dictating our perceptions of reality and knowledge (Popkewitz, 1981b:301). Dominant conceptions of science influence the questions we ask about education, our definitions of intelligence, the phenomena we deem worthy or unworthy of study, and ultimately the very fabric of school life. An example of this influence is in order. Take the discussion of 'basics education' which has permeated educational conversations for the last fifteen years. The discussion of the basics has often been tacitly informed by a positivistic epistemology with its accompanying set of assumptions, concerns, and *way of knowing*. The everyday use of the term 'basics' implies a view of knowledge which is grounded in scientific realism. Knowledge is an entity which is out there, quantifiable, measurable, and capable of being purchased, distributed, and acquired. 'Basics talk' assumes the desire of educators to be efficient, objective, dispassionate, business-like, and accountable.

The basics mind-set promotes a technical view of knowledge — i.e., information which is essential, neutral, and detached from the knower. There is a specific body of knowledge to be learned, the technical view asserts, and there are specific methods of teaching and learning it. The conversation about the basics is impatient with uncertainty, the concern with the genesis of knowledge, epistemological quibbling, and the complex interaction between knower and known. The positivistic search for certainty and knowledge rooted in Habermas's technical interest (which in this case serves the imperative of technological progress) lays the foundation on which the house of basics-talk has been constructed. In other words, basics-talk is legitimized by the positivistic conception of scientific methodology (van Manen, 1978:56–7).

An example of the positivistic view of educational knowledge as physical scientific knowledge may be helpful at this point. The immediate origin or many of the research-based reforms of the last twenty-five years can be traced to the Great Society education programs of the Johnson administration. Before they would appropriate the funds to implement compensatory programs for disadvantaged students Congress demanded a rigid system of accountability. Thus, evaluation of some form was deemed essential.

The system of evaluation which was adopted reflected the ideological assumptions of systems analysis and cost-benefit analysis techniques which gained popularity in the Pentagon in the mid-1960s. The positivistic epistemology of the systems analysts imposed a physical scientific view of knowledge on educational research that continues to help define the parameters of educational inquiry. The identification of efficient educational programs became a central concern of the federal leaders in education at the time (House, 1978:388).

Senator Robert Kennedy was in part responsible for the accountability features which would accompany compensatory programs. Kennedy demanded a scientific system of reporting the effects of the new programs. Economically disadvantaged parents, especially poor black parents, he argued, deserved access to the statistics on how their children were doing. The Senator reasoned that these statistics (in the form of standardized test scores) would hold school officials accountable to their constituents. With its faith in the validity of test scores, Kennedy's plan was undoubtedly flawed. But his purpose was to help parents of children in need of compensatory education become informed participants in the educational process.

Kennedy's intentions were lost, however, when President Johnson announced in August 1965 that he was introducing the Planning, Programming, and Budgeting System (PPBS) throughout the federal bureaucracies. In the Department of Health, Education, and Welfare (HEW) a new office was created, entitled the Assistant Secretary for Program Evaluation. It was filled by William Gorham who had helped implement PPBS in the Department of Defense. Along with his assistants Alice Rivlin (who would later take Gorham's place) and Robert Grosse, Gorham attempted to 'develop goals that could be stated, measured, and evaluated in cost-benefit terms'. Gorham, Rivlin, and Grosse were not interested in Senator Kennedy's attempt to make the schools responsive to local parents. They viewed the evaluation problem as a research effort to identify efficient approaches to educating disadvantaged children (House, 1978:389).

Congress passed the Elementary and Secondary Education Act with all of its accountability provisions. Gorham, Rivlin, and Grosse saw Title I which emerged from it as a 'natural experiment' which would facilitate the identification of the most effective methods of teaching. These 'best methods' would be passed on to teachers and administrators so that resources would ultimately be allocated in an efficient manner. They would remedy teachers' ignorance of what works — scientific research would provide the positive knowledge needed to improve teaching practice.

Problems emerged, however. Even though the systems analysts had won the battle to require an evaluation stipulation for all subsequent social and educational legislation, they came to find out that educators were not equipped to provide the uniform data necessary to complete the cost-benefit analysis procedures necessary to determine which programs were efficient. Programs, the systems analysts argued, would have to be arranged in a manner that would facilitate evaluation. This attempt spread to other levels of government in the following years. Educational research was thus profoundly affected. Indeed, educational practice was affected. State after state has adopted reform movements which incorporated positivistic systems analysis-based assumptions about educational evaluation, knowledge, and research. A closer examination of these assumptions is in order.

Alice Rivlin soon emerged as the most important theoretician and spokesperson for the systems analysts. In 1971 she laid out her assumptions about social and educational research quite explicitly in *Systematic Thinking for Social Action*. Before any policy-producing research can take place, Rivlin argued, educational experts must identify the objectives of education. Such a pronouncement is reminiscent of the accountant's advice on how to become a millionaire who pays no taxes — first, get a million dollars. Neither task is deemed problematic. The deep differences over educational goals which divide the public and educators are ignored. Rivlin is guided by the assumption that educational experts can dictate educational objectives because of the social consensus over what schools should do. 'I believe there is a wide measure of agreement in the nation ... about desirable directions of change', Rivlin wrote. Differences between the right, the middle, and the left over social and educational policies do not involve the objectives of such policies. Rivlin and her systems analysts soulmates did not see a world where different groups competed for power and resources. The educational interests of rich and poor, management and labor, black and white, and men and women were basically the same. The historical and contextual nature of social scientific knowledge was not understood by Rivlin (Rivlin, 1971:46–7).

The important goals of education are not only easily identified, Rivlin continued, but they are capable of being measured. Reading proficiency, mathematical competencies, and the acquired knowledge of certain subjects can be illustrated by standardized test scores. Thus, she reasoned, we need to 'focus on these measurable outcomes' and how best to produce them. Goals are already determined; let us turn our attention to the identification of the most efficient methods of improving our scores (Rivlin, 1971:69–70). When faced with the failure of her evaluation studies in 1968 and 1969 to detect a cause-effect relationship between educational policies and test score improvement, Rivlin did not abandon her attempt to identify efficient methods. The problem, she argued, was that social services and education were not organized to answer properly questions of methodological efficiency. That, she concluded, would have to change (House, 1978:392).

Indeed, the goals of evaluation began to change. Once evaluations were designed to measure the success of programs; now the programs were designed to insure the success of the evaluations. In the process, Rivlin called for more governmental control of all aspects of the programs — design through evaluation. Teachers, she reasoned, did not possess the expertise to produce efficient and effective products. Ignorance of productive techniques and methodologies was the basis of the problem of delivering good education, Rivlin maintained. Experts were charged with the task of establishing a 'production function', i.e., the identification of a functional relationship between resources employed and results produced. 'Stable relationships', Rivlin wrote, 'exist between these outcomes and the 'inputs' to the educational process: different types of teachers, facilities, equipment, curriculum, and teaching methods'. Just as the engineer sought regular relationships between inputs and outputs, Rivlin's social researcher would seek similar associations in the world of education. The knowledge of education produced would be certain — it would be verifiable (Rivlin, 1971:70; House, 1978:392–5).

Rivlin's use of physical scientific and manufacturing analogies is noteworthy. Educational methods and children were viewed in the same way as raw materials in manufacturing. The analyst would arrange the methods and the children in various combinations in order to ascertain the grouping that would provide the best output. The best output in the manufacturing process was the product; in education it was the test score. The Pentagon origins of the systems analysis methods were highlighted by the phrase heard frequently in HEW during the late 1960s: 'We want the biggest bang for the buck'. What was good for missile systems and manufacturing was also good for social services and education.

Immersed in the positivistic view of knowledge of the 'Pentagon boys', Rivlin was hard pressed to understand the mind of the educator. Some of the educators she encountered were 'frightened by words like "input" and "output" production function'. School people simply do not understand the necessity of good record-keeping, she complained. Without good record-keeping it is impossible to make sense of standardized test results. Her effort to institute national standardized testing met with 'illogical' resistance. 'National testing', she reported in frustration, 'is a bugaboo of school people'. She appealed to 'commonsense'. Surely, we can measure our success in a logical way, she wrote. We can take into account changes in test scores, drop-out rates, attitudes, and so forth and use our data to determine connections between success and the methods employed. 'It seemed logical', Rivlin recollected. Most people agreed (Rivlin, 1971:80–2).

Rivlin applied this mind-set to the study of the Title I programs, but the data provided by the schools, she lamented, proved to be too scanty and imprecise. It was not merely that the programs were not designed to allow for evaluation, but, as Ernest House argues, the *'world'* was not organized properly to yield information about production functions'. It was too complex, too messy, to allow for precise identification of cause-effect relationships; it was too ambiguous, too contradictory to allow for positive knowledge. Such realities, however, did not deter Rivlin. The problem, she argued, was not with their paradigm, not with the foundations on which her research and evaluation studies were built — the problem was with the design of the Title I programs. Even with more rigorous evaluation methods, Rivlin maintained, experts would still face limitations on what they could learn about the programs. To yield information for evaluation the programs would have to be designed more scientifically. 'There was no experimental design. There were no control groups'. School people, Rivlin continued, made 'no attempt to define promising methods or approaches and try them out in enough places to test their operation under different conditions'. School people would have to learn the techniques of the physical scientific laboratory (Rivlin, 1971, pp. 83–4).

We have no choice, Rivlin argued, we must design social and educational programs as laboratory experiments — this is the *only* way to gather the information necessary to improve the effectiveness of social and educational service. The physical science approach will work, she maintained. All we have to do is delineate the treatment precisely and then control all extraneous influences. Habermas's notion of the technical interest is pervasive in this context. The knowledge which Rivlin hoped to produce would enable social scientists to duplicate conditions and to reproduce results. Thus, educational events could be predicted and controlled (Rivlin, 1971:108).

Control would be centralized in the hands of federal bureaucratic agencies. Educational laboratory experiments (Rivlin called them systematic innovations) would not happen spontaneously. An experimental strategy would take careful planning, research-based organization, and adequate funding formulae devised by a cadre of federal experts. Worshipping the cult of the expert, Rivlin wanted empirically-trained bureaucrats to design curricula, teacher training methods, and teacher recruitment policies. The voices of individual teachers were to be silenced. It will work, Rivlin proclaimed. The implementation of such policies requires centralization of decision-making, and Rivlin believed that in the last half of the twentieth century America was achieving that goal. State governments are achieving more and more control over local schools, she observed. Big-city school systems are sufficiently centralized to carry out systematic innovation on a major scale. It would take little prodding, Rivlin wrote, to encourage a success-oriented school superintendent to engage in systematic innovation. Once he was provided with the 'best new ideas in curriculum and approaches' the leader would 'map out a plan for trying the most promising ideas in a systematic way in his own system ... Why does it not happen this way?' the perplexed Rivlin wanted to know (Rivlin, 1971:92–3).

Rivlin admitted that such centralization could possibly result in bureaucratic red tape and rigidity. But there was a way to avoid such outcomes, she asserted. Accountability procedures must not focus on compliance with inputs, e.g., teaching methods, curricular arrangement, and detailed guidelines. Evaluators must focus their research on outputs, e.g., standardized test scores, drop-out rates, and school attendance statistics. Federal grant monies could be used to reward those systems which improved measurements of outcomes. School leaders would be rewarded, Rivlin maintained, just like plant managers in large corporations who are 'promoted according to sales and profits'.

Rivlin's faith in positivistic research methods and conceptions of knowledge has profound implications for those of us concerned with making teaching good work. Educational experts from the systems analyst school seek to impose research-based techniques on teachers in the place of the knowledge of teaching derived from experience, apprenticeship, and study of educational purpose. Such context-stripped research-based knowledge cannot substitute for professional knowledge — especially when teachers are researchers. Much of this professional knowledge is tacit rather than overt and can only be acquired through years of practice. Rivlin's positivistic vision of knowledge, many would argue, confuses Michael Polanyi's notion of tacit knowledge with scientific generalizations and methodological rules. If teaching could proceed only on the basis of scientific rules, teachers would be paralyzed. Teaching is like speaking, for if a speaker was to rely on research-based, formulized rules he or she would be mute (House, 1978:400; Rivlin, 1971:126–7).

The centralization of decision-making power in the hands of educational experts results in the reduction of teachers to mere executors of the experts' conceptualization of the teaching act. Teacher power and self-direction is thus undermined. Rivlin and her colleagues have expressed little embarrassment over the autocratic, controlling features of their social science. Systems analyst Charles Schultze, who would become Head of the Council of Economic Advisors in the Carter administration, openly wrote of the need to control local administrators and practitioners in order to secure their allegiance to the goals set by the experts. Fidelity to the goals would be insured by building in a set of incentives for those who comply and 'penalties [for those] who thwart social objectives' (Rivlin, 1971:121).

Arthur Wirth is not comfortable with such views of knowledge, research, and humanity itself. The positivist physical science tradition is not adequate for the study of human affairs, he argues. It treats human problems as if they can be solved only by 'one right way' — provided by rigorous application of physical science techniques. When positivism and its view of knowledge are combined with inquiry into human life, the main interest becomes the identification of the natural laws of human behavior. Once identified these laws are used to predict and control. The result of Alice Rivlin's research orientation, he reasons, is to 'translate the life world into a mathematical form'. 'Is there not something about human life that is violated deeply by such efforts?', Wirth asks (Wirth, 1983:113–39).

Henry Giroux picks up where Arthur Wirth leaves off. Arguing that knowledge is an entity which must be constantly challenged, redefined, and negotiated by all participants in social and educational settings, Giroux counsels teachers to resist the domination of the educational experts. In order to resist, teachers (and their students) must gain the ability to unveil the truth claims of the experts and to uncover the genesis of knowledge which has become official. To be critical teachers must analyze how knowledge conceals or distorts the social, political, and economic status quo. In other words, Giroux draws upon Habermas and his notion of the emancipatory interest of knowledge which leads to freedom from dominant forces and distorted communication (Giroux, 1981:104, 108, 113).

Stanley Aronowitz and Giroux use Chester Finn as a example of an educational researcher who is caught in Habermas's technical interest and the use of physical scientific, positivistic definitions of social knowledge (Aronowitz and Giroux, 1985:4). Finn argues that educators must use testing as a method insure quality in American schools. 'Hesitant to pass judgment on lifestyles, cultures, and forms of behavior', Finn writes, 'we have invited relativism into the curriculum and pedagogy'. Finn accepts the existence of a set of absolute standards which lay the foundation for a form of objective measurement of progress (Finn, 1982:32). Finn is the contemporary bearer of Rivlin and Schultze's legacy: let the experts determine the definition of quality and the goals of schooling. The cult of the expert is alive and well as teachers continue to search for their voice in the educational workplace. Knowledge of teaching practice is commodified, packaged and distributed to teachers. Teachers, in turn, are expected to take the pre-packaged knowledge of the various subjects and 'dish it out' to their passive students. If successful, students will become 'culturally literate' and 'vocationally competent'.

The educational results of the application of physical scientific views

of social and educational knowledge are often quite unfortunate. Aronowitz and Giroux charge that Finn and his soulmates have renounced the
critical intent of knowledge acquisition and education in general (Aronowitz and Giroux, 1985:9). This critical intent involves an understanding of
who we are and the forces which have shaped us. It concerns the ability to
connect the formal knowledge of schooling with the ever-changing conditions under which everyday life takes place. The ability *to connect* is
central to the critical intent of education. The evaluation techniques required by Rivlin's experimental programs are incapable of measuring the
student's or the teacher's ability to make these connections. The only
knowledge it is capable of measuring is the fragments of data which by
themselves grant us little insight into the nature of reality. In order to
compare educational techniques efficiently curricula must be standardized
and focused on the measurable. By definition the critical intent of knowledge acquisition cannot be included — it is much too imprecise, too
much subject to individual variation. The wisdom of Dewey and his
speculations on the nature of school knowledge are rendered irrelevant
by Rivlin and Finn. Consider a few of Dewey's speculations on school
knowledge and their incompatibility with the schooling-as-manufacturing
metaphors we have investigated.

Dewey was uncomfortable with what school reformers of the 1970s
and 1980s would come to call basics knowledge — a form of knowledge
we referred to previously as essential, neutral, and detached from the
knower. It is something external, Dewey wrote in 1916, a body of cogni-
tions an individual might store in a warehouse. Operating under this view
of knowledge, study becomes a process where one draws on what is in
storage. Such a perspective misses an important point, Dewey argued.
'The function of knowledge', he said, 'was to make one experience freely
available in other experiences'. At this point Dewey distinguished between
knowledge and habit. His distinction is valuable, for Dewey's description
of habit sharpens our understanding of the type of 'knowledge' which is
taught in schools when they are managed by physical scientific, positivistic research models.

When a learner has formed a habit, he or she has gained the ability to
use an experience so that effective action can be taken when he or she
faces a similar situation in the future. This is valuable, Dewey argued, for
everyone will face similar situations in the process of living. A child who
learns to solve long division problems will certainly be faced with such
problems again and again. But habit is not enough; it makes no allowance
for change of conditions, for novelty. An individual who has learned a
habit is not prepared for change and thus is vulnerable to confusion when
faced with a previously unencountered problem. The habituated skill of
the mechanic will desert him, Dewey wrote, 'when something unexpected
occurs in the running of the machine'. The man, on the other hand, who
understands the machine is the man 'who knows what he is about'. This

mechanic understands the conditions which allow a certain habit to work, and is capable of initiating action which will adapt the habit to new conditions. The type of teaching and the type of schools which engender such types of thought are far distanced from the basics schools which view all knowledge as empirically measurable.

Dewey provides another example of the difference between habit and his definition of knowledge. A primitive group of humans watch a flaming comet streak across the sky. Frightened by the spectacle, they react to it in the same way they react to other events which threaten their security. They try to scare it away as if it were a wild animal. They scream, beat gongs, and brandish weapons — reactions which to us seem absurd. The actions are so ridiculous to us that we fail to comprehend the fact that the primitives are 'falling back upon a habit in a way which exhibits its limitations'. We do not act the same way since we see the comet not as an isolated event but as part of a process. We see its connections with the astronomical system and, based on our *knowledge*, respond to its *connections* and not simply to its immediate occurrence. Knowledge based on connections, then, would view an experience as a vantage point from which a problem presented by a new experience could be considered (Dewey, 1916:335–41).

To Dewey the *content* of knowledge is what has happened, i.e., what is considered finished and settled. But the *reference* of knowledge, he argued, is the future. Knowledge in the Deweyan sense provides the means of understanding what is happening in the present and what is to be done about it. It is this aspect of Dewey's theory of knowledge which informs Aronowitz and Giroux's notion of the critical intent of education — in their words, 'the ability to connect contemporary experience to the received information that others have gained through their generalized experience' (Aronowitz and Giroux, 1985:9).

The basics proponents and the systems analysts intent on precisely measuring the 'output' of education continue to misunderstand the inexact and ever-changing nature of knowledge based on connections. Many educational thinkers, Dewey contended, deny the future reference of knowledge. These thinkers regard knowledge as an entity complete in itself. Dewey's Hegelian background, with its emphasis on the dialectic, helped move his view of knowledge beyond the 'knowledge in isolation' format. The dialectical notion of process was omnipresent in his view of the nature of knowledge. Knowledge from this perspective could never be viewed outside the context of its etymology and its relationship to other information. We only have to call to mind, Dewey wrote, what passes in our schools as acquisition of knowledge to understand how it lacks any meaningful connection with the experience of students. A person, he concluded, is reasonable in the degree to which he or she sees an event not as something isolated 'but in its connection with the common experience of mankind' (Dewey, 1916:342–3). Alice Rivlin, the systems analysts,

Chester Finn, and the basics proponents have been hard pressed to measure such a form of knowledge. Here again, positivism fails in an educational context.

When action research was rediscovered in the United Kingdom in the 1970s, the motivation for its resuscitation involved the growing acceptance of the positivistic view of knowledge with its emphasis on pre-specified measurable learning outcomes and its degradation of the role of teacher as a self-directed professional. Teachers were beginning to question the usefulness of positivism's abstract generalizations in the concrete and ambiguous situations in which they operated on a daily basis. The teachers and researchers who conceptualized this teacher-as-researcher movement began to reformulate the notion of educational research, which, they maintained, is different from empirical research just as practitioner knowledge is different from traditional scientific knowledge (Elliott, 1989a, p. 5).

Educational action research is on-going in conception rather than aimed toward the achievement of generalizable conclusions. The conclusions of the teacher as researcher would never be more than tentative generalizations always subject to revision because of their recognition of continuous contextual change and the divergence of differing teaching situations. Such research would differ from positivistic research in that it would not seek traditional methods of verification or replication — teacher research would find itself in a never-ending state of revision. In the traditional positivistic framework, the action researchers argued, too much evidence vital to the appreciation of the complexity and ambiguity of human learning situations is abandoned in the attempt to meet scientific requirements of verifiable knowledge (Elliott, 1981:1; Longstreet, 1982:147–9).

In the traditional positivistic paradigm the need for replicable generalization constricts all other purposes to which educational research might be applied. Educational research, the action researchers argue in the spirit of Dewey, must be judged afresh in new situations. General rules are not substitutes for actual experience — they are guides to reflection gleaned from experience. What constitutes an appropriate teacher action is not pre-ordained by an education deity — it is a matter of personal judgment in a particular situation. 'Generalization' takes on a different meaning for the teacher researcher than it does for the empirical researcher. Constantly confronting the idiosyncrasy of one unique situation after another, the teacher researcher would be guilty of a crude and impractical reductionism if he or she claimed to have sorted out cause and effect relationships in the classroom (Elliott, 1989a:1; Lincoln and Guba, 1985:181).

The goals of teacher research do not involve the identification of cause-effect relationships between classroom variables. From the teachers-as-researchers' perspective teaching itself is thought of as a form of research which attempts to understand the process of translating larger educational values into modes of daily practice. Such a process requires that a teacher develop an understanding of educational purpose, perferably one which is aware of its dependence upon an awareness of larger social purpose. The teacher researcher thus attempts to continuously evaluate his or her strategies for implementing those educational values deemed of worth. In the process such action research hopefully helps to redefine the crude forms of teacher evaluation presently employed by administrators and supervisors. The structure of bad work cannot hold when critical teacher research becomes common — it is simply out of philosophical alignment with the democratic grounding of teachers-as-researchers critically conceived.

It should come as no suprise to teacher educators that teachers often react quite negatively to attempts to feed them theory. Theory, in the eyes of many teachers, represents their disenfranchisement in the educational workplace, it signifies the power of researchers to define what counts as valid knowledge. Theory is threatening to teachers because it is generated by a group of status-superior outside experts who use a set of certified, official procedures to inquire into teacher practices. From these procedures generalizations are produced which often serve to delegitimize the experience of teachers.

Here theory is used in a technical context — theory about teaching as a technical act, teaching as practical skills. These practical skills of teaching cannot be ignored; indeed, they are essential to successful practice. Many educators have argued that theoretical knowledge of practical skills can be useful only after a practitioner has a set of lived classroom experiences to build on. Teachers do not gain initial knowledge of practical skills by devoting themselves to a study of the theoretical domain — one does not grasp a theoretical principle about education and then put it to use in his or her classroom. Teacher educators might want to keep these ideas in mind in designing their curricula (Torney-Purta, 1985:73; Elliott, 1989a:1).

Critical teacher research must walk very carefully around this problem of theory. Critical teacher research does not view teaching as simply a technical act, and as a result does not seek theoretical generalizations about the proper techniques to employ in the classroom. Thus, it certainly rejects positivistic attempts to generate generalizable theory about proper classroom practice. Critical teacher research especially rejects the attempt to use action research in education to produce generalizable theory. Nevertheless, critical teacher research is very concerned with the notion of the theoretical at the level of social vision and its connection to educational purpose — social theoretical questions of ethics, justice, and democracy are very important to critical researchers. William Pinar and Madeleine Grumet have written of a reconceptualized notion of theorizing, viewing it as a contemplative activity which does not seek an immediate translation into practice. Reconceptualized theory, they write, interrupts taken-for-granted understandings of our work, it allows the demands of the practical to assume a depth and complexity that respects the human condition (Pinar and Grumet, 1988:98–9). Freed from positivism, liberated from its capture by the domain of the expert, theory in critical teacher research aids practitioners in their attempt to contemplate and appreciate the complexity of their task.

But obviously not all that passes as action research in education has escaped the clutches of positivism, much has not considered the democratic implications of the research act. Many school projects have viewed teacher researchers as implementors of theoretical strategies devised by researcher experts or administrators. Teachers test how well particular strategies work through analysis of particular techniques in their own classrooms. Promoted as teacher-friendly, these projects in the name of good work actually promote a very restricted view of the role of teachers. Teachers are supporting actors, they are not capable of playing lead roles, i.e., in developing critical perspectives at the level of ideas (Connelly and Ben-Peretz, 1980:98–100). Practitioners, in this context, are still seen as mere executors. Advocates of teacher research who support this implementation orientation are quite naive when it comes to the realm of ideology. They do not realize that the act of selecting problems for teachers to research is an ideological act, an act that trivializes the role of teacher. When administrators select problems for teacher researchers to explore, they negate the critical dimension of action research.

When the critical dimension of teacher research is negated the teacher-as-researcher movement can become quite a trivial enterprise. Uncritical educational action research seeks direct applications of information gleaned to specific situations — a cookbook style of technical thinking is encouraged, characterized by recipe-following teachers. Such thinking does not allow for complex reconceptualizations of knowledge and as a result fails to understand the ambiguities and the ideological structures of the classroom. Teachers, in this context, retreat to cause–effect analysis, failing to grasp the interactive intricacy of a classroom. The point that educational problems are better understood when considered in a relational way that transcends simple linearity is missed. Thus, teacher research becomes a reifying institutional function, as teachers, like their administrators and supervisors, fail to reveal the ways that the educational bureaucracy and the assumptions which support it constrain one's ability to devise new and more emancipatory understandings of how schools work (Orteza, 1988:31; McKernan, 1988:154–7).

Teacher research is coopted, its democratic edge is blunted. It becomes a popular grassroots movement that can be supported by the power hierarchy — it does not threaten, nor is it threatened. Asking trivial questions, the movement presents no radical challenge or offers no transformative vision of educational purpose, as it acts in ignorance of deep structures of schooling such as the positivistic view of educational knowledge. Teachers are assumed to be couriers, that is, information deliverers and are accorded a corresponding lack of status in the workplace (Ruddick, 1989:9; Ponzio, 1985:39–43). Uncritical educational action research fails to recognize that inquiry must always subject its findings to assessment and some form of critical analysis — and critical analysis is always dangerous in its unpredictability and transformative character.

This data analysis aspect of critical teacher research must always be directed toward an understanding of self. In this critical context it must analyze the ideological forces which frame our views of ourselves as teachers and democratic agents. How does ideology, for instance, work to define our relationship with the teaching workplace? Teacher researchers as critical analysts search for patterns and underlying themes. As argued in Chapter 2, a system of meaning is developed which helps us separate the significant from the insignificant. This system of meaning in critical educational action research is, of course, derived from critical ways of knowing — feminist theory as a prime example. Feminist epistemology has taught us that we cannot grant dominance either to subject or context in educational research. Traditional androcentric ways of knowing such as positivism have denigrated the importance of context, thus allowing for a decontextualized research which produces a dissociated body of information and theory about education. Traditional Marxism denigrated the importance of the subject, granting dominance to context (i.e., economic base) thus producing a form of economic determinism. The feminist system of meaning grants us an analytic device which allows us to expose such ideological influences in our schools, our classrooms, our consciousnesses. Through critical action research we thus come to understand the insidious ways that ideology shapes our self-images, our definitions of professionalism.

Chapter 5

Purposes of Research: The Concept of Instrumental Rationality

In a natural context unaffected by the ideology of positivism teachers decide what needs to be learned in their classes, how to help children learn it, and how such learning might then be assessed. In a positivistic system we know that the quality of our teaching and student learning will be tested and measured even if it is never clearly specified what exactly constitutes the purpose of testing. Even if the tests serve to fragment, narrow, deflect, and trivialize the curriculum, we still must use them because accurate scientific measurement takes precedence over such curricular considerations. This positivistic obsession with measurement, exemplified by the basics-talk discussion in Chapter 4, forces us to assume for the sake of testing efficiency that there is a specific body of knowledge to be learned, and there are specific methods of teaching and learning it.

Such an assumption forces us to accept without question that the specific body of knowledge to be learned is valid, that it belongs in our classrooms. Teachers and educational researchers need not trouble themselves with inquiry about the constituent interests of this knowledge. Educational researchers need only concern themselves with empirical investigations of how best to teach this information. If we manipulate this variable in this specific way, do students acquire more or less of the knowledge? Thus, many would argue, educational issues in this positivistic framework are reduced to technical issues. Questions of ends or purposes are subservient to questions of means or techniques. Critical theorists have labelled this tendency 'instrumental rationality'. Advocates of critical qualitative approaches to educational research argue that the purpose of educational activity must always be an integral aspect of the research process.

When teacher researchers separate purpose from educational research the tendency to break learning into discrete pieces considered in isolation is perpetuated. In the instrumental rationality of James Mill's 'mental mechanics', through Edward Tichener's structuralism, to behavioral objectives and componential objectives, educators have assumed that the whole was never more than merely the sum of the parts. Houses from this perspective are no more than the nails and lumber that go into them, and education is no more than the average number of objectives mastered. Many educators have referred to this fragmentation process as 'bitting'. It is not hard to imagine a classroom caught in the bitting process. Students copy information from chalkboards and overhead projectors and skim textbooks to find information fragments that would answer both the questions in the study guides and the multiple choice tests. Children listen (when they're not talking); they respond when called upon; they read fragments of the textbook; they write short responses to questions provided on worksheets. They rarely plan or initiate anything of length or conceptualize their own projects. They rarely even write essays. They are learning to be deskilled, to be passive, to be citizens who are governed, not citizens who govern. They are being taught not to seek deep structures which move events, but to examine only the surface level of appearance. They will not understand the concept of consciousness construction or the subtlety of the process of hegemony. Ideology will remain a foreign abstraction in their eyes. Those students who will transcend such blindnesses will make their emancipatory journey in spite of their classroom experiences, finding analytic inspiration outside the school context. Instrumentally-rational research serves to perpetuate the most pernicious effects of bureaucratized school practices (Bracy, 1987:684).

Just as positivism negates our view of how instruction and evaluation might take place in a natural setting, it also shapes our view of how teachers might naturally relate to the research act. In a positivistic, instrumentally-rational context we know that research produces theories which are applied to achieve specific goals. Positivistic research sets up a context where the factory model division of labor is reproduced: the researcher conceptualizes the teaching act and produces theory; the practitioner executes the directives of the researcher and applies theory. The teacher is alerted to some weak component of his or her subjective theory of education by the researcher's comparison of it to a research-grounded scientific theory. The researcher provides the teacher with a choice of scientifically-validated teaching strategies. The teacher exercises his or her professional autonomy selecting, applying, and then practicing a strategy in a supervised training session where contextual variables have been controlled.

All phases of such a process depend on an instrumentally rational concern with the measurable results of particular strategies. Does the strategy serve to raise test scores? No questions are asked of issues such as: the worth of raising the scores, the tacit view of intelligence embedded in them, the educational and political side effects of viewing their improvement as the primary goal of teaching. Value dimensions, ideological dimensions of human practice escape the vision of instrumental rationality. No room for uncertainty or spontaneous innovation exists; instrumental rationality demands that research cannot begin until agreement exists on all definitions and that a well-formed problem has been established. Research and thus teaching will proceed in line with the dictates of the well-formed problem — in modern schools the improvement of test scores often constitutes the problem. Research is reduced to the attempt to find relationships between specific teaching skills and test score improvement. We make 'remarkable' findings which are passed along to teacher education students — for example, the more time students study a particular subject, the greater the possibility that they will raise their test scores in that subject. Such a logocentrism, an embrace of reason accompanied by the exclusion of the affective, the emotional aspects of learning and knowing, forces us to focus on the least important aspects of the educational process — aspects which are inevitably the most measurable (Kroath, 1989:60–1; Eisner, 1984:450; Schon, 1987:6).

A medical analogy might be in order. In the instrumentally-rational world of positivistic medicine doctors are subjected to some of the same forces as teachers. Technological innovation in medicine has produced machines which inexorably fix the attention of both doctor and patient to those aspects of an illness which are measurable. Human dimensions of the illness which are at least of equal importance are neglected. Doctors must rebel if they are to serve their patients effectively; they must not allow a science of measurability to dictate what techniques they use, no matter how effective the technique might be in addressing the particular variable measured by the high-tech equipment purchased at great cost by the hospital administrators. The doctor must never lose sight of the patient as a human being with unmeasurable but yet important feelings, insights, pains, and anxieties (Wiggins 1989:687). In education the technology of the standardized tests often moves us to forget that students are human beings with unmeasurable but yet important characteristics.

We cannot suppress the concept that science is more than merely a method. Indeed, it is a philosophy. Moreover, reason embraces a corpus of qualities which transcend mere calculation — it cannot, in other words, be reduced to a formula for problem solving. Positivistic researchers, their opponents argue, focus on the rigor (commitment to the established rules for conducting inquiry) of research at the expense of touching reality. William James captured this idea almost one hundred years ago when he chided scientists of his day about their excessive love of method. Science, he wrote, 'has fallen so deeply in love with method that . . . she has ceased to care for truth by itself at all'. Anticipating one of the central tenets in the critique of instrumental rationality, James argued that scientists pursued their technically verifiable truth with such a vengeance that they forgot their 'duty to mankind' — i.e., technical means took precedence over human ends. Human passions, he concluded, are more powerful than technical rules, as the heart understands that which reason cannot comprehend.

Technical elegance for research is insufficient in our struggle to understand. The positivistic concept of technical elegance has redefined the very way we look at reason and what it means to be reasonable. Reason has as much to do with *what* we think as with *how* we think. It is as concerned with the substance of our thought as it is with its form. Habermas and Marcuse have maintained that positivistic instrumental rationality has focused our research strategies on the how and the form to the neglect of the what and the substance. Thus, the science of education becomes a technology which is focused on moving us to educational outcomes that we take for granted. These outcomes typically maintain existing power relationships, Habermas and Marcuse argue, as they disregard the ways in which current forms of schooling affect human life (Habermas, 1971; Habermas, 1973; Marcuse, 1964; James, 1956).

Research based on instrumental rationality fails to comprehend the importance of the existential conditions in which problems take shape. As a result, the information emerging from such inquiry loses a significant portion of its meaning. By focusing on the technical, research is fragmented and thus loses sight of any holistic sense (Giarelli and Chambliss, 1984:38). By spending more time on task and by identifying before hand the competencies which students will master during class, teachers may indeed increase the amount of knowledge inserted into each student's mind. Questions concerning the worth of such knowledge and whose interests it serves, however, are irrelevant to the process. Instrumentally-rational researchers focusing on a quantitative measurement of the knowledge component of such a classroom might ignore the very essence of the educational experience. The relationship of the knowledge to the existential worlds of the students is a question which is infrequently asked in an instrumentally-rational research context.

When they overlook the content of teaching, positivistic researchers acquire a very thin view of the nature of the educational process. In asking a question about, say, the causes of student learning in a classroom a far more in-depth understanding would be necessary if the researchers were to suggest policy changes on the basis of the understanding gained through research. This use of thin knowledge of education to support policy changes and methodological changes often reflects modern educational practice. Modern empirical investigations often eventuate in a set of rules for pedagogical planning and management of a classroom. These rules are often cited as inviolate because of their hard scientific basis. Not only are there research methodological questions about the efficacy of such rules, but there are also questions about the general relationship between research findings and the process by which rules for practice are developed. If we fail to ask these questions, positivistic researchers may transform value-laden issues of policy into merely technical issues which can be resolved empirically (Macmillan and Garrison, 1984:17; Donmoyer, 1985:19).

The effect, then, of educational research based on instrumental rationality, Edith Baldwin writes, is educational policy marked by an emphasis on control and conformity. Researchers strive to understand systems of causal laws and the ways the variables relate to one another. Such understanding, Baldwin contends, lead to a perspective which assumes that certain variables may be manipulated to achieve certain outcomes. Control and thus conformity are deemed desirable and rendered possible by such research orientations.

Teachers are profoundly affected by such attitudes. They are taught to accept passively and to apply empirical knowledge gathered by professional researchers. Manageable bits of facts are the building blocks of knowledge, and these pieces of knowledge can be efficiently transmitted to students. Modern reform movements are often grounded in instrumentally-rational research. Teachers have curricular choices only when their decisions contribute to a more efficient and controllable system. Science is geared toward the administration of human beings. The moral implications of goals such as control and efficiency are eliminated from consideration. Educational practitioners, grounding their actions on the research base, act upon the belief that the laws of social life are well-known and devoid of ambiguity (Baldwin, 1987:17; Popkewitz, 1981b:310).

For example, modern educational reform movements are often justified by curricular research which accepts without question the goals of certain programs. The primary task of such research is to help explain how the teaching techniques which are employed contributed to the accomplishment of the predetermined objectives. Questions on which inquiry is based might include: Was the course material learned or not?; Did teachers consider the pre-packaged teaching material clear and easily useable?; Did students understand the course goals?; and, How well did students achieve the course goals? By assuming the validity of the course goals, researchers tacitly promoted an *ad hoc* curriculum theory which supported the ideological and pedagogical assumptions of the designers of curriculum materials (Popkewitz, 1981b:304).

The instrumentally-rational, positivistic researcher must be able to measure precisely whether or not predetermined objectives have been met. Maxine Greene writes of the instrumental rationality of reform movements which have emerged from the National Commission on Excellence in Education's *A Nation at Risk*. Teachers, the report argues, should be evaluated in light of the knowledge provided by the research base on teacher effectiveness. Decisions on teacher salary, promotion, tenure, and retention should be based on these evaluations. Greene maintains that the governing definition of effectiveness is so closely linked to the researchers' use of test scores and *measurable* achievement that discussion about the complex nature of effectiveness is discouraged.

Moral aspects of effectiveness were removed from the evaluation procedure. Questions about justice, humanity, compassion and their relationship to effective teaching were deemed out of place when judging a teacher's worth. The effective teacher, or master teacher, is a master of means; he or she is not to be concerned with moral or ethical ends. In other words, Greene argues, efficiency takes precedence over moral vision. Concern for 'should' or 'ought' disappears, as 'effective' teachers properly organize their materials, devise their pre-operational sets, incorporate their mnemonic devices, and apply their innovative monitoring procedures (Greene, 1985:18–19, 21).

Who are we to question the research which has identified the good teacher as one who is prompt and orderly, reviews materials, asks specific questions, expresses enthusiasm and uses body behavior (smiles and gestures) which display interest, and spends more time on task? Who are we to question the research instruments which have been devised to measure precisely the degree to which teachers' behavior matches the verified 'effective teacher' behavior? Robert Sherman in an assessment of Florida's master teacher plan argues that single-minded focus on these isolated components of effective teaching diverts our attention from the forest to the trees. In his studies of great teachers in history and literature, Sherman points out that almost every one of these criteria of effective teaching is violated by one great teacher or another (Sherman, 1985:14–15). The failure of twentieth-century educational researchers to focus on ends and purposes has undermined the value and applicability of much of our effort to understand the educational process.

In the latter portion of the nineteenth century American society was reeling from the socio-economic changes wrought by industrialization. Factory work had changed the lives of millions of Americans, the fabric of economic life with its mass markets had altered the existence of almost everyone, and labor unrest and violence on the part of the new industrial workers had struck fear in the hearts of the well-to-do. Taylor, the industrial engineer, argued that his scientific methods could bring about a rational society, an efficient workplace, higher productivity, and more docile workers (Fay, 1975:19, 44–5).

Using a rigorous methodology Taylor conducted empirical inquiry to identify inefficient aspects of the production process. Time-and-motion studies used a stop-watch to isolate all the moves and procedures in a specific task. After he identified all the possible time-saving changes, he tried them out with groups he had designated first class workers. Testing his procedures with the first class workers, Taylor refined the specifics. Once satisfied with the steps, the procedure was standardized and taught to other workers. Each worker was provided with an instruction card which described in detail the job, how it was to be accomplished, and the exact time he had to do it. There was only one way to do a job, Taylor argued, and that could be determined only through scientific research on the job by experts. One type of man, therefore, was required to analyze and plan the work, another entirely different type was needed to execute it. As Taylor told a mechanic working under him: '[you're] not supposed to think; there are other people paid for thinking around here' (Wirth, 1983:12).

This is an excellent example of instrumental rationality. The *means* of improving worker efficiency and productivity take precedence over the *end* of respect for human dignity. Taylor's perspective on the uses of social research was enthusiastically received not only by industrial leaders but by educational leaders as well. It was in the first decades of the twentieth century that the goals of schools and the goals of business and industry began to merge. Reports commissioned by business organizations indicated that students who did not stay in school did not make good workers. Since most schools held on to the classical curriculum while neglecting so-called 'practical' vocational studies, the business reports argued that even children who possessed a formal education were not being supplied with 'industrial intelligence'. Students who acquired this industrial intelligence would gain certain technical skills and social attitudes such as the desire to contribute to the good of the community, the ability to take orders, respect for authority, the disposition to follow directions, and the desire to be productive workers. Workers holding such attitudes would contribute to an orderly and stable workplace, free from the unhealthy consequences of labor–management disputes. Working toward the same goals, business and education adopted similar organizational strategies. The principles of scientific management were beginning to be seen as the panacea not only for business but for education as well (Church and Sedlak, 1976:192, 204, 256, 297, 302, 314).

Taylor's research was implemented in industry and was then transferred directly to American schools as it became the prototype for educational administration. An examination of the application of Taylorism's impact on American schools clearly illustrates the manner in which instrumentally-rational science became the guiding light in American educational policy. First, we will examine Taylor's system of scientific management and then we will survey its educational expression.

Taylor's research indicated that a new role for management was needed. Under his system industrial managers would plan and control every aspect of the manufacturing process in detail. Controlling the process involved the reduction of the role of the laborer to the point that he had only one basic responsibility — to do what he or she was told. The need for the judgment of the worker, Taylor claimed, would be eliminated in his system. Thus, a deskilling process was rationalized; the conception of work was separated from its execution. Human beings were viewed as components of a larger system; men and women were simply factors in a physical scientific system. The notion of human dignity or the fact that humans are conscious beings was not considered by Taylor's research and the policies which emerged from it.

91

Taylor divided his system of scientific management into several components. From these components educational-administration theorists divided the basic principles behind what came to be known as scientific education. The first component of the Taylor system concerned the development of a means of measuring the quality of an employee's work — 'management based on measurement', he called it. In education this component shows up in the need for the school to measure the achievement of all students and teachers. In order to make this possible the goals and outcomes of schooling must be conceived in measurable terms. In the process the instrumental rationality of scientific management comes to dictate educational purpose and teacher role.

The second component involved standardization. Once the efficiency researcher determined the *best* way a particular job was performed, then all workers would perform the job that way. Everyone would gain, Taylor claimed, as workers would perform their tasks with more efficiency and less frustration, productivity would be increased, and management would experience higher profits. In education this component emerges in the standardization of curriculum and teacher method seen by many educational leaders as necessary to an efficient school system. Teachers whose jobs are standardized can be monitored far more closely. Incompetency, it is argued, can be quickly identified, for when a supervisor walks into a standardized classroom he or she knows precisely what *should* be occurring. Again, teacher control of the conceptualization of the teaching act is diminished.

The third element of his plan Taylor called the 'task idea'. It was necessary Taylor argued, for management to set specific measurable tasks for each worker everyday. Standardized and measurable, these precisely stated work objectives would keep workers on task as they would always know what was expected of them. Management by objectives would emerge decades later as a more sophisticated expression of the task idea. When the language of behavioral psychology was added to the idea, behavioral objectives would be the result (Callahan, 1962:25–34).

Taylor's notion of the task idea seems like a prototype of Madeline Hunter's research-based teaching/supervision model which has become so popular in American schools in the last few years. Hunter's self-described 'scientific' model assumes a predetermined, prescribed version of teaching based on 'seven essential steps'. Hunter-oriented teachers no matter what their subject, would follow these specific, measurable steps in every lesson. Supervisor evaluation would be simplified and streamlined, as administrative personnel came to define quality instruction as that which conforms to Hunter's model and, her supporters argue, thereby facilitate accountability. Teachers, proponents contend, 'will know what behaviors are expected of them, and they will be able to perform accordingly.'

The range of behaviors which may be deemed good teaching are considerably narrowed under Hunter's plan. Supervisors admit that creative lessons which fail to follow the model must be evaluated as unsatisfactory. Thus, rewards for teaching are not based on reasoned notions of competence and creativity but on adherence to format, i.e., teacher compliance. Like the workers in Taylor's efficient factory, the Hunter system strips teachers of their role in the conceptualization of the teaching act. Teachers become executors of managerial plans. Managers concern themselves with devising strategies which keep teachers on task. This instrumentally-rational system is justified on its scientific basis and is thus shielded from interrogation because of its *objective* status (Garman and Hazi, 1988:670–2).

Taylor labelled the fourth element of his plan 'functional foremanship'. After standardization of the job had occurred, it was necessary that workers be supervised to insure that they carried out the standardized method. The traditional arrangement of one foreman keeping watch over a shop-full of employees was insufficient, Taylor argued. Under functional foremanship this one foreman would be replaced by 'eight different bosses'. If the conception of the job was to be controlled by management then employers had to make sure that their drone workers were controlled at every point in their work. In education one might note the proliferation of supervisory and administrative personnel in recent years. Teachers often feel like the victimized workers in industries managed by Taylor's principles. As workers' or teachers' control of the conceptualization of their jobs is reduced, the need for more administrators increases.

By 1911 educators all around the United States were calling for the development of educational principles grounded on Taylor's research. At the NEA convention held in Chicago in 1912, the positive response to the call was obvious. Many of the sessions took their themes from the mentality of business efficiency and scientific management: 'By What Standards or Tests Shall the Efficiency of a School or System of Schools Be Measured?'; 'Standards of Measuring the Efficiency of Normal School Students'; 'A Study in Adolescent Efficiency'; 'The Principles of Scientific Management Applied to Teaching Music in the Public Schools'.

As the Taylor system picked up steam in educational institutions, educational aims had to be trivialized as they were made sufficiently measurable to fit the demands of the new system. Add to this the fact that schoolmen spent little time identifying problematic factors. For all his *naiveté* Taylor devoted great effort to the analysis of the problems of industrial production. The administrators who applied scientific management to education typically did not have Taylor's research background. Neither did they have the time and resources for thorough research. The result of their efforts were pitifully naive programs which terrorized teachers and stifled students.

Taking their inspiration from Taylorite research strategies as they were applied in the study of business and industry, educators began to employ factory metaphors in their discussions of the educational process.

Pupils were seen as the 'raw material of the business of education'. The school building was termed 'the plant'. The school boards and the teaching staff were the 'directorate and the working force'. Society's expectations of education were called the 'problem of the market'. When the language of business had become the lexicon of the school, the business domination of schools was complete.

In an educational system which employed factory language and shared the ideological assumptions of business, it is not surprising that descisions were made on the basis of quantifiable notions of efficiency. There are so many components of education that research can measure, administrators argued, that it would be silly to worry about those few things that cannot be measured. Decisions in curriculum development were made on the basis of the dollar value of teacher-pupil ratio — not on educational considerations. Because of small class sizes a subject like Greek could never be described as efficient; it was therefore dropped from most curricula. The outcomes of the so-called educational efficiency experts' research were always the same: increase the number of classes per teacher; increase class size; cut teachers' salaries; and reduce the number of classes offered so that fewer teachers would be needed.

The researchers in business and industry, educational administrators concluded, can best determine the goals of schooling. Thus, the function of educational leaders was not to formulate educational policy but to carry out the desires of business leaders. Soon the argument was made that it was a waste of time for school administrators to study social and cultural contextual questions or history or philosophy. Administration theorist Frank Spaulding summed up this crudely practical, acontextual view of the education of the administrator: he (sic) would not borrow his perspective from 'Hegel or Herbart, Harris or Hall'. The educational leader should be like the great captain of industry who merely 'projects an idea ahead, then works up to it.'

By removing educational administrative research and education from the qualitative realm of social context and surrounding it with the trappings of physical science and business, administration theorists succeeded in improving their own status as well as the status of school leaders. Because the public was impressed with the trappings of hard science and business terminology, educational leaders were rewarded for devoting most of their efforts to matters of efficiency and measurement. No matter how hard it may be, administrative theorists argued, it is necessary for educational leaders to establish quantifiable standards in the intangible as well as the more concrete fields of study. In this way educational leaders could improve their public images because it would be possible to report research on educational progress in comparative numerical terminology which everyone could understand.

By the second and third decades of the twentieth century the training of educational administrators reflected these trends. Administrator educa-

tion stressed the technical: courses stressed procedures in processing records and reports, finance, cost accounting, child accounting, and general
business management. Statistical research methodology was added to the
administrators' curriculum and served to provide the profession with a
more scientific appearance. Based on the work of Edward Thorndike,
school leaders learned statistical research methods which allowed them to
evaluate the many standardized tests that were beginning to be used in the
second and third decades of the century. Studies of the textbooks utilized
in administration courses in much of the twentieth century indicate that
the courses were virtually unconcerned with the larger social purposes
that educational administation must confront. Topics addressed in the
most popular administration textbooks until late in the 1940s included
toilet paper, toilet bowl cleaners, roach powders, towel services, and the
purpose of painting, to name only a few. Obviously, the emphasis of
administrator education (and the policies such administrators often implemented) was on *means* (the achievement of efficiency) rather than *ends*
(an understanding of educational purpose as it relates to political and
philosophical questions concerning the nature of a good and just society)
(Callahan, 1962).

Such an instrumentally-rational system could not have developed
without a corps of technically-trained administrators. An educational culture based on positivistic assumptions had worked to preclude questioning
of the goals of educational leadership. The fact that such a technicist
orientation could result in large part from the way we have defined the
nature of educational science has escaped most educational analysts and
certainly the public. The forces which work to shape educational and
social vision are often shaded from view. It is essential that educators,
especially teachers who are researchers, understand such forces.

It is extremely difficult to understand such ideological forces using an
instrumentally-rational, positivistic orientation to educational research.
Such a research perspective has attempted to measure ambiguous educational processes by focusing only on quantified educational outcomes. The
resulting ideological innocence supports the power relations of the status
quo, the mythology of classlessness, the equality of opportunity, the
political neutrality of school, and financial success as a direct consequence
of an individual's initiative. When positivistic research focuses on educational outcomes, the importance of cognitive processes is exaggerated and
their role in learning is decontextualized. This decontextualization, this
separation of cognitive processes from situations which give them meaning
— why, for example, might we want to develop our cognitive abilities? —
gives us a simple-minded view of both educational purpose and the actual
effect of schools on the lives of its students and teachers. As students and
as teachers we are molded by dominant ideology, yet we rarely understand the character of the constraints that ideology enforces on our
psyches and our bodies. Indeed, we are too often unaware of the possibil-

ity which exists for all humans to transcend such limitations and to move in an emancipatory direction. In many ways the democratic critique of educational research as merely outcome measurement is rather simple — how can we possibly assume that schools can maintain a separate identity unaffected by the processes of power, capital accumulation, racial, gender, and class relationships? (Kickbusch, 1985:47–53).

Outcome-measures tell us a little about a specific condition, but they fail to tell us about the most important aspect of the educational research act — the description of the situation which contributed to the creation of the condition. The situation which brought about the condition must be understood before we can understand or ameliorate the condition. Instrumentally-rational outcome measures are like a thermometer which reports body temperature but cannot tell us what has brought about a fever. When we view research as mere outcome measurement and fail to explore just what it is that educational research should do, we are left vulnerable to a bevy of abuses of research data. We assess teacher effectiveness, assign students to curriculum tracks and specific classes, and decide which schools receive excellence awards on the basis of research data. As a result, we sometimes reward the most conventional teachers, assign creative students to non-academic curricula, and decorate schools which possess a large percentage of upper-middle class students. In all of these cases research strategies which look only at outcomes, not processes, are employed. In all cases the outcomes measured only partially reflect the texture, complexity, and quality of the process: what is good teaching?; what makes a good student?; what does a good school do? (Richards, 1988:496; Elliott, 1989a:4).

When we rely too heavily on traditional outcome research our view of the educational process is seriously affected. Our ability to theorize purpose, to understand the way our educational goals are socially constructed, is severely limited. We begin to equate talent with the outcomes we have chosen to measure. Our view of ability or intelligence becomes exclusive, as it regards only previously defined skills as worthwhile — a common consequence of instrumental rationality. Adult accomplishments, for example, were found to be unrelated to test scores, suggesting that there are many kinds of talent related to later success that, although unmeasured by research instruments and thus unaddressed by schools, could be nurtured in educational situations. School knowledge is made into something that it is not — preparation for life. Instead it is merely preparation for tests. When instruction is directed by outcome measurements students are denied the opportunity to learn how to interpret, to decode, to organize knowledge in a way which reflects their own passions and experiences. All learning is reduced to a concern with right or wrong answers. Challenging material cannot be addressed in instrumentally-rational schools because it often does not lend itself to an outcome-based, right or wrong answer framework. Students are enculturated to the system, soon coming to recognize that ways of knowing which do not lend themselves to such a motif are not very important in the everyday life of school (Munday and Davis, 1974:i; Duke, 1985:674).

The outcome measurement of instrumentally-rational research leads to a factory-model, Tayloristic view of knowledge. Like work in turn-of-the-century factories, central office staffs take apart the curriculum, sequencing knowledge, numbering it, and sub-numbering it — e.g., performance objective one, activity seven. Teacher lesson plans are required to match an official format and to fit particular objectives and proficiencies. Subjects like English with a diverse range of content are reduced to measurable proficiencies involving reading comprehension and grammar. Social studies and science are reconstructed into fragments of facts (factoids) and arbitrary pieces of jargon. Measurability thus takes precedence over substance and significance. Deeper, more complex, more existentially significant questions are set aside because we cannot control contextual variables. If the goal of education is to produce a kind of thinking that sees beyond surface appearances, focuses both on solving problems and imagining unthought-of problems to solve, then research centered around outcome measures does not tell us much about our successes and failures. Such a research orientation tends to force teachers to direct their attention to isolated skills and quantifiable entities that render the entire process inauthentic, inert. If teachers, students, and schools, for example, are assessed on the basis of how much homework is assigned, teachers will be leaned upon to increase homework assignments. It doesn't take an astute observer to figure out that if the homework is repetitive memory work students will learn little and feel more alienated, more uninterested in school.

Outcome-directed research often conveys an inappropriate message to teachers, administrators, and the public, sometimes with dangerous consequences. When researchers, for example, studied airline performance, they asked which airline had the best record for being on time. When such a factor is analyzed outside a variety of contextual factors, e.g., safety, serious consequences may result from airlines scrambling to achieve a better on-time record. Along the same line, researchers who evaluate teachers on the basis of particular outcomes may miss the brilliance of their lessons if they do not take into account particular contextual factors. Knowing a student's special needs may move a teacher to abandon a particular content objective in order to provide a pupil with a much needed success experience. The validation of the student's ability may mean far more to both the long-term emotional and learning needs of the child than would a short-term factual understanding (McNeil, 1988, p. 484; McNay, 1988, p. 360; David, 1988, p. 500).

Teachers often understand the negative effects of the types of evaluation which emerge from an instrumentally-rational conception of research. Many times teachers have to divide their classes into two segments: one which is challenging and thought provoking and another which teaches simplified, context-stripped information for student use on proficiency tests. High school biology teachers have reported that they teach a text-bookish, misleadingly simplified version of photosynthesis for proficiency tests and then a real lesson which explains why their test-based description doesn't explain the actual complexity of the process. This form of teacher resistance to the malformations of instrumental rationality taught students a valuable lesson — the official content of the proficiency test-guided curriculum negated the ambiguity of physical reality and provided only partial and misleading information about the world. In the name of educational reform, state educational agencies unable to see beyond the instrumental rationality of positivistic research establish policies which require teachers to focus on simple skills that are easily tested — not on critical, more sophisticated thinking styles and creative activity.

Thus, outcome-directed research based unwittingly on Taylor's efficiency procedures for pacing assembly lines remakes teaching into a set of generic behaviors. Drawing upon scientific management and a simplification of cognitive psychology, teacher evaluation based on such a research model devises lists of behaviors teachers must exhibit. I have been legally required as a student teacher supervisor to use South Carolina's mandated teacher assessment instrument (the Assessment of Performance in Teaching — the APT) to evaluate my practice teachers. The instrument reduces teaching to 51 performances which must be passed by the state's teachers and student teachers. Word always circulates among the student teachers that for the APT observation a certain type of lesson is required — a lesson unlike the student teacher's natural teaching style. Thus, on APT evaluation day the lesson an observer sees is quite different (and usually less challenging) than the norm. The APT assessors and evaluators in similar evaluation models do not need to possess subject-matter expertise in the classes they observe. Such knowledge would be irrelevant because the teaching skills are generic — verified technical acts which emanate from the empirical research base. Thus, teachers can achieve perfect scores on the assessment instrument even though their understanding of the subject is weak and their lesson is boring and trivial. Teaching may be judged on the basis of whether or not simple-minded activities are consistent with ill-conceived goals, whether or not all the materials that are to be used in the lesson (e.g., chalk, chalkboard, overhead projector, etc.) are listed in the lesson plan, or whether or not a teacher uses a student's name to illustrate a point in the lesson. These are actually three of the 51 performances mandated by the South Carolina State Department of Education's APT. Thus, teachers and evaluators are reduced to puppets of the tyrannical instrument (Haney and Madaus, 1989:684; McNeil, 1988:483–4).

Linda McNeil writes of the effects of these outcome research-driven evaluations on teachers. On days when they are evaluated creative teachers often teach very traditional lessons because evaluators would not understand a critical and creative lesson. Because of such demeaning requirements many teachers have for the first time felt the need to engage in political action. They are ready to organize to try to reclaim control of teaching from the technocrats who in the name of scientific research take away teacher's prerogatives to do what they know their students need — to be free from the oversimplified rote learning required by the standardized tests. In this positivistic context the best practices of teachers are rarely linked with assessment procedures. McNeil provides an excellent example of teacher frustration and administrative blindness. In a workshop designed to engage students in the role of active, creative workers in the classroom, one teacher questioned how such an effort could be accomplished in light of the instrumentally-rational system of assessment used by the school. A principal responded that it would be easy. If students were engaged in a project, the principal assured her, an evaluator would just come back at a more appropriate time. The principal, designers, and implementors of teacher evaluation strategies confuse technique for teaching and management for pedagogy. It is the best teachers who are frustrated by this situation, the best teachers who begin to think about leaving. When a teacher's student proficiency test scores are tied to career advancement and merit pay, creative teachers make up their minds — they have to leave teaching or at least the school district (McNeil, 1988:484–5).

In the form of outcome-driven research instrumental rationality has weakened the voice of teachers, while centralizing the governance of schools. Because it has the blessing of the scientific cult of objectivity, teachers, administrators, and community members cannot see the positivistic dimensions of educational policy emanating from such research. Teaching which is legitimized by positivistic research is increasingly controlled by centralized agencies far away from the school. Questions such as what is taught, how it is taught, by whom, to whom, and for what purposes are answered less by teachers than by bureaucratic functionaries. Those who define what constitutes educational research will control the purposes of education, the shape of schools, and what is viewed as good teaching. Indeed, one of the greatest dangers of technocratically-reformed schools of the late twentieth century is that by supporting merely one view of educational excellence the very assumptions on which a pluralistic, egalitarian, democratic society is based are undetermined. Questions of ethics and justice are neglected by policies emanating from a research tradition which by nature cannot address them. Such questions are relegated to the fuzzy realm of personal judgment — a realm which must always be subservient to the authority of impartial scientific analysis (Salganik, 1985:609; Porter, 1988:503).

In the industrialized workplace of the twentieth century analysts have often found that the evaluation of work has been the primary mechanism through which employers have controlled employees. Thus, the assumptions which guide researchers in their construction of evaluation instruments take on greater importance than many of us might have realized. Teachers do not use objective test results or highly technical evaluation instruments to judge their own teaching. Since the advent of technocratic reforms teachers and their workplace supervisors have more and more come to hold different conceptions of the way teaching should be carried out — a situation which opens the door to a range of potential conflicts. Educational leaders tend to emphasize task uniformity, while teachers tend to value task diversity. After the implementation, for example, of Tennessee's Master Teacher Plan, established on an outcome-based model of research, teachers voiced strong displeasure because of the conflicting visions of the teaching task. Tennessee teachers were troubled by their loss of professional autonomy which impeded their ability to provide appropriate instruction. The standardized procedures and curriculum which were justified by the knowledge base of empirical research moved teacher concerns away from the needs of individual students (Rosenholtz, 1987:536–8). The Tennessee master teacher experience illustrates one of the central concerns of critical teacher research and of this book: policymakers in education too often lack an understanding of the assumptions which underlie a research act and the pedagogical and political consequences of particular views of what constitutes research. If educational leaders do not understand these aspects of research, then teachers must teach them. The teacher-as-researcher movement may reverse the typical flow of communications in the educational hierarchy — teachers may speak with an authoritative voice to their managers.

As teachers come to speak with a more authoritative voice, they will feel more freedom to express their opinion of the instrumentally-rational research they have read. Such research, teachers argue, seems quite irrelevant to their purposes and needs. Positivistic research has contributed neither to the clarification of educational problems or the formulation of solutions to them. The precision of positivistic research and its emphasis on prediction have little application in the everyday classroom. Such teacher perspectives lay the foundation for a culture gap between practitioners and researchers. In the last couple of decades teachers have increasingly perceived that educational researchers have less and less to say that would be helpful to their everyday life. Research and practice are separate entities — researchers are captives of their epistemologies and their culture's own agenda (Orteza, 1988:34; Longstreet, 1982:143; Oldroyd, 1985:113; Schon, 1987:10). Researchers are captives in the sense that they have asked only those questions which were answerable by empirical methods of hard science. One discipline or paradigm is not adequate to the task of understanding the network of the intricate and ambiguous human relationships which make up a classroom. Researchers need a multi-dimensional set of research strategies to understand such classroom interactions and the relationship between the classroom and the deep structures of the larger society. In the instrumental rationality of much educational research the attempt to translate such intricate relationships into numbers often renders the data gathered meaningless in the eyes of practitioners. Until researchers free themselves from the oppressive culture of positivism their research will remain irrelevant to teacher practice (McNay, 1988:360; Orteza, 1988:34; David, 1988:500).

Many positivistic research studies depend on observation within strictly controlled teaching situations that has little to do with everyday classrooms. What teachers perceive as the irrelevance of such research often relates to what Lee Shulman labeled 'task validity', i.e., the degree to which the environment in a laboratory is analogous to the complex environment of the classroom. Informed by their practical knowledge, teachers have intuitively questioned the generalizability of laboratory research findings to the natural setting of the classroom. Teachers may have suspected the inapplicability, but the research establishment was not so insightful. The positivistic mainstream assumed that laboratory research findings were the source of solutions which could be applied in every classroom setting (Doyle, 1977:175; Ponzio, 1985:40). Positivistic researchers failed to understand that every classroom possessed a culture of its own — a culture which defines the rules of discourse in classroom situations. Meanings are negotiated around who should talk, and what are the consequences of particular behaviors.

Thus, the meanings of specific classroom events depend on a researcher's knowledge of what happened previously — how classroom meanings, codes, and conventions were negotiated. Thus, for a positivistic researcher to walk into a class without an understanding of the previously negotiated meanings and expect to make sense of the situation is unrealistic; it is even more unrealistic for him or her to expect that generalizations applicable to other classrooms can be made from this incomplete and often misleading snapshot of a classroom. To understand the complexity of the classroom, alternative research methods must be employed. This realization has sparked the mushrooming acceptance of qualitative, naturalistic research. Contrary to positivism's attempt to make quick and clean observations devoid of context, this research orientation places a high priority on detailed, long-term observation of behavior in natural settings. Qualitative, naturalistic researchers realize that the space between teaching and learning outcomes is shaped by a cornucopia of variables. Because of this complexity the attempt to explain divergence in student performance by reference to a few generalizable aspects of teacher action is reductionistic and misleading (Doyle, 1977:179–88). Who is better suited to make long-term, detailed, multi-dimensional observation of classroom behavior than a teacher?

Research which seeks to improve teaching teaching does not fit the objective positivist paradigm. Teachers who do research will never approach the act of inquiry without an agenda — they will be prejudiced because they live and work in the schools. These prejudices are not an impediment, however, they are part of the relevant understandings teachers have acquired from their experience. In conjunction with their classroom inquiry, these understandings can lead to more sophisticated reflection and reflective action. The tenets of action research do not allow this teacher reflection to be cannibalized by instrumental rationality. Teacher research assumes that no one has a more intimate knowledge of students than do teachers. The teacher is the individual who hears students speak day after day, monitors their work, listens to their problems, applauds their successes. Who is better equipped to determine the grounds on which students are evaluated? (Altrichter and Posch, 1989:25–6; Madaus, 1985:615).

Even though teachers occupy this unique vantage point and possess special forms of educational knowledge, they are still vulnerable to the demands of an instrumentally-rational culture of positivism. The technocratic system of surveillance and workplace hegemony spawned by the culture is very difficult for teachers to resist. I listen to my teacher-graduate students who are excited by an emancipatory vision of the teaching act express despair over the power and ubiquity of the technocratic management model which crushes their dreams. To survive teachers resist the techno-teaching model imposed on them by instrumentally-rational reforms; but just as with Paul Willis's lads, the form their resistance takes may be emancipatory or it may exacerbate their domination. The practical knowledge teachers extract from their experience is undoubtedly valuable, and it is often used by teachers as an alternative, a form of resistance to the accountability strategies shaped by positivism. But without a mechanism for questioning and sophisticating such knowledge it becomes a reactionary form of resistance, a static, regressive response to the positivistic attack on teacher integrity. It is perceived by politicians and the general public as a manifestation of teacher incompetence. As such it serves to justify tighter controls and the extension of technical reforms. We have no choice, political leaders contend, these incompetent teachers must be held accountable. In order to insure 'quality education' the reins are tightened — the public, politicians insist, deserve scientific assurances that teachers are teaching the 'basics'. The culture of positivism thus perpetuates itself.

Advocates of critical action research maintain that emancipatory forms of resistance to the malformations of techno-teaching exist. Although positivist administrators and political leaders will oppose it, an action research-based resistance which seeks alliance with critical democratic groups within the community poses an emancipatory alternative to both the static traditional craft culture grounded on an unexamined practical teacher knowledge and the instrumental rationality of the town-down technical reform movement. Teachers operating in this critical action research orientation which seeks solidarity with democratic social groups draw upon our notion of subjugated knowledges to develop a system of meaning, a source of authority to which they appeal for professional guidance. While their practical knowledge serves as an invaluable source of insight into the conduct of their professional lives, teachers develop methods of inquiry into their own teaching while collaborating with groups outside of the educational establishment who offer special perspectives on the effects and consequences of schooling. Collaboration with such groups may spur teachers to ask questions of their practices which they had never before considered: Do I unconsciously respond to the children of the dispossessed differently than I do the children of the privileged?; Do I condemn the children of the dispossessed with low expectation?; Do I operate with a different set of rules for students from different status backgrounds?; Do I respect the form of knowledge (subjugated knowledge) that many of my students bring to school or do I equate education with the eradication of such ways of knowing?; Does my classroom encourage an active view of citizenship or does it view citizenship as a passive form of rule following?

When teachers begin to understand the perspectives and subjugated knowledges of the marginalized and use such frames of reality to formulate research questions in their own practices, the positivistic managerialism of the school workplace cannot survive. The creative forms of resistance which emerge from such emancipatory orientations liberate the teacher from the role of obedient functionary of the state to that of a self-directed professional. Teachers will no longer simply follow the empty definitions of excellence (which usually involve test score improvement) emanating from political and educational leaders. Critical teacher researchers empowered by their solidarity with democratic groups will demand a clarification of educational excellence — excellence for whom and for what purpose. Is it an excellence based on an economic resurgence spurred by more productive but less self-directed workers?; or is it an excellence which revolves around an emancipatory vision of self-directed citizens alert to the way power works to construct our consciousnesses and which is motivated by a well-defined conception of pragmatic social justice? Research models which define school success in terms of a narrow definition of student achievement are not consistent with this teacher-driven reconceptualization of excellence. Teacher research grounded on an emancipatory system of meaning is essential to the realization of this democratic reconceptualization of the teacher workplace (Duke, 1985:674; Elliott, 1989a:9–14).

Critical conceptions of the teacher as researcher must avoid the pressure of the positivistic culture of schooling to devise slick packages of 'how to do critical action research'. Advocates of critical action research must walk a tightrope here. While avoiding step-by-step models of the 'proper' methods of educational action research, they must at the same time be sufficiently concrete and specific to provide guidance to teachers who might have no conception of how to begin their lives as practitioner researchers. While I am no Flying Wallenda, I will attempt to walk that tightrope in the following paragraphs. I do not mean to be glib when I argue that there are as many ways to conduct educational action research as there are creative teachers. Indeed, there are numerous forms of data collection. As we teach we are constantly collecting data from different sources, in different ways, and for different purposes. The value of critical teacher research is to bring these data collection techniques to our consciousness, to refine them, to extend them through exposure to the ways other teachers and researchers have employed them, and to act on them in a way that is consistent with the system of meaning we have constructed. As teachers bring their data collection techniques to their consciousness, techniques that may prove helpful would include recording field-notes and subsequent reflection about them, audio and visual recordings of classroom events or of students away from the classroom, and interviews of students by teachers (Wood, 1988:138; Torney, 1985:73).

An important aspect of the teacher research process involves the attempt to discern patterns and insights from such data. This analysis can be conducted by the teacher alone or in conjunction with other teachers. One of the most difficult, yet vital, portions of the process revolves around the teacher's attempt to distinguish what data is significant and what is noise. Often times that which has been regarded as noise by traditional researchers may be heard differently by a practitioner. A public address system, typically ignored by instrumentally-rational research, may take on new significance to the teacher researcher. A female elementary teacher may hear a gender-related condescension toward a predominately female staff coming across in the edicts issued by the male principal over the P.A. What was once background noise that had to be filtered out of 'real' educational research becomes an important manifestation of the power dynamics which operate in the elementary school workplace. Before their acquaintance with critical action research, many teachers may have viewed their research act as primarily concerned with deriving information about students and the factors which lead to enhanced performance. After bringing the research process to critical consciousness a variety of topics are open to teacher inquiry. Utilizing a systematized mode of analysis which produces previously unthought of insights, the teacher perceives deep structures which shape and grant meaning to classroom events (James and Ebbutt, 1981:90; Wood, 1988:146).

The benefits of critical action research go beyond the effort to escape the blinders of instrumental rationality and to gain insight into the dynamics of their classrooms. When teachers listen to their students and elicit their opinions and perspectives, a variety of benefits are derived. Students who are allowed to express thought previously suppressed for fear of negative judgment or retribution experience a form of catharsis. This catharsis allows for a healthier, more authentic, teacher-student relationship which inevitably leads to better communication and mutual understanding. The student, and in many cases the teacher, is confirmed, his or her experiences validated. If for no other reason, the student feels a greater sense of self-worth resulting from the attention and interest displayed by the teacher researcher. Such teacher-questioning of students induces pupils to organize their thoughts that were previously unsystematized in order to render them understandable to the teacher. Thus, an element of interpretation is necessary — an interpretation which is relatively easy to elicit from students because of its connection to their lived worlds (Reinharz, 1979:318).

Daniel Duke extends this concept of teachers interviewing students — he labels the process 'debriefing'. Students are asked questions which move them to recollect and reconstruct previous experiences. From this information, Duke argues, teachers can make valuable decisions about how to improve their courses and develop curriculum in a way that is more responsive to student needs. Few examples exist in the literature of curriculum research which make use of student perceptions of what they have learned and what it means to them. Instead of asking students what they have learned, instrumentally-rational research has settled for empirical observations of student classroom behavior or student responses to standardized tests or highly structured survey instruments. Duke lists seven debriefing questions teachers can use for student interviews: 1) What did you learn in the class?; 2) You just told me what you learned. What do you think learning is?; 3) Now that you've defined learning, is there anything you learned in class that you didn't mention in question one?; 4) What do you know as a result of taking the class that you didn't know before taking it?; 5) What can you do as a result of taking the class that you couldn't do before taking it?; 6) What one point did the teacher emphasize the most during the course?; 7) You tell me that you can reduce what you learned in an entire course to a few minutes. Is that all you learned in the course? (Duke, 1977:157–8). Thus, teacher research becomes a valuable teaching tool. As they reconstruct their own experiences by answering Duke's debriefing questions, students take responsibility for organizing, interpreting, and making sense of their academic lives (Duke, 1985:674).

Paulo Freire is very instructive in our attempt as critical action researchers to involve our students in our research. When we act on Freire's conception of inquiry, teacher research becomes a powerful teaching tool, a learning experience for students. Freire maintains that there are no traditionally-defined objects of his educational research — he insists on involving the people he studies as subjects, i.e., as partners in the process. He immerses himself in their ways of thinking and levels of perception, encouraging them all along to begin thinking about their own thinking. This method of critical research, which involves the study and criticism of the research process, is also a pedagogical process. Everyone involved, not just the researcher, joins in the process of investigation, examination, criticism, and re-investigation — everyone learns to see more critically, to think at a higher level, to recognize the forces which subtly work to shape their lives. Critical action researchers can put Freire's methods to work in their own classrooms. In the process of conducting their own research, they can teach students the research techniques that they have learned. Students may be encouraged to employ fieldwork skills such as observing, interviewing, picture-taking, videoing, tape-recording, note-taking and life history collecting. In the process students learn and sophisticate the traditional skills we value in curriculum: reading, writing, arithmetic, listening, interpreting, and thinking. An excellent example of such student research is the Foxfire approach developed in Georgia twenty-five years ago where students learned research skills by going into the community and collecting local folklore (Freire, 1972:134–7).

As they conduct this type of research, Freire contends, the researchers (be they teachers or students) are educating and being educated along with their students. When we return to the research site to put into practice the results of our inquiry, we are not only educating and being educated but we are researching again. The teacher research process, thus, is never ending, never complete. When we implement the plans which emerge from the research, we change the consciousness of both our students and ourselves — a change which initiates a new set of questions and a new phase of research. Of course, Freire's critical, democratic concept of research is anathema to the instrumental rationality of positivistic researchers. His invitation to those being examined to participate in the formulation, criticism, and reformulation of research provides a direct challenge to the positivistic cult of the expert. At the same time, it provides critical educational action researchers with a sense of direction, an orientation which transforms our idea of research from mere data gathering into a consciousness-raising, transformative pedagogical technique (Freire, 1972:135–7).

Central to this notion of emancipatory action research is an appreciation and a utilization of the student's perception of schooling. Before Freire's approach can work, teachers must understand what is happening in the minds of their students. Such an approach comes directly out of a critical theoretical notion of intersubjectivity which rejects scientistic methods of understanding human behavior. Freire, Habermas, and other critical analysts seek to uncover the social construction of consciousness focusing on motives, values, and emotions. Operating within this critical context the teacher researcher studies students as if they were texts to be deciphered. The teacher researcher approaches them with an active imagination and a willingness to view students as socially-constructed beings (Grady and Wells, 1985–86:35).

When teachers have approached action research from this perspective they have uncovered some interesting information. In a British action research project, for example, teachers used student diaries, interviews, dialogues, and shadowing (following pupils as they pursue their daily routines at school) to uncover a student preoccupation with what was labelled a second-order curriculum. This curriculum involved matters of student dress, conforming to school rules, strategies of coping with boredom and failure, and methods of assuming their respective roles in the school pecking order. Teacher researchers found that much of this second-order curriculum worked to contradict the stated aims of the school to respect the individuality of students, to encourage sophisticated thinking, and to engender positive self-concepts. Students often perceived that the daily lessons of teacher (the intentional curriculum) were based on a set of assumptions quite different from the assumptions which guided out-of-class teacher interactions with students. The anger and hostility which resulted from such inconsistency are typically misunderstood by teachers. Only in an action research context which values the perceptions of students could such student emotions be understood and addressed (Oldroyd, 1985:117).

One of the most important techniques teacher researchers have used to gain access to student perceptions and their (teachers') own understandings of them involves keeping student and teacher journals. As teachers keep track of their practices, understandings, research strategies, and research interpretations, their ability to act on their reflections is enhanced. Michael Armstrong writes of how as a teacher researcher he would write every evening about what happened in his class that day. He structured his journal writing around the question, 'What were the most significant events of the day?'. He followed this description with his own observations, interpretations, and speculations about the events. Typically, he wrote about particular incidents which illuminated the nature of the children's learning. To excavate student perceptions that are often hidden from the teacher, often concealed from even the student's own consciousness, teacher researchers may want to read parts of their own journals to students. Such an act of teacher disclosure of self may spark a meta-analytical process which initiates student and teacher thinking about their own thinking. As a result, closer, more authentic student-teacher and student-student relationships may develop which allow for more revealing social interactions, more sophisticated learning activities, and more opportunities to connect academic learning with the lived experience of students and teachers.

In such a context classroom change becomes a negotiated process based on the shared perceptions of students and teachers. The positivistic view of change as a means of power-coercion is abandoned — such a perspective simply does not fit the culture of a classroom where teachers and students attend to, reflect and act upon the perceptions of one another. In such classrooms empowered teachers released from the control of instrumentally-rational administrative surveillance procedures pass more and more responsibility to their students. Along with such responsibility students gain more opportunities to think for themselves, to engage in their own research, and in the process to become educated in a critically-defined way. Such an education would allow students to perceive themselves as significant agents in the life of the society. In such a situation learning is seen as an act of social participation, i.e., citizenship (Wood, 1988:138; Armstrong, 1981:17; Oldroyd, 1985:116–17).

Of course, as an author of a book on the teacher as researcher, I believe that teachers have much to gain from an understanding of action research. But, as I tried to convey in Chapter 2, educational action research conceived outside of a larger system of meaning simply becomes one more educational fad whose popularity, like the child-centeredness and the back-to-basics movements, waxes and wanes periodically. When critically-grounded in an emancipatory system of meaning, action research may be one of many strategies employed to empower teachers and to sophisticate the project of public schooling. It may help us avoid the tendency of teachers to fall prey to the deadening routinization of school, the anti-intellectual culture of schools which stifles teacher interaction as professionals, the victimization motif which induces teachers to see themselves as powerless objects of administrative tyranny devoid of a professional decision-making prerogative. Without some form of critical intervention teachers encounter the same situations over and over again, seeing what they expect to see, and constantly reconstructing the classroom in its own image (Ruddick, 1989:7).

To avoid a slick step-by-step prescription of quick and easy methods of initiating critical teacher research, here are a set of tentative guidelines for teachers interested in incorporating critical action research into their teaching.

1 *Constructing a system of meaning.* Critical action research begins with the teacher's construction of a tentative system of meaning, a source of authority to which they look for philosophical guidance in considering the purpose not only of their research but of their teaching. From my perspective critical theory, feminist theory, postmodern analysis, liberation theology, Deweyan educational theory, Afro-centric epistemology, and indigenous peoples' knowledge serve as starting points in our construction and ongoing reconstruction of a system of meaning.

2 *Understanding dominant research methods and their effects.* Armed with this emancipatory system of meaning, critical teacher researchers are empowered to expose the assumptions of existing research orientations, to critique the verified knowledge base that emerges from them, and to reveal the ideological effects of such

processes on teachers, schools, and the culture's view of education. Once the assumptions and effects of such research strategies are revealed, critical action researchers can begin to see those aspects of education which the strategies ignore. Many times critical research will begin its inquiry at the locations invisible to instrumentally-rational research.

3   *Selecting what to study.* Guided by their emancipatory system of meaning and their rejection of instrumentally-rational research and the educational practices justified by it, critical teacher researchers begin to see their schools and classrooms from unique angles which reveal problems often unperceived by less-prepared practitioners. Teacher decisions about what to study emerge from this ability to see familiar settings from the outside looking in.

4   *Acquiring a variety of research strategies.* Acquaintance with the literature of qualitative inquiry provides the teacher researcher with a diverse battery of inquiry methods. Different methods may be employed for different purposes in divergent situations, thus promoting research flexibility and the potential for unique teacher insight.

5   *Making sense of information collected.* Again, the system of meaning developed by the critical teacher researcher is invaluable to the action research process. In this case the system of meaning allows the teacher researcher to identify previously unrecognized patterns in the data collected in the classroom, school, and community. Bolstered by the emancipatory system of meaning the teacher researcher is able to uncover relationships among classroom, school, and community which serve to change the focus of one's professional life. Teachers may ask: Why do I react this way to these particular students?; Why do I feel that I must cover this body of information?; Why did this particular student behavior anger me so?

6   *Gaining awareness of the tacit theories and assumptions which guide practice.* Critical action researchers turn their inquiry on themselves seeking to uncover the forces that construct their own consciousnesses. In this process teachers attempt to develop a dialectic of distance which simultaneously puts them closely in touch with their thoughts and feelings about their teaching, while at the same time granting them the analytical ability to see themselves from a critical distance — a distance which allows them a view of their relationship to wider social and ideological forces. As teacher researchers view themselves as part of a wider cultural panorama, relationships are revealed which help them to see how they come to believe and act. Aided by the dialectic of distance, teachers study themselves as they would the students in their classrooms.

7 *Viewing teaching as an emancipatory, praxiological act.* Critical action research is incompatible with a view of teaching as a technical act of information delivery. Critical action research requires a pedagogy of personal and social transformation. The mere act of developing a system of meaning which guides research design, selection of research methods, interpretation of research, action based on research, and personal analysis of consciousness construction cannot help but alter a teacher's way of seeing, of reading the world. Thus, critical action research cannot claim neutrality. It can never avoid initiating challenges to the undemocratic, scientifically-managed, instrumentally-rational workplace of teaching. When adopted, critical teacher research enters into the fray. It is enlisted in the struggles to reclaim educational inquiry from the instrumental rationality of much educational research, to redefine knowledge in a way which exposes the political consequences of positivism, and to save the dignity of teaching from the culture of narrow accountability (Bogdan and Biklen, 1982:209–10; Oldroyd and Tiller, 1987:18; Kroath, 1989:61–8; Longstreet, 1982:149; Torney, 1985:74).

Chapter 6

The Quest for Certainty

Julian Jaynes in his *Origin of Consciousness in the Breakdown of the Bicameral Mind* has presented a grand theory of the development of human consciousness and the relationship between that development of human history. After the breakdown of the bicameral mind (In Western civilization c.12 BC) in which the right hemisphere of the human brain comprehended reality and then transmitted or 'told' men and women about it in the familiar language of a 'god', mankind searched in vain for the certainty provided by these aural hallucinations. No longer, Jaynes contends, were humans blessed by divine intervention in their lives, and, as a result, they were beset by anxieties and tensions resulting from the need for conscious decision-making. Human history thus became a quest for certainty, a search for new forms of authority.

The main themes of the last four millennia in Western culture (the same themes are present in other cultures but in differing time-frames) emerge when studied in this Jaynesian context. In the late second millennium BC, many stopped hearing the voices of the gods. By the end of the first millennium BC, those men and women (the prophets and the oracles) who still heard the voices were dying away. From the time of Chirst until 1000 AD, it was the transcripts of the testimonies of the oracles and prophets which provided our authorization and our volition. In the last 1000 years these writings began to lose their authority (Jaynes, 1976). During this millennium the church found itself challenged by science. Contrary to popular belief the two forces clashed not over the existence of the divine but over the proper path to divine certainty. Indeed, the scientific revolution was driven by a desire to uncover hidden divinity, i.e., a divine plan for the universe. With the coming of the Enlightenment and nineteenth-century scientific materialism this search for a divine plan ran into an ironic detour. The romantic search for God's hand was dismissed as scientists began to posit that there was no room for the divine in a cold, rational universe. Darwin's thesis that it was evolution not divine wisdom which created nature implied that there was no authorization from the outside. Man (sic) had to depend on his own volition.

This breakdown of divine authorization is reminiscent of the breakdown of the bicameral mind at the end of the second millennium BC. We are inundated with substitutes as more and more people have become aware of the breakdown: meditation, sensitivity-training groups, mind control, scientology, and many others. Indeed, the types of organized religion which have flourished in recent years (e.g., fundamentalism) have ignored the great questions raised by social, cultural, and scientific events of the last few centuries. They have allowed little, if any, inquiry into questions concerning evolution, anthropology of religion, or the psychological quest for certainty.

Furthermore, science itself takes on a quasi-religious role, as it seeks certainty in the ruins of traditional religion. Taking its cue from traditional religion science has developed an 'infallible dogma'. Science strives to be a force which explains everything, soothes our uncertainty, provides a ritual (a research methodology) which if followed grants a pathway to truth and releases humans from the need for cultivating their own self-direction. Positivistic science has often sought, in the same manner as traditional religion, the Final Answer and the One Truth (Kincheloe *et al.*, 1987:14–18).

Critical theorists have argued that these scientific tendencies affect all aspects of a culture. As previously mentioned, Henry Giroux (drawing upon the work of Horkheimer, Adorno, Marcuse, and Habermas) has contended that when positivistic science is combined with the forces of domination in a society a 'culture of positivism' is formed (Horkheimer, 1974). This culture of positivism informs the way we approach all problems — both technical and human. Giroux and the critical theorists maintain that the positivistic culture assumes that certainty exists and that there are final answers in the world of humans. The critical perspective argues that there is no certainty in the world of human affairs and it is high time we abandon the search. The quest for certainty in the social realm often focuses our attention on the trivial — on that which can be easily measured. Rarely do the most significant questions of human affairs lend themselves to quantification and the pseudo-certainty which often accompanies numbers.

If Jaynes' thesis is correct social and educational researchers find themselves as players in a larger historical context where human beings have searched for certainty in an attempt to regain a lost security. The instrumental rationality that we have analyzed reflects this tendency, as positivistic researchers have searched for a method (a means) which is never-changing, an anchor in a stormy sea of ambiguity. Some analysts would argue that the critique of positivism moves humans and their search for knowledge into a new era. In the post-positivistic age, they argue, mankind (sic) will no longer be crippled by the quest for certainty. As a result, humans would find greater comfort with ambiguity. In their pursuit of knowledge researchers would abandon the search for an Absolute

Method, utilizing a wide diversity of research methods to study a wide diversity of topics. Let us examine in more detail the quest for certainty in educational research.

Positivistic researchers argue that social research should be designed to accumulate evidence which will allow us to make sense of the social world in a systematic fashion. In this process we will find and modify laws while extending existing ones. Once again we see the physical science model informing social and educational research, as positivistic researchers argue the point that all sciences are unified — i.e., the classical method of the physical sciences is applicable in all research contexts, education included (Smith, 1983:12).

There is great security in this unity of science position. Researchers have been frightened by the prospect of diversified conceptual frameworks and research strategies. When we give credence to a variety of methods of seeking and validating information, many researchers argue that belief, meaning, experience, and knowledge become muddled and confused. Therefore, positivistic researchers have traditionally presented a case for rigorous methodology. Rigor implies conceptual clarity and consistency and the elimination of bias — i.e., the human input of the researcher. Most importantly, rigorous research limits the way in which information might be interpreted, *one* way being the ideal. To facilitate rigorous research, proponents have called for a universal language of ideas in which all research problems could be formulated. In this manner debate over linguistic meaning would be eliminated and objectivity would be insured. Thus, the natural order could be described with great accuracy as the problems of observer bias and language imprecision would be solved (Eisner, 1983:23).

This belief in an underlying natural order where there is regularity in the way humans act exerts a profound impact upon the way humans approach research. These regularities or social laws, positivists maintain, are best expressed through quantitative analysis and the language of mathematics. Mathematics plays the role of the universal language of ideas which eliminates human bias and imprecision. The *raison d'être* for educational research within this tradition, therefore, is to develop theories which give coherent expression to human regularities.

The assumptions of social regularity and certainty behind this positivistic research tradition influence social practice. What began as a research method slowly evolves into a view of the world which includes descriptions of how humans should behave, believe, and experience. Educational science which is grounded in positivistic research assumes that the laws of society and the knowledge of human existence have been verified and are ready to be inserted into the minds of children. Educational 'engineers' devise curricula and organizational strategies for schools as if there were no ambiguities or uncertainties in the social and educational world. Children in these circumstances, anti-positivists charge, are controlled and manipulated like animals in a biology laboratory. The sacred rituals (methods) of science grant these practices an aura of legitimacy and sanctity (Popkewitz, 1981:301, 309).

Anti-positivists argue that the attempt to alleviate anxiety produced by the questioning of scientific unity causes researchers to hold fast to positivistic formats. In the larger Jaynesian historical context marked by the quest for certainty science has traditionally played the role of the new religion while scientific methodology has been substituted for church liturgy. In this quest for authorization and certainty humans have often sought rules, orders, and structures. Numerous studies have indicated that positivistic science attracts more 'authoritarian personality types' (Adorno, *et al.*, 1950) than do the arts, humanities, and non-positivistic science (Oxtoby and Smith, 1970:87–100). That such authoritarian personalities are attracted to the positivistic sciences should not be surprising, as positivism accepts a rationally ordered universe, seeks to discover universal laws and patterns, and attempts to provide absolute explanations of phenomena (Head, 1979:40).

Elliot Eisner believes that the quest for certainty is hopeless, for if we can learn anything from science it is that our ideas about the world change and that they will continue to change in the coming years. The chance of arriving at some juncture in human history where research will become unnecessary because we will understand the nature of reality is slim. There are no social and educational laws and thus no certainty — and we should get used to it. There is unlikely to be any single research strategy or theoretical view that will allow us to grasp the whole of reality.

Given such prospects, the anti-positivists tell us, researchers should welcome a proliferation of research paradigms and take advantage of the new angles they provide for viewing the world. This research pluralism or eclecticism, they argue, will take our understanding of the world to previously unexplored dimensions. Those who accept research pluralism will recognize that divergent theoretical systems and research paradigms designate different phenomena as data and that what we consider reality cannot be separated from the methodological procedures employed to produce those conclusions (Eisner, 1983:23–4).

The path to such eclecticism, however, is beset with obstacles. Indeed, philosophers of social science speak of a crisis in social inquiry. It is a crisis with roots in two attempts: 1) the fight to free social science from the positivistic quest for certainty; and 2) the struggle by those freed from the first quest to figure out what to do with their freedom — i.e., to cope with the choices presented by research pluralism.

Evidence of the crisis is manifested by an inability to agree upon standard criteria for judging the progress of a field of study. With so many approaches to research available, social scientists find it increasingly difficult to make evaluations across the wide range of activities undertaken in the name of their discipline. Maybe even more disconcerting is the inability of researchers in social sciences to understand the assumptions, aims, and languages of one another. Yet, what is the alternative? The attempt to bond our studies in a common language with shared assumptions takes us back to a positivistic quest for a universally understood language of research — an Esperanto of inquiry, if you will.

Shared aims, anti-positivists maintain, stifle our creativity and research freedom. Much of the great physical and social scientific research seemed aimless to the patriarchs of the disciplines when it was first encountered. In the most healthy scientific situation there is generally little consensus about what the next step should involve, which method should be utilized to pursue the next step, or how exactly success should be measured. The price of our abandonment of the quest for certainty is untidy diversity, but the world itself (especially the social and educational world) is not all that neat (Smith, 1983:12; Eisner, 1983:14).

Barbara Frankel states it well, arguing that those who are disturbed by this untidiness are simply lamenting the 'confusion and noise' foisted upon social science by the 'humanness of human beings'. Like the librarian who dreams of the tidiness of a library without patrons, Frankel's neo-positivists fantasize a spick and span social science where researchers are all identical, unbiased, infallible measuring instruments. Research would be so much easier, they dream, if researchers and the researched didn't have to interact through the imprecise medium of verbal language, disagree over standards of success, and find themselves separated by divergent value structures (Shweder and Fiske, 1986:1–2). At this rate, they warn, we will never really 'know' anything.

Psychologist Donald Fiske argues that we can achieve greater certainty than many eclecticists believe and that unification of science is possible. Indeed, if social science is to progress in its attempt to describe reality, we must focus our attention on its unification. Agreeing that different methods of science research produce different forms of knowledge, Fiske argues that there is no reason that the different forms of knowledge cannot be brought together. We have unrelated bodies of knowledge, Fiske argues, because we have not developed an adequate general theory of social knowledge.

We must search for ways of integrating divergent research methodologies, he says. Researchers must disregard the pessimists who doubt such integration is possible and develop systems of meta-analysis which provide strategies for pulling together data obtained by different methodologies. Once meta-analysis pulls together diverse data, it must compare and analyze the facts so that researchers can decide their next steps. Thus, Fiske believes that universal scientific aims are possible and necessary in the struggle to overcome the confusion of research eclecticism.

One of the most important ways of escaping the uncertainty of eclectic social science, Fiske argues, is to delimit precisely what it is that social science wants to know. Pointing to physics, Fiske reflects E.P. Wigner's observation that progress in physics has been due to a restriction of the discipline's concern to the attempt to explain the 'regularities in the behavior of objects'. Nobel Laureate Wigner argued that this 'specification of the explainable may have been the greatest discovery of physics so far'.

There are obvious implications here for social scientists, Fiske asserts. Social science has simply had too high a level of expectations, as it has attempted to understand broad, vague entities such as intelligence and culture. We must focus our research on the regularities in the behavior of social objects. Strongly disagreeing with anti-positivists such as Frankel and Eisner, Fiske argues that social laws exist and can be discovered. The regularities to which he refers are the building blocks of social laws. In other words, Fiske contends that our search for the laws of society must start small with microscopic methods of investigation. The objects of social inquiry, he says, must be small objects and short temporal periods. Fiske is confident that years and years of such microscopic research will eventuate in an accurate portrayal of social reality (Frankel, 1986:354–5).

Fiske cannot accept a postmodern conception of disorder. It is this positivistic discomfort with uncertainty which motivates the construction of logocentric designs: build more jails and get the deviants into them; re-establish old-fashioned discipline and solve school management problems; allow administrators to determine what textbooks teachers should use and adopt them; inquire into what strategies improve test scores then require teachers to use them; give principals and deans more responsibility to fire people; pass a law or a constitutional amendment which requires citizens to respect the flag; do research that is simple, orderly, and elegant, and produces verifiable data; devise questionnaires that soothe our quest for certainty by subtly requiring respondents to answer questions in ways that prove that the world is stable and predictable; as a research analyst, assume that the word and the deed are consistent. All of these designs are based on the assumption of common frames of reference. The fact that they are arrived upon in a way which reflects the tacit dominant ideology of a time and place is not considered in the quest for certain knowledge of the world of education. Thus, in its assurance, its refusal to examine the assumptions which guide it, the quest for certainty often obscures more than it uncovers (Gordon, Miller and Rollock, 1990:15).

Jacques Derrida ridicules the certainty with which science makes 'valid' arguments. Such arguments always begin with primitive and undefined terms and premises, he contends, and to ignore this situation is to seek a fictional security. Meaning, like an eroding hillside, slowly dissolves until language and texts take on a configuration quite different from their original state. A reader in 1952 may have derived a different meaning from a phrase than does a reader of the same phrase in 1992. Meaning derived from research data or frames of reference which serve as the starting place for educational inquiry cannot help but reflect the ideology and social frames which surround them. Unexamined frames of reference lead to claims of scientific certainty which perpetuate privilege for the privileged and oppression for the oppressed (Cherryholmes, 1988:121).

These ideas have important implications for teacher researchers when they attempt to make sense of existing educational research and when they begin to formulate the questions they wish to explore themselves. Teacher research and practice, for example, cannot be conceived as mere problem solving, because a problem does not unambiguously present itself. A problem is, as we have already maintained, identified as a result of particular ideologies and social frames (Altrichter and Posch, 1989:25–6). This situation serves to illustrate the value of our notion of critical constructivism discussed in Chapter 2. A Piagetian level of formal thinking with its emphasis on problem solving is insufficient for the critical teacher researcher. Such a level of thinking does not allow researchers to explore the origins of problems, the assumptions which move us to define some situations as problems and others as not problems, or the source of authority which guides us in our formulation of criteria for judging which problems merit our research time. This is where our critical constructivist notion of post-formal thinking helps us understand the complexity of our role as teacher researchers. Employing such a thinking style we begin to uncover the hidden ways ideology shapes the questions which rest at the foundation of our research. Thus, we see far more clearly the shaky foundation on which the quest for certainty rests.

Consider for a moment how our faith in the constancy of meaning shapes our lives as teachers. The meanings researchers attribute to terms such as reading, teaching, and learning influence the forms our evaluations of teachers, students, and schools take. For example, think about a researcher seeking to determine whether a constructivist method of teaching science produces more learning than an inquiry method. The researcher begins the study by identifying what learning is and what behaviors should be examined to determine whether it has or has not taken place. There is nothing objective about such a process; absolute, certain knowledge does not emerge from such a study. The knowledge which does emerge is inherently conditional — dependent on an acceptance of a variety of assumptions about the goals of science education, the definition of a good student, the nature of learning, etc. As Robert Donmoyer argues, these research issues are always questions of meaning. As our perspective on research fashions our teacher evaluation strategies, the designation of who is a competent or who is an incompetent teacher is contingent on the system of meaning on which researchers operate.

Donmoyer writes of a school district's attempt to evaluate a whole language teacher he knows. Everyone in the system, including individuals who do not embrace a whole language approach, regard him as an excellent teacher. However, when administrators attempted to evaluate him on the basis of a new evaluation instrument a problem developed. The supervisor came to his classroom several times to evaluate the teacher but always left without doing so. The evaluator kept waiting for the teacher to 'teach' — teaching, according to the research on which the system of evaluation was based, involved standing in front of students and delivering information. The researchers who developed the instruments used by the supervisors assumed a constant, one-dimensional meaning of teaching and learning. Donmoyer concludes that researchers must consider questions of meaning, diverse constructions of both learning and the teaching act. No research project, no curriculum, no evaluation instrument should be developed before different conceptions of what it means to teach are considered (Donmoyer, forthcoming a:4–7).

Once again we are confronted with the danger of the quest for certainty, the search for a universal knowledge applicable in all situations. The teacher evaluations, the curricula developed, the ability grouping which come out of this sacred educational science are clothed in the garb of technical expertise (Cherryholmes, 1988:121). The force field of certainty surrounds them, rendering them inpenetrable to the misgivings of those directly affected: creative teachers with negative evaluations; individuals from low status cultures whose experiences, whose subjugated knowledges, are absent from school curricula; brilliant students with unique learning styles whose talents are not appreciated by the culture of the schools nor measured by standardized tests. Contrary to the assumptions of the positivistic cult of certainty which too often shapes school practice, meanings are never closed but remain forever open — open to negotiation. Interpretations are never final because humans are incapable, thankfully, of a final perception. A student may be taught and evaluated by a gaggle of teachers, but only one may recognize the genius previously overlooked. Knowledge doesn't age well; it often turns to vinegar. New facts come to light, fresh interpretations uncover new relationships which render traditional accounts *passé*. Albert Einstein as a student is viewed as a failure, as a scientist, the genius. Yesterday's certainties are tomorrow's superstitions. Deliver me from the dreary universe where everything can be known (Slaughter, 1989:267; Reinharz, 1979:366; Lincoln and Guba, 1985:184). Such is the world of the camp science fiction movie where a time traveller changes one event, and scientists in charge of the time travel project 'know' that if this particular event is changed then a particular set of consequences will result. Such cinematic depictions illustrate the simplicity and determinism of positivistic science's quest for certainty.

The certainty of modernity has created a host of rigid dichotomies that affect the educational research act and educational practice: objective reality and subjective experience, fact and imagination, truth and opinion, neutrality and partisanship, logic and emotion, secular and sacred, and public and private. The cause-effect linearity of modernist positivism, with its emphasis on decontextualized problem solving, sets the agenda for what we consider important about the educational process. From the perspective of Ilya Prigogine, the 1977 Nobel Prize winner in chemistry and proponent of postmodernist chaos theory, such linearity not only determines what we consider important about the world but distorts our view of the world in the process. Prigogine argues that unstable dissipative structures are far more common than structures that are stable (Prigogine and Stengers, 1984:209). The recognition of these unstable dissipative structures is a major step in the human attempt to make sense of the physical and social world. We need to move beyond both modernity's simplistic linearity and its yearning for certainty and adopt more sophisticated tools of analysis.

A postmodern mode of analysis assumes that the world is complex, characterized by a web-like configuration of interacting forces. Scientists, like everyone else, are inside, not outside, the web. As we realized in Chapter 2, the knower and the known are inseparable — they are both a part of the web of reality. No one in this web-like configuration of the universe can achieve a God-like perspective — no one can totally escape the web and look back at it from afar. We all must confess our subjectivity; we must recognize our limited vantage point. To recognize how our particular view of the web shapes our conception of educational reality, we need to understand our historicity. Cause–effect educational research tends to ignore the way our historicity (our place in space and time) works to construct our consciousness; as a result, our concept of social activity and of the educational process is reduced to a static frame. Thus, the positivistic researcher feels empowered to make predictions, to settle questions, to ignore the dialectical process in which all social activity is grounded. From this perspective linear mathematics controls the variables, eliminates extraneous perturbations, and paints a Norman Rockwell portrait of the schoolhouse (Doll, 1989:244–7; Slaughter, 1989:265).

Prigogine and postmodern analysts realize that such simplicity does not work. A so-called 'extraneous perturbation' falling into the complex interactions we have referred to as the web of reality, can produce an expanding, exponential effect. Inconsequential entities can have a profound effect in a non-linear universe. The shape of the physical and social world depends of the smallest part. The part in a sense is the whole, for via the action of any particular part the whole in the form of transformative change may be seen. To exclude such considerations is to miss the nature of the interactions which constitute reality. The development of a postmodern reconceptualization of educational research does not mean that we simplistically reject all empirical science — obviously there are questions in education which involve counting, figuring percentages, averages, etc. It does mean, however, that we conceive of such empirical questions as one part of the web, i.e., the interactive configuration. A postmodern reconceptualization of educational research means recognizing, as Dewey did, as feminist epistemology does, that the knower and the known are intimately connected, that a science which separates fact from value, purpose, and belief is a pseudo-science divorced from the *Lebenswelt*, the lived world of human consciousness. Such a reconceptualization reminds us as teacher researchers that we can display our findings and argue for their value, but always with one hesitation, a stutter, a tentativeness — never as the truth (Besag, 1986b:21; Doll, 1989:247–8; Briggs and Peat, 1989).

'So what?', many teachers interested in action research may ask, We just want to learn the five steps to classroom research, they argue. Why all this talk about the postmodernist response to the quest for certainty? As with the other themes of this book, the reason that such explorations are important involves the way they shape our professional consciousness. The models of teaching we are taught, the definitions of research which support our inquiry, the angles from which we view intelligence, the modes of learning which shape the way we think all emerge from the certainty of modernism. Like reality itself schools and classrooms are complex webs of interactions, codes, and signifiers in which both teachers and students are interlaced. Just as postmodernism asserts that there is no single, privileged way to see the world, there is no one way of seeing the classroom, seeing intelligence, seeing teacher or pupil success. Once teachers escape the entrapment of the positivistic way of seeing, they come to value and thus pursue new frames of reference in regard to their students, their classrooms, their workplaces. They begin to look at their lessons from the perspective of their students — their black students, their Hispanic students, their white students, their poor students, their middle and upper middle class students, their traditionally successful students, their unsuccessful students. They examine their teaching from the vantage point of their colleagues or an outside lay observer from the community. Thus, they step out of their teacher bodies looking down on themselves and their students as outsiders. As they hover above themselves they examine their teacher education with its emphasis on bulletin board construction, behavioral objective writing, discussion skill development, and classroom management. They begin to see that such professional training reflects the certainty of modernity, as it assumes that professional actions are reducible to a set of skills applicable to all situations (Nixon, 1981:195–6).

But if science can't be certain, and if we come to realize that our particular location in the web influences what we see, how then can educational research be of any value? Many teachers become quite anxious upon such realizations and without reflection assert that research is a waste of time, capable only of yielding opinion. They have been educated in a culture of positivism which teaches that knowledge is universally applicable, always superior to the 'softness' of opinion. Critical qualitative researchers, of course, try to alleviate teacher anxiety with the observation that even though educational inquiry has value dimensions, even though it is not absolute, it can be helpful. Critical action research, for example, can be viewed as a postmodern science of becoming. Certainty and prediction can be replaced with a notion of anticipation — the imaginative construction of the possible. Prediction is predicated on a positivistic body of empirical data and cause–effect relationships; anticipation takes empirical data into account but then moves into another dimension of the imagination. The quest for control of educational phenomena is abandoned as is the search for a precise reflection of educational reality. Postmodern research is always tentative. It is nothing more than a temporary perspective on a particular segment of the educational world, concerned with the humble process of anticipation with all of its attendant qualifications (Lincoln and Guba, 1985:184; Noblit, 1985:97; Reinharz, 1979:366).

When teachers as researchers gain the analytical ability to transcend this positivistic certainty, they begin to remake their world of practice in a way which reveals the deep structures which have determined their professional lives. Here again the notion of critical constructivism re-enters our analysis, at teacher researchers gain what can be labelled reflexive awareness. It may seem insignificant to those trapped in the culture of positivism, but the critical constructivist ability to step back from the world as we are accustomed to perceiving it and to see the ways our perception is constructed through linguistic codes, cultural signs, and embedded ideology is a giant step in learning to research, to teach, indeed, to think. We are required to construct our perception of the world anew, not just in a random way but in a manner which relativizes what appears natural, which opens to question that which seems real. We ask questions of how that which is came to be, whose interests do particular institutional arrangements serve, and from where do our own frames of reference come. In other words, we are engaging in a critical construction of the world and our relation to it. In an educational context practitioners can through action research critically construct, i.e., remake, their professional lives around the asking and answering of such questions. Facts are no longer simply 'what they are'; the truth of beliefs is not simply testable by its correspondence to these facts. Professional knowledge does not rest on the foundation of the proven. To engage in critical action research is to take part in a process of world making. To remake, to rename our world we seek guidance from our system of meaning, our emancipatory, democratic source of authority (Slaughter, 1989:264; Schon, 1987:36).

In this critical constructivist process Newtonian-like generalizations do not negate our critical system of meaning — human action is constructed not caused (Donmoyer, *forthcoming* b:5–6). For example, if scientists 'prove' via statistical techniques that one particular action results in one particular outcome, such a form of knowledge does not invalidate the larger principles, the ethical precepts which guide our actions. Educational researchers, for instance, determine a statistical correlation between ability grouping and the improvement of standardized test score averages in a set of schools. Are we to infer from this that ability grouping is a scientifically proven, effective educational technique? The answer is no because of several issues of interpretation, ethics, and justice which emerge from our democratic system of meaning. Are standardized test score improvements valid indicators of student progress? What segments of the student population improved their test scores? the worst students? the average students? the best students? What strategies did teachers use to improve the scores? Did socio-economic class play a role in the way the ability groups were divided?

Thus, the way we interpret such a study depends on the way we construct our system of meaning. The empirical data derived from the study are not simple irrefutable facts — they do not constitute certainty. They represent hidden assumptions — assumptions the critical action researcher must dig out and expose to the light of day. Ability grouping, therefore, is not necessarily the proven way to bring about educational improvement. As Einstein and Heisenberg pointed out long ago, what we see is not what we see but what we perceive. The knowledge that the world yields has to be interpreted by men and women who are a part of that world. What we call information always involves an act of human judgment (Besag, 1986b:21). In the case of ability grouping our perception of the proof of its success is quite dependent on what part of the web of reality we are entangled: from whose perspective do we see the effects of ability grouping?; what constitutes an educational improvement?; are there facets of schooling that might be more important than fact accumulation?; what happens to students placed in low ability groups? Such questions do not show up in many empirical studies. Without a critically constructed system of meaning, they will remain unasked.

The quest for certainty, action research, and the way we think are intricately entwined. It might help us visualize our notion of a critical constructivist form of research if we look at it as the highest of three levels of research cognition: Level 1, puzzle solving research; Level 2, self-monitoring, reflective research; Level 3, critical constructivist research.

First-level research revolves around the concept that puzzles are well-structured problems. All aspects necessary for a solution to a puzzle are knowable and there is a particular procedure for solving it. The role of the researcher is to learn this procedure and then to go about solving puzzles. Educational problems, thus, are viewed as puzzles for which particular solutions may be inductively agreed upon after researchers have all been exposed to a common set of empirical observations. Certainty is deemed possible because puzzles push researchers into one way of thinking — a correct pathway to a solution exists, the goal of the research act is to find it. Research as puzzle solving does not require the consideration of alternative strategies; such a view of research often blinds the inquirer to information which ostensibly does not relate to the solution of the puzzle. The attempt to verify or refute existing educational theories is a form of puzzle solving — the rules are all established *a priori*. Indeed, puzzle solving as a mode of research has little to do with the everyday world of schooling because educational decision making rarely presents itself in the form of puzzles.

Level 2 research involves a form of meta-cognition where researchers reflect on their level one research activities. Such reflection may involve the identification of mistakes and the analysis of alternative strategies and data-gathering tools in the attempt to solve the puzzle. New variables may be found which sophisticate the research process, new forms of research which provide unique perspectives on the puzzle may be applied. The third level of research draws upon our notion of critical constructivism as it opens the door to epistemological considerations. Here, researchers examine the criteria of knowing, and the certainty of knowing, asking questions about the nature of problems themselves. An important difference between the levels of research cognition involves the Level 2 analysis of the problem solving potential of a particular research strategy and the Level 3 questioning of whether or not particular research questions allow for a solution we know for certain to be correct.

Most research in educational situations involves ill-structured problems. Puzzles and ill-structured problems are different epistemologically, that is in the ways they can be known. To argue that the act of teaching is a puzzle problem is to trivialize its multi-dimensional complexity — teacher education too often treats it as such. Differences in these epistemological assumptions become very important when teacher researchers begin to consider the types of questions they want to ask about their teaching. Here again we turn to our system of meaning to help us select our questions. We critically construct our epistemological compass which guides us through the morass of research conventionalism and its level one and two assumptions about the existence of an objective reality, a puzzle-filled universe that is absolutely knowable and known. Level 3 teacher research with its postmodern rejection of certainty transcends the conventional view of inquiry which accepts the universal applicability of the educational knowledge base. There is a correct way, conventionalists assume, to set up a fifth grade math class.

Each level of research is necessary to the understanding of the next. Indeed, there are puzzle-like questions in education that lend themselves to empirical analysis. A form of meta-cognition is undoubtedly valuable to the sophistication of such empirical questions. But such forms of research cognition do researchers little good when we begin to look at ill-defined questions such as: What is the relationship between school performance and social class?; and, How do definitions of intelligence affect that relationship?. To approach the problem researchers must gather empirical evidence about school performance and its relationship to social class. Also important is empirical data on the ways that intelligence tends to be defined by particular groups. The gathering of such information is a level one research activity. In the process of finding such evidence researchers may gain a meta-awareness of problems in their samples and of better (maybe more qualitative ways) of understanding the complexity of the various relationships. To make sense of the data acquired we must move to a Level 3, critical constructivist form of research. Here we draw upon our critical sense of meaning to understand the significance of the evidence collected. What do we ask of it? For what purposes might we put it to use? Now that we understand certain aspects of the relationships between school performance, social class, and definitions of intelligence, what might we do in schools that we are not now doing? Our data seems to tell us that social class background influences students' perceptions of what role schools are supposed to play in their lives. Students from lower socio-economic class homes not only tend to make lower grades but hold different definitions of school success than middle and upper-middle class students. We have discovered that the definitions of intelligence used by school leaders better match the middle and upper-middle class students' definitions of intelligence than they do lower socio-economic class students.

With this information in hand, what do we do? Drawing on a critical system of meaning which has reconceptualized the concept of justice, rendering it more than a legalistic notion, we may seek to engage teachers in a dialogue about how different socio-economic groups come to define intelligence and what we as teachers have to learn from such conflicting definitions. In the process teachers may come to see intelligence in a context which enhances understanding of the inherent inability of educational psychologists and educational leaders to provide a universally-applicable, certain answer to the question, 'what is intelligence?'. What we define as intelligence often depends on where we are standing in the web of reality — from what socio-economic location? from what gender location? from what racial or ethnic location? Such analysis turns teachers' thoughts about intelligence inward, encouraging them to examine their own definitions and the impact such definitions make on the ways they approach students from different backgrounds. Such analysis induces teachers to consider how their approaches affect school performance of diverse students, their self-concepts, and their view of the role of schools in their lives. Thus, without this third level of analysis the research act ends before its meaning can be explored.

It is here at Level 3 that teacher researchers learn to think about their professional lives in a post-formal way: What are the significant questions which come out of research data?; What are the purposes of our professional lives?; What does it mean to possess knowledge about educational activities? It is at Level 3 that we must consider the nature of the research problem and adopt a type of thinking which is contextually appropriate. In the example concerning school performance, socio-economic class, and definitions of intelligence educational research as puzzle solving is entirely inappropriate. Although Level 1 and Level 2 questions are a part of our example and are certainly important, such questions of this type hold implicit dimensions which might be examined at a critical constructivist level of research. These Level 3 questions yield results which are entirely unpredictable, often leading to higher stages of consciousness and awareness on the part of the researcher. At these higher stages of consciousness multiple answers of equal validity to research questions may co-exist. By definition the higher state of consciousness which emerges from Level 3 analysis demands a loss of a certain degree of comfort and certainty (Kitchner, 1983:222–8; Altrichter and Posch, 1989:22; Slaughter, 1989:264–5). Again referring to our example, we can never again be sure of just what intelligence is; we can never rest comfortably with particular conceptions of school success; we can never assume that we hold a privileged perspective on such matters from outside the web of reality — we, too, are flies entangled in a particular part of the web. But if we are conscious of our position there is no reason for despair. We are human agents capable of much more than simply following rules to solve pre-defined problems. We are active interpreters and negotiators involved in an exciting process of cultural reconstruction and educational reconceptualization. If we hold the power to reconstruct our own consciousnesses, then we are capable of reinterpreting our traditions and reinventing our futures together in solidarity with other self-directed human agents.

Practitioner thinking, of course, is intricately connected to these levels of research cognition. The teacher researchers who operate at a critical constructivist level seem to be more tolerant, flexible, and adaptive, and employ a wider repertoire of teaching models. They tend to be more self-directed and better equipped to handle paradox, contradiction, and conceptual complexity. The teacher researcher operating at a critical constructivist level enters into a post-conventional world where certainty is sacrificed in the recognition of discrepancies between surface appearances and inner reality. Such a recognition allows a teacher researcher to use action inquiry as a vehicle to overcome bureaucratic definitions of his or her deskilled role in the workplace. Action research in this context transcends mere teacher monitoring of the implementation of administrative edicts; it involves the analysis of structural effects of schooling and the generation of new knowledge (Oja and Ham, 1984:171–3, 180–1).

Level 3 teacher research adopts a progressive view of knowledge which assumes that even as data is being collected it is being subjected to critical analysis. A more positivistic view of knowledge assumes that only after one knows the facts is he or she ready to analyze. Such a view misses the important point that what we designate as the facts is an act of interpretation — in the case of positivistic research it is an unconscious act of interpretation. Knowledge derived from research in a level three critical constructivist orientation is not a static or inert entity — privileged groups with the authority to certify knowledge have often taken this viewpoint. Critical constructivist research proceeds tentatively, ever mindful of ambiguity and uncertainty. When we know for certain, little need exists to pursue alternative ways of knowing. 'Deviant ways of seeing' are dismissed as irrelevant — they are not viewed as an important source of new insight and socio-educational innovation (Romanish, 1986:49–50; Schon, 1987:18).

This view of research cognition as critical constructivism revolutionizes the way we view teaching and the education of teachers. The negative consequences of the quest for certainty are avoided, as teacher researchers and teacher educators begin to imagine and construct new ways of thinking about teaching and teacher education. If the act of teaching was known and constant, teachers could act on empirical generalizations and teacher educators would know exactly what teachers needed to know to perform successfully. But teaching is not constant and predictable — it always takes place in a microcosm of uncertainty. Thus, what we call valuable practitioner knowledge is elusive. How to teach teachers what to do in conditions of uncertainty is even more elusive. The positivism of professional schools of education in the early twentieth century used science to eliminate the uncertainty of professional practice and replace it with empirical knowledge about the teaching act. The cult of the expert in the educational sphere precluded an admission of uncertainty. The uniqueness of particular teaching situations was ignored by educational researchers/experts whose clients demanded official knowledge — knowledge which specified the scientifically-sanctioned 'right way' to proceed (Schon, 1987:6, 11–13, 171). In a culture which relies on the expert for guidance, uncertainty doesn't play well — indeed, recognition of complexity and attendant certainty are the accoutrements of strength, of positive, affirmative leadership. The higher our levels of research cognition, the weaker our perspectives often appear to a culture which has been conditioned to buy into a quest for certainty. This cruel irony tends to impede the attempt to teach sophisticated, critical thinking and to retard the movement to put teachers into positions of control over their workplaces.

Chapter 7

Verifiability

Positivistic social sciences are concerned with developing verifiable knowledge. The logical positivists of the Vienna Circle developed the verifiability principle of meaning which contended that something is meaningful only if it is verified through the senses (empirically). The verifiability principle necessitates the use of operational definitions to specify that which is under study (Popkewitz, 1981b:307; Phillips, 1983:5). An operational definition assigns meaning to an entity by enumerating the activities (operations) necessary to its measurement. The operational definition serves as a manual of instructions for a researcher, granting him or her a list of activities necessary to the research process. Fred Kerlinger gives an example of an operational definition of intelligence: 'Intelligence ... is scores on X intelligence test, or intelligence is what X intelligence test measures (Kerlinger, 1973:31).

The positivistic impulse and the behavioristic research traditions merge with Thorndike's argument that anything which exists, exists in some amount and can thus be measured. Such an idea when applied to education focuses research on statistical analysis of quantified variables. If the objects of positivistic research in education can always be quantified, then anti-positivists argue that quantifiability becomes an essential precondition for that which is to be studied. Thus, given enough time the truth or falsity of the findings of educational research can be established — i.e., data can ultimately be verified in a quantifiable manner (Macmillian and Garrison, 1984:17; Donmoyer, 1985:16).

Denis Phillips claims that the verifiability principle of the logical positivists died long ago, choking to death under its own weight. It was never clear about how to verify scientific principles — using its own criteria for meaning, a principle was not verifiable through the senses. Instead of criticizing and misrepresenting positivism, Phillips argues, eclecticists such as Eisner and Giroux should begin devising methods of verifying knowledge and separating fact from belief.

Phillips represents a host of social science and education researchers who express great discomfort with eclecticist, qualitative research. If what counts as knowledge is perpetually determined by values and interests and if objectivity is always socially agreed upon, what is left to protect us from relativism? If individuals can invent their microcosms, how can researchers distinguish truth from fiction? We have gone far enough, Phillips and his supporters argue. In our rejection of positivism we have thrown out the baby with the bathwater and in the process, they argue, we have done away with the concept of a mistake. The attempt to verify data is complicated by the post-Kuhnian proliferation of research strategies. Positivists are horrified by the breakdown of knowledge; anti-positivists are heartened by the possibility of new forms of understanding (Phillips, 1983:7–12).

A breakdown of knowledge? No way of determining a mistake? You must be kidding, research eclecticists taunt their critics. Proponents of pluralistic methods contend that different research methods produce different perspectives, that different theories couch their observations in divergent terms, that different world views lead to different conclusions. The result of these contentions, they assert, does not lead to the conclusion that there is no way of knowing when someone has made a mistake. Positivists want a single way to validate a statement. In many ways, the eclecticists argue, positivists are like religious fundamentalists in their belief that there is only one way to heaven — validation (Smith, 1983:ll; Eisner, 1983:13; Phillips, 1983:12).

Those of us who hold the validity of a variety of ways of approaching reality, eclecticists contend, have not abandoned rationality — logocentrism yes, rationality, no. We must be aware of alternative paradigms and develop rational methods of selecting one as we contemplate our research. If empirical evidence, for example, is not appropriate for assessing the worth of information, then some other basis for validation or some critical reconceptualization of the term must be developed. Generally, researchers in education have not considered the question of alternative paradigms and the rational search for alternative methods of validation. Often educational researchers have found themselves unable to see beyond empirical validation of their research data. Mistakes are determined via empirical methods or not at all.

In the attempt to transcend empirical methods of validation, researchers need guidance. One of the best ways to initiate thinking about a reconceptualization, a redefinition of validation might involve discussion of different orders of mistakes. First-order mistakes result when evidence cannot support conclusions that are arrived upon through the use of a particular language. Examples of such mistakes would involve problems of researchers concerned with traditional experimental and correlational design, e.g., inappropriate generalization and inadequate sample size. Second-order mistakes come about when language employed to state propositions is inappropriate for particular purposes. A good example of such a mistake would be Newtonian physics, as its language is inadequate when we travel at the speed of light. Third-order mistakes involve the inadequacy of the purposes of the research. An example of a concern with third-order mistakes is Henry Giroux's critique of mainstream educational research. Giroux's critique is not primarily concerned with methodology or language; the focus of the critique is on questions of overall purpose. The analysis of third-order mistakes helps researchers choose between competing paradigms (Eisner, 1983:13). Such orders of mistakes are similar to our concept of the levels of research cognition.

Positivists argue that the only way to avoid mistakes is through the application of a rigorous research methodology, i.e., one that follows a strict set of objective procedures which separate the researcher from that being researched. In order to be meaningful, the argument goes, social inquiry must be rigorous. Indeed, positivists see the pursuit of rigor as the most effective means to validation. The basis of rigorous research is, of course, quantification. Unambiguous and precise, rigorous quantitative research reduces subjective influences and minimizes the ways in which information might be interpreted.

Positivists have traditionally preferred quantitative to qualitative data because of the search for methodological rigor and thus freedom from the distortion of human subjectivity. Among most social science researchers quantitative research might at first glance appear to be a superior means to approach validation. Let us follow an argument presented by Kenneth R. Howe which raises some questions about this assumption.

'Mrs. Johnson's class contains 29 students', is an example of an observation sentence in which the data is low in fallibility. The phrase, low fallibility, means that there will be a high degree of agreement as to the accuracy of the data by observers regardless of their world views and backgrounds.

'Mrs. Johnson's class was more valuable than most middle school classes in that students, through Mrs. Johnson's assistance, began to understand their own personal histories and in the process made an important step toward self-direction'. Here the data is quite distanced from a simple observation statement and has high fallibility, meaning that intersubjective agreement as to its accuracy will be low. Thus, it has been often stated that quantitative data is superior to qualitative data relative to the criterion of fallibility. Howe argues that this judgment cannot be generalized and just the opposite ordering of fallibility is often the case in social and educational research.

To prove his point, Howe offers the example of the testing of a research instrument designed to evaluate attitudes. Of course, the basic aim of such a research instrument is to gather quantitative data about attitudes. Experience teaches us over and over again that measurements of attitude are afflicted by problems of interpretation. These interpretive problems are often so severe that the validity of the data obtained from the instrument is questionable. Because of the imprecision of language, differences of interpretation of the instrument's questions by researchers and respondents, different criteria on the part of the respondents for marking the intensity of response (1-strongly agree, 2-agree, 3-no opinion, 4-disagree, 5-strongly disagree), conflicting assessments of both the meaning of the respondents' replies and the social forces which shaped them, and the diverse interests of the researchers interpreting the attitudinal scales, such quantitative research tends to be highly fallible — to say the least, certainty is elusive.

The only way to lessen the fallibility, Howe argues, is to induce respondents to discuss the instrument. Researchers must ask for and listen to the opinions of the respondents about the meaning of their responses and how the instrument might be interpreted. Such opinions are, of course, qualitative data and are very distanced from simple observation statements. But, this subjective data is being used in this case to reduce the fallibility of the quantitative data collected. Thus, in this situation the qualitative method is less fallible than the quantitative method (Howe, 1985:13–14).

Validation is thus rendered more problematic than many quantitative-empirical researchers would prefer. There is less certainty and more fallibility in survey data-gathering, correlational studies, and control treatment experiments than educational researchers would like to admit. Many philosophers of educational research wince when Fred Kerlinger argues that research methods are procedures on which beliefs have no effects. Techniques of inquiry, he maintains, are skills which exist independent of the predispositions, politics, and commitments of those people who do research.

Many philosophers of research not only doubt Kerlinger's protestations of the possibility of objectivity, but they even doubt that empirical researchers themselves really follow the rigorous methodological steps advocated by researchers like Kerlinger. Actual research, they argue, is often quite different from the so-called reconstructed logics that writers of textbooks on educational research espouse. Real-life field researchers use what is termed logic-in use, which refers to the reasonable, flexible, and expedient means often employed when undertaking a project. The logic-in-use research process is often a capricious journey with side trips and lots of dead-end streets. These detours, however, are usually omitted when it comes time to write up and justify research findings. The intuitive leaps, the thinking which gave birth to the research question, the values which moved the researcher to pursue a particular question are usually not included in the reconstructed logics of educational research. The final reports, many analysts would argue, are idealized versions of what researchers believe pure scientific method and the most rational form of research should be (Howe, 1985:13–14; Donmoyer, 1985:13–19).

Research eclecticists do not want the search for empirical validation, methodological rigor, or data infallibility to sabotage the search for significance. To be rigorous is one thing, to focus on significant reality is something else. If the rigorous method is not suited to the subject matter, it contributes little to understanding. Methodology should not be criticized as ambiguous and vague, if the problems to which it is applied are ambiguous and vague. And this is the condition of educational research — the problems of the educational world are complex, not given to simple description, and rarely reducible to only a few variables. The inability of a research orientation to produce infallible research outcomes is not a mark of failure; it reflects the inherent properties of the reality under scrutiny and the types of complex questions that the students of the discipline ask about the meaning of that complex reality (Kerlinger, 1973:12–15; Soltis, 1984:6).

Consider the question of the control of variables in this context. Take, for example, the hundreds of studies conducted on classroom discipline in the last thirty years. In addition to problems of sample size, of the relationship between what is defined as good discipline and desirable educational achievements, and of cause and effect, the control of variables in discipline research presents special difficulties. Literally thousands of unmentioned factors have a significant influence on what happens in any classroom (Fiske and Shweder, 1986:13; Barrow, 1984:153). One student may respond to a specific teacher's disciplinary action in one manner, not because of the disciplinary action itself, but because he or she is accustomed to a certain type of disciplinary action at home. An American Indian child, for example, raised in a permissive home may interpret a subtle, mildly coercive, non-corporal disciplinary act very differently from a black child raised in a strict home where the rod is not spared. To the Indian child, the disciplinary action is understandable and consistent with prior experience; to the black child it is a sign of the teacher's weakness.

Another child reacts differently to the subtle, mildly coercive disciplinary act because of the nature of his or her relationship with the teacher. A student, whose parents are long-time acquaintances of the teacher, knows the teacher as a trusted friend. When confronted with corrective action of any kind, this student may feel very embarrassed because he or she is unaccustomed to conflict in his or her relationship with the teacher. What appears to the researcher as a mild admonishment elicits a great deal of embarrassment from the student. Another student is affected by the presence of an outside observer and reacts in a way that is inconsistent with prior behavior. There is no way that the observer can account for all of the possible variables which may affect what is being observed (Barrow, 1984:153).

The various facets of a student's or a teacher's nature, of every individual's background, of every context, and of all the interrelationships and combinations of these factors, may be the key elements in helping explain what is going on in a classroom. The point is that the uniqueness of the combination of the factors may constitute the explanation for what is happening in Mr. King's tenth grade English class on March 12, 1993; if it is unique, then it cannot be used as a basis for generalization. If variables cannot be controlled, data certainly cannot be validated in any empirical sense.

Much research on teaching is validated, non-empiricists argue, only by means of the analytic and the arbitrary. The analytic means of validation involves that which is true by definition; the arbitrary is that which is significant only in the particular case, and thus is arbitrary, not a constant which lends itself to generalization (Barrow 1984:186). Kieran Egan illustrates the analytic and the arbitrary methods of validation using a couple of examples. He writes of a hypothesis set up for empirical validation: lists of facts presented in an ordered way are easier to learn than facts presented in an unordered way. The task of the empirical researcher is to validate or not validate this hypothesis.

Couched within the hypothesis, however, is an analytic element, i.e., something that by necessity is already true. It is already true that a body of facts that is ordered in some manner is easier to learn than one which is not because of the conceptual relationship between learning and order. It is a logical impossibility to learn a list of facts which possesses no pattern or order. The process of learning imposes an order on the list. Understanding, a corollary of learning, involves the shaping of that which is learned. Even rote learning involves the imposition of pattern even if the pattern is only based on sound. One does not need to formulate an empirical study to discover that. Yet, study after educational study seeks to validate hypotheses such as the more time on task a student spends, the more he or she learns. Why bother?

Following Egan's examples, the important questions thus become: What do we mean by ordering?; When does something become ordered?; and What types of ordering facilitate the learning process? Obviously, different configurations of facts may appear ordered to different people. Bob looks at a list of numbers which are apparently random; Martha looks at them and sees her telephone number. This is where Egan's conception of arbitrary validation appears. Empirical research finds that some children learn some lists better than others and vice versa. Researchers give some children ordered lists and others unordered lists, but, as we already understand, all learned lists are ordered in some way. The differences in the list learning of the different children has to do with their divergent conceptions of what is and is not ordered. The child who can learn list A more easily than list B apparently sees more order in list A than in list B. Empirical researchers have often missed this point as they observe the child. The investigators impute an ability of the child to learn an unordered list — it is a list unordered from the *researcher's* perspective. In other words, the child saw order where the researcher did not. There is nothing to be validated or generalized from such research. If researchers find that certain factual list arrangements enhance student learning in one specific context in one specific study, it does not follow that another student will experience similar learning enhancement. His or her perception of order may be quite different.

Another example of the problematic nature of empirical validation of research on teaching involves inquiries into the relationship between teaching style and student performance. Typically, researchers attempt to validate relationships between so-called styles of teaching and standardized test score improvement. In addition to questions such as the control of important variables and the reliability of standardized tests, the question of the validity of the categorization of teaching styles emerges. Critical researchers make the argument that the attempt to reduce teaching styles to, say, two or three categories is futile. In practice no teacher will clearly represent one category. In other words, no teacher will display only the characteristics of a formal teacher as opposed to an informal teacher. All teachers to some extent are formal in some regards and informal in others. When disagreements over the characteristics of the different styles appear, the validity of the categories is called into further question.

When observers classify the same teacher differently the conclusions drawn from the data will, of course, be significantly affected. In order to manage the data of such studies, teaching styles must be reduced to a minimal number of categories. While it may be profitable to classify cars or hats in terms of styles, it is probably unwise to classify loving or teaching in such a manner — especially when we feel the necessity to lay out only two or three types. Empirical validation is such contexts is a pipe dream, logically impossible because of the complexity of the reality of human experience (Barrow, 1984:192).

Where does all of this leave validation? We must reconstruct our thinking about the meaning and applicability of the concept of validation in the context of educational research, eclecticists argue. Our goal in research is not merely to validate the statistical relationship of variables but is to understand, to make intelligible, and to preserve the cohesiveness of the phenomena being studied. This process may better be accomplished by portraying patterns rather than by discovering causes. As a result, a researcher may be more concerned with choosing a language where signification and the concern with meaning take precedence over statistical significance. Indeed, eclecticists may be more concerned with unique events than with repetitive ones that allow researchers to manipulate quantifiable variables. Proponents of research pluralism are less concerned with reducing the world to atomistic parts which can be quantified than with the attempt to create a social synthesis which leads to a new level of understanding. The level of understanding that can be obtained is limited only by the vision of researcher (Frankel, 1986:356–7). Before we can reach those new levels of understanding, before we can attain Level 3 critical constructivist research cognition, we must reconceptualize the notion of verifiability. In the process of this reconceptualization we might draw insight from the limitations of the traditional positivistic definitions of verifiability. We have already discussed how setting influences human behavior. The 'place' (Kincheloe and Pinar, 1991) in which social activity, consciousness construction, and schooling occurs cannot be dismissed by the inquirer. When researchers attempt to remove human activity from its place, its natural setting, serious consequences result. Contrived settings, often positivistic laboratory situations, are set up by researchers who hold similar implicit assumptions, ask similar questions, and look for similar outcome measurements. Is it suprising that such settings are perceived to generate regularities in individual behavior — regularities which form the basis for verified generalizations? (Wilson, 1977:247–8).

Such a system of verification, of truth claim for research findings, tells us little about how the world works, how consciousness is constructed, how schools operate. A process of verification which is conducted in a non-naturalistic, artificial venue attends only to particular, measurable, isolated variables. Such variables are sometimes so isolated, so insignificant in light of the multitude of other variables not explored that the results of the inquiry are irrelevant. The validity claims of such research are, to say the least, questionable. Positivistic laboratory researchers present verified knowledge about how a particular technique produces success in teaching; understanding their process of verification we may hold justifiable skepticism that such a technique will prove successful in a real school, in the everyday classroom that teachers inhabit. Remove this concept for a moment from the educational world and think of it in a zoological context. Ethologists have written of similar insights into research on animals. Research conducted in animal labs or zoos produces data on wildlife that has little to do with how they behave in natural settings. Zoos, labs, and questionnaires in a sense become unique settings in their own right with their own dynamics and peculiar forces which help mold behavior (Orteza, 1988:26; Wilson, 1977:248).

Positivistic researchers in their search for verifiable data fail to recognize that their controlled situations take on this Frankenstein life of their own. Such blindness precludes understanding of the often hidden processes by which settings shape behavior. Both the physical arrangements of the settings and the subjects internalized expectations of what is allowable generate forces which help fashion research findings. In natural settings such as schools participant behavior cannot be understood without careful attention to the participant's relationship to the traditions, norms, roles, and values which are inseparable from the lived world of the institutions. The inability of positivistic researchers to say very much that is meaningful about school life is due in part to their lack of regard for these often invisible, but foundational aspects of organizational life. Research removed from the natural setting cannot account for such aspects of organizational life because they are not present in the contrived laboratory situation — hence, the truth value of the knowledge produced is undermined (Eisner, 1984:450; Wilson, 1977:247–8).

If the truth value of research is indeed undermined, positivistic researchers find themselves in a crisis of verification. Critical teacher research seeks a way out of this crisis; the way out involves our attempt to reconceptualize the notion of verifiability. One place to start is to distinguish traditional positivistic verifiability from a more critical, qualitative perspective. As we have already argued, traditional positivistic verifiability is rational, based on a mathematical set of assumptions; we might conceive of the critical, qualitative orientation in a more emotionally empathetic, artistic frame. Where positivistic verifiability rests on a rational proof built upon literal, intended meaning, a critical qualitative perspective always involves a less certain approach characterized by participant reflection and emotional involvement. With these general statements in mind the central question emerges: How do we judge the quality of of inquiry carried out by critical teacher researchers? (Reinharz, 1979:361; Lincoln and Guba, 1985:11).

The question is complex — validity is probably an inappropriate word in the non-positivistic context. We need to move beyond the attempt to develop critical qualitative research criteria that parallel those of the positivist paradigm. Qualitative researchers have sometimes failed to move research to a higher level of cognition when they have allowed the positivistic tradition to dictate their vocabulary, their grammar, and their criteria for research quality. To a critical constructivist teacher researcher validity means much more than the traditional definitions of internal and external validity usually associated with the concept. Positivism has traditionally defined internal validity as the extent to which a researcher's observations and measurements are true descriptions of a particular reality; external validity has been defined as the degree to which such descriptions can be accurately compared to other groups. Is trustworthiness a more appropriate word to use in a critical constructivist research lexicon? Maybe such a word is helpful because it connotes and signifies a different set of assumptions about research purposes than does the term 'validity'. Let us consider what criteria might be used to assess the trustworthiness of critical constructivist teacher research.

1 *Credibility of portrayals of constructed realities.* Critical teacher researchers reject the positivistic notion of internal validity which is based on the assumption that a tangible, knowable reality exists and research descriptions accurately portray that reality. Our reconceptualization of validity discards the concept of internal validity replacing it with the notion of credibility of the researcher's portrayals of constructed realities. Such a category recognizes the postmodern concept that the world is not explicable in

terms of simplistic cause–effect relationships. The universe can be viewed from multiple perspectives which are constructions of the human mind. There is no absolute benchmark to which we can turn for certainty and comfort — we award credibility only when the constructions are plausible to those who constructed them. And even then there may be disagreement, for the researcher may see ideological distortions in the constructions of those researched — distortions which those researched may not see themselves. Indeed, the researched may argue that the word 'distortion' is entirely inappropriate when applied to them. Thus, no scale can measure the trustworthiness of critical constructivist research, no TQ ('trustworthiness quotient') can be developed.

2　*Anticipatory accommodation.* Here critical constructivist researchers reject the positivistic notion of external validity. The ability to make pristine generalizations from one research study to another again accepts a one-dimensional, cause–effect universe. In a positivistic context all that is needed to ensure transferability is to understand with a high level of internal validity something about a particular classroom and to know that the make-up of this classroom is representative of another classroom to which the generalization is being applied. The positivist would argue that the generalization derived from the first classroom is valid in all classrooms within that same population. Time or context factors are irrelevant in the positivistic context. Many qualitative researchers have argued that this positivistic concept of external validity is far too simplistic and assert that if generalizations are to be made, if we are to be able to apply findings in context A to context B, we must make sure that the contexts being compared are empirically similar. This is an important step (it moves us from Level 1 puzzle solving to Level 2 reflective research cognition) for it alerts us to the misleading nature of what passes for positivistic, nomothetic generalization. But another step, maybe a leap, is necessary. Our notion of transferability of research findings from one context to another is still quite constricted by this Level 2 qualitative perspective. If we accept a Piagetian notion of cognitive constructivism, we begin to see that in everyday situations humans don't make generalizations in this positivistic way. Piaget's notion of accommodation seems appropriate in this context as it as asserts that humans reshape cognitive structures to accommodate unique aspects of what is being perceived in new contexts. In other words, through our knowledge of a variety of comparable contexts we begin to understand their similarities and differences — we learn from our comparisons of different contexts. Prediction, the goal of both Level 1 and Level 2 research, is not the desired outcome, i.e., anticipatory accommodation. We will explore this concept (this criterion) in more detail later in this Chapter when we analyze the nature of generalizability. With these two criteria of trustworthiness we begin our reconceptualization of validity at a critical constructivist level.

Positivists may argue that our reconceptualization of validity is little more than an attempt to destroy our ability to truly know anything. Expressed in such language the charge may be true. But just because we may not be able to *truly* know anything (i.e., to know with certainty), this does not mean that we can't pursue knowledge and judge the quality of our pursuit within certain limits — limits that are a product of our theoretical base, our prior assumptions. From a critical action research perspective traditional efforts to achieve validated knowledge insofar as they seek to establish distance between the researcher and that which is researched actually impede our understanding and insight. We *can* pursue knowledge by promoting a closeness between researcher and researched — a closeness based on a lengthy interaction which explores the etiology of the phenomenon and seeks to discover relationships between its history and present context. As we cultivate this closeness we make use of our most powerful ways of knowing — our subjectivities and intuitions. We use our images and symbols to help explain the phenomenon we have grown to know so intimately. Our intuition is more than an occasional flash of insight; it is a tool which allows us to see the forest, the trees, and the wood and the simultaneous, multidimensional relationships among them. Research which promotes such insight, which can be used to improve our practice, is of a higher quality than that which holds internal and external validity but tells us little that we didn't already know or could use in our professional lives.

The concept of generalizability provides a key to our attempt to redefine verifiability. If critical teacher researchers can derive insight into one educational context from the analysis of another, they have made an important start in their attempt to understand what reconceptualized verifiability might mean. The restricted concept of positivistic generalizability is inappropriate for the critical educational action researcher. Practitioner fields such as teaching, counselling, and social work are concerned with individuals not aggregates, and as a result do not need empirically verified knowledge in the same way that a chemist would need it. Verified, statistically significant information from studies with large randomly selected samples, Robert Donmoyer writes, says little to particular individuals in particular situations. Thinking in terms of critical constructivism with its anticipatory accommodation, teacher researchers will always have to decide whether a research generalization is relevant to a particular student, whether the generalization needs to be fine tuned to accommodate the student's uniqueness, or whether the generalization is irrelevant to certain students in certain classrooms. Critical constructivist teacher researchers realize that verified generalizations can never tell teachers what to do; but research on teaching can help teachers raise questions and consider possibilities (Donmoyer, *forthcoming a*:2–11).

It is at this point that we can clearly see the value of action research, as it forces us as teachers to reconceptualize the notion of verifiability. It induces us to think about what knowledge in one context says to us about another situation. This concept of transferability involves more than a simple thought process. As critical teacher researchers we constantly confront the issue of the trustworthiness of our action research. What does it tell us about other situations in our own professional lives?, in other teachers' professional lives? Does it help us expand our repertoire of social constructions and the complexity of our understanding of them? Does it help us accommodate new situations in our attempt to make sense of our professional microcosm? The value of critical action research begins to become apparent: in the spirit of critical constructivism it helps us formulate questions rather than providing answers to previously constructed puzzles.

Thus, the notion of external validity is transcended; the way we compare our action research to other groups is more in terms of a heuristic (a means of furthering investigation, questioning our practice) rather than in terms of mathematical probability. If we fail to reconsider the positivistic notion of external validity, teachers will continue to argue that research has little relevance for them, that researchers (those mysterious experts sitting in the ivory towers) hold a naive and idealistic view of the real world of the classroom. Teachers intuitively know that classrooms with their many significant and peripheral variables, their chaos, are not a good place to replicate (validate) research. Validation of this type demands that the same conditions found in the original situation exist in the second situation — we can't cross the same river twice, teachers intuit. Consider what a naive view of validation teacher researchers would hold if they, like positivist researchers, attempted to externally validate research in our classrooms. Operating in this way teachers would attempt to teach a student to read using only validated general principles of reading pedagogy. Teacher spontaneity and creativity based on understandings of the unique experience of the student would be suppressed because it might not jibe with the generalized pedagogical principles (Orteza, 1988:26; Lincoln and Guba, 1985:114).

To the positivist, generalizations are the *raison d'être* of research. All this talk about particularity (i.e., the unique experience of the learner) and anticipatory accommodation seems rather fatuous to the positivist who questions the worth of inquiry which does not seek to validate generalizations. Our critical constructivist notion of anticipatory accommodation, of course, moves beyond a positivist concern with generalization. At the same time, however, it moves beyond a desire to know only the unique. We want to assimilate in the Piagetian sense — i.e., we want to understand

the commonalities of particular categories. As we seek these commonalities we are searching in a way for valid generalizations. But assimilation
without accommodation never moves beyond lower levels of research
cognition — we must understand the unique, the particularistic aspects of
our lived worlds, our classrooms in order to make a difference in the lives
of our students, to connect their particular experience to the world at
large. If we live in an instrumentally-rational world of research for the
purpose of prediction and control, our concern with the dialectic of
particularity and generalization is certainly misguided. Uniqueness and
particularity complicate the attempt to derive validated laws which can be
applied to the effort to predict and thus control human behavior. The
positivistic concept of validated generalizations reeks of determinism and
totalitarian forms of government. Researchers become partners of the
guardians, as they provide these law-givers with the validated generalizations which make it unnecessary to consider the particulars of each case.
What is good for one citizen is good for all — at least citizens in that
particular classification, sampling. What is good for one student is good
for all — at least students in that particular classification, sampling
(Lincoln and Guba, 1985:110–11). I cannot repress the Orwellian images
surrounding the positivistic view of validation.

If teachers take seriously the positivistic perspective toward the production and use of validated generalizations, they are rendered virtually
helpless by unusual or unique situations. Teachers find themselves in
much the same situation as Jack Nicholson did in the famous diner scene
in *Five Easy Pieces*. The diner had devised a set of generalizations for all
situations. When Nicholson placed a unique order, the waitress acting on
the diner's established generalizations didn't know what to do. The particularity of Nicholson's unique order could not be *accommodated* by the
'positivistic' generalizations of the diner. In a bureaucratized world which
operates on positivistic validated generalizations, we often face similar
conflicts in everyday life. Indeed, Burger King builds an entire advertising
campaign around the concept of 'have it your way', meaning that they can
perform the extraordinary feat of making a hamburger with pickles or
without, with lettuce or without, etc. This attention to particularity is so
unusual in the late twentieth century that it must be broadcast to all who
will listen. Positivistic science has created a way of seeing which denies the
researcher's and the researched's uniqueness to the point that they are
replaceable and interchangeable with any other researcher or subject —
late capitalist alienation conquers, depersonalization ensues.

There will always be a Jack Nicholson requesting the unexpected, the
chicken salad sandwich without the chicken salad; there will always be
contingencies, fissures, disjunctions, and disruptions. But in the quest for
certainty, the search for validated knowledge, researchers study groups
of things, not single things (Reinharz, 1979:114; Lincoln and Guba,
1985:114). The essence of the particular is missed when it is treated as a

sample of a species or a type — it is not itself, it is a representative. Viewed in this way the particularistic, the individualistic has no proper name; it is alienated and anonymous. A child is interesting to the positivistic researcher only as he or she represents something other than himself or herself. A theory of place as a category of particularity fights this reductionist tendency of positivistic generalization, of external validation. Place is the entity which brings the particularistic into focus; a sense of place sharpens our understanding of the individual and the psychic and social forces which direct him or her. Without place our appreciation of such particularistic forces is ever fuzzy and depersonalized. Place with its attention to local conditions renders positivistic external validation impossible. There are always differences in context from place to place, and even a single place differs over time (Kincheloe and Pinar, 1991:1–23). The notion of positivistic validation exerts a direct effect on our attempt to promote teachers as self-directed researchers. Teachers as researchers are taught to distrust the generalizability of their work. How could it be applicable to other situations when it is unscientific? It does not lend itself to statistical aggregation and thus falls short of the demands of external validity. Because such research falls short of the rigor of positivistic generalizability, teachers must turn to the authority of the traditional school hierarchy with its top-down flow of power. The status quo is thus legitimized as teachers are unable to validate their own research — they must follow the edicts derived from 'truly' scientific studies of the experts. Expert research is replicable in the positivistic sense; the personal insight of anticipatory accommodation is not (Elliott, 1989a:15–16; Besag, 1986a:12). The culture of positivism exalts validation that is rationalistic, propositional, and law-like. The trustworthiness criterion, anticipatory accommodation, is suspect in the positivistic culture because its foundation rests upon intuition, direct experience, and vicarious experience. What good is an educational insight derived from anticipatory accomodation, positivists ask, when it represents merely a time-and context-bound working hypothesis. Give us validated facts, the positivists demand (Lincoln and Guba, 1985:120).

When we think of how we learn from experience, we realize the limitations of the positivist quest for validated generalizations. In this context diversity between settings becomes a liability not an asset — the opposite should be the case. Critical constructivist researchers see diversity between settings as an opportunity for cognitive growth. Novelty of setting can sophisticate our research cognition, as it forces us to accommodate new situations. The teacher researcher, in the language of Piagetian schema theory, through accommodation begins to integrate his or her understanding of a concept to account for more and more diversity and to differentiate those understandings in a way that highlights distinctions in the meaning and application of the concept. A teacher researcher attempting to explore the meaning of intelligence, for example, would assimilate an understanding of the concept based on his or her own experience. The teacher would accommodate the concept as he or she began to examine students who were labelled unintelligent but upon a second look exhibited characteristics which in an unconventional way seemed sophisticated. The teacher would then integrate this recognition of exception (accommodation) into a broader definition of intelligence. The process of differentiation in this context would involve the teacher's ability to discover new kinds of intelligence among his or her students and to categorize these different forms of intelligence for future use. In a sense, this process of assimilating, accommodating, integrating, and differentiating is the operation that Howard Gardner followed in developing his theory of multiple intelligences. Such a process would not be constrained by a positivistic notion of verifiability but would unleash the researcher's creative powers (Flavell, 1977:7; Donmoyer, *forthcoming a*:23–4; Reinharz, 1979:116).

Once again our system of meaning helps us conceptualize the purposes and processes of our research. Because we value the insight gained from the recognition of the dialectic of particularity and generalization — the attempt to move beyond our assimilated experience, the struggle to expose the way ideology constrains our desire for self-direction, the effort to confront the way power reproduces itself in the construction of human consciousness, we ask questions about validation that those unacquainted with our system of meaning might never consider. Instead of allowing ourselves to be controlled by a positivistic concern with external validity, we seek, through a comparison of our own action research to the research of others, an integration which provides us with a higher level of understanding of particular aspects of our classrooms, of education in general. In the process of constructing a new integration we begin to reconceptualize our purposes as teachers. Thus, teacher researchers don't need to seek positivistic validation because they have to live with their findings. The professional activity of critical action researchers is shaped and grounded by their inquiry — theirs is applied research. Traditional positivistic researchers are satisfied with tests of statistical significance, often ignoring the test of lived experience. Validated information from a positivistic perspective tells us 'about' something, shunning the attempt to construct a system of meaning which helps us conceptualize the purposes research might serve and the nature of the relationship of knowledge to the construction of a teacher's or a student's consciousness (Reinharz, 1979:362).

Positivistic research does not worry about validating knowledge in a way in which people usually experience it — the thought processes of positivism are in many ways a perversion of how humans validate information and make judgments in everyday life. Such an unnatural mode of thinking, of validation does not work to extend, to integrate our understandings. When we simply validate knowledge 'about' something we fail to ask questions related to our system of meaning. In other words such a positivistic form of validation serves to keep us on a level of research assimilation (much like Level 1 puzzle solving research cognition), where we validate information merely in terms of familiar cognitive techniques. Without help from our system of meaning researchers may never ask the questions which move us to a level of research accommodation. This is where we begin to redefine validation, where we recognize that our assimilations are sometimes constructed not as much by ourselves but by dominant ideological forces within the society. This is how power is reproduced; dominant ideology blocks our recognitions of exceptions, our attempt to modify our assimilated understanding of the world of education. At this point we progress to Level 2, self-monitoring, reflective research and then on to Level 3, critical constructivist research; here validation takes on a new meaning as we gain awareness of the relationships among our system of meaning, our research findings, and our everyday experiences as teachers (Donmoyer, *forthcoming a*:28–31; Lincoln and Guba, 1985:120).

Chapter 8

The Value of the Qualitative Dimension

Ever since positivists applied physical science methods to social science research there has been a struggle to address those aspects of the human condition that need not just counting but understanding. The information that social scientists collect may include observed behavior, documents, and artifacts, but these source materials cannot be separated from the meanings granted them by past, present, and future human agents. The qualitative dimension of research attempts to appreciate this human meaning. As long as educational researchers base their inquiries around concepts with such diverse meanings as, say, intelligence, qualitative judgment will (or at least *should*) remain a central concern of educational research (Holland and Mansell, 1983:102–3; Howe, 1985:14–15).

Qualitative research is distinguished from quantitative research in that quantitative research is concerned with frequency while qualitative research is concerned with abstract characteristics of events. Qualitative researchers maintain that many natural properties cannot be expressed in quantitative terms — indeed, they will lose their reality if expressed simply in terms of frequency. Knowledge of human beings involves the understanding of qualities which cannot be described through the exclusive use of numbers. As qualitative researchers direct their attention to the meanings given to events by participants, they come to understand more than what a list of descriptions or a table of statistics could support. When positivistic researchers focus inquiry exclusively on a quantitative dimension, research in the social sciences is narrowed to those aspects which lend themselves to numerical expression. Instead of focusing on a student's attitude toward learning or his or her creativity, much educational research will instead direct its energy to achievement — an operationally defined achievement based on standardized tests at that (Willers, 1987:5; Popkewitz, 1981a:308).

Qualitative researchers are not attempting to argue that there is no need for quantitative research in education. Quantitative research is very important in a variety of educational contexts, for it often serves as a check on qualitative data. Well-executed quantitative research with an understanding of context and a concern with purpose can provide important insight into certain human affairs. Quantitative methods allow us to focus on variables of interest, and the use of mathematical symbols permits an economical summary of information.

This economy is illustrated by the attempt to perform arithmetic functions in English without the help of mathematical symbols. Many questions in education are dependent upon comparisons of specific variables. Using quantification such comparisons are rendered manageable and degrees of difference can be determined. All of these benefits and more can be derived from quantitative methods, as long as quantitative researchers are aware of the qualitative dimensions to all quantitative research. All quantitative research grows out of a qualitative context, i.e., it is shaped by paradigms, values, political tendencies, and ideologies. The problem with quantitative research in education is that it is not always aware of this qualitative dimension. Thus, to improve their 'trade' quantitative researchers must address three essential questions before, during, and after the inquiry process: 1) What is the relationship of the investigator to the investigated?; 2) What is the relationship between facts and values?; and 3) What is the goal of the investigation? (Howe, 1985:15; Sherman, Webb, and Andrews, 1984:33; Smith, 1983:6).

Philosophers of research have found the attempt to describe the universal concerns of qualitative research to be quite difficult. Because of its abstract nature different qualitative researchers will promote different goals for their research. Typically holding an eclecticist position the qualitative researcher will purposely seek divergent research strategies and goals. Recognizing this diversity as a part of the qualitative culture, Robert Sherman, Rodman Webb, and Sam Andrews set out on the difficult quest to identify the general characteristics of qualitative research. They conclude that certain characteristics can indeed be identified in most qualitative research.

One of the most important aspects of qualitative research is its concern with context. 'Context stripping' is an unfortunate feature of science, and, as such, scientific methods which do not consciously work to avoid this stripping distort the reality they attempt to portray. Human experience is shaped in particular contexts and cannot be understood if removed from those contexts. Thus, qualitative research attempts to be as naturalistic as possible, meaning that contexts must not be constructed or modified. Research must take place in the normal, everyday context of the researched. Ethnography, for example, is a quintessential form of qualitative research, as it studies events as they evolve in natural settings.

Qualitative research views experience holistically, as researchers explore all aspects of an experience. As individuals explore human situations they must attend to the variety of factors which shape them. The underlying complexities of school experience, so often missed by quantitative researchers, must be addressed by the qualitative researcher in his or her quest for holism. The connections which tie experiences together and often provide their significance in human affairs are essential features of holistic qualitative research.

One of the most important characteristics of qualitative inquiry is the belief that methods of inquiry must be appropriate to the aims of inquiry. Qualitative researchers take seriously Aristotle's point that each 'science' has relevant methods which are uncovered when inquiry takes place in the discipline's unique subject matter. This does not mean that qualitative researchers do not borrow or share different methods — they are typically eclecticists. The research methods that they employ may be diverse, but they will be consistent with the general aims of qualitative inquiry. Instead of intervening in experience by removing it from its natural setting or by structuring the 'important' aspects of the experience quantitatively, qualitative research looks for social and cultural patterns of experience, or relationships among various occurrences, or the significance of such events as they affect specific human purposes.

Qualitative research, Sherman, Webb, and Andrews argue, is concerned with experience as it is 'lived', 'felt', or 'undergone'. This concern with phenomenological consciousness is an essential aspect of qualitative research. Qualitative thinking involves the feeling and appreciation dimension of human activity which, of course, borders on the aesthetic dimension. Thus, qualitative research attempts to appreciate human experience in a manner which is empathetic to the human actors who feel it or live it. Ethnography as a mode of qualitative research succeeds to the degree it enables one to understand what goes on in a society or a social circumstance as well as the participants. The readers of high quality ethnography should feel that if they were to find themselves in the school described they would have a keen understanding of the forces which moved, say, the principal to act in a certain way.

Another common aspect of qualitative research involves the idea of making judgments. The function of this appraising aspect of qualitative research is to describe the essential qualities of events, to interpret the meanings and relationships among those events, and to appraise the significance of these events in the larger picture of social and educational concerns. In making these types of judgments qualitative research must be explicit about the social values and human interests on which its appraisals are grounded. Without such explicit delineation of this grounding, qualitative research falls prey to the same demons it criticizes in much quantitative research (Sherman, Webb, and Andrews, 1983:25–8).

With such concerns paramount in the minds of qualitative researchers common problems of educational research can be addressed. Awareness of context, holism, aims, consciousness, and appraisal can prevent educational researchers from simplistically transforming value-laden policy issues into technical questions with empirical answers. It can free researchers from the futile search for empirical answers to non-empirical questions. It can release researchers from slavish adherence to unanswerable questions of truth and falsity so that they might focus more on both the desirability of the purposes their research promotes and methods of appraising the value and credibility of research purposes in general (Donmoyer, 1985:19).

Teacher researchers use qualitative research perspectives to enrich their own unavoidably subjective view of the lived world of education. After involving ourselves in action research do we possess new and better ways of seeing educational events? Are we better able to conceptualize educational questions in general and questions about our practice in particular? Can we transcend the empty rhetoric and the cliches which often dominate education-talk, e.g., we're here for the children, we believe in quality education for everyone, our school system seeks to provide educational excellence? Does our qualitative teacher research equip us, in the spirit of anticipatory accommodation, to apply insight gained from one context to another? The purposes of qualitative research are multi-dimensional, as the inquiry attempts to engender understanding on three levels simultaneously: the issue being researched, the research process itself, and the researcher. When qualitative research is framed by our notion of critical constructivism, it becomes praxiological in the sense that it seeks to change for the better (within the context provided by our system of meaning) the issue being researched, the research process, and the researcher. It moves them in an emancipatory, democratic direction (Donmoyer, 1987:358–9; Reinharz, 1979:368).

Such a critical constructivist perspective on the purposes of qualitative inquiry values teacher empowerment, believes in human agency (i.e., the capacity of individuals to change their own lives), and trusts that teacher workplaces can become growth-inducing, humane environments. By providing techniques which allow us to see from new perspectives what schools and the contexts in which they operate are like and why they have come to be that way, qualitative research teaches action researchers to heighten their consciousnesses of themselves as players on the educational stage, to take themselves less for granted, and to view themselves as objects of study. As teachers watch themselves be educators, they ask questions such as: Who do I call on in class?; Who do I criticize and from whom do I withhold criticism?; Where in the school do I hang out?; Where do I stand when I'm teaching?; How do I arrange my room?; Do I respond differently to the misbehavior of different students? Such a perspective grants teachers a dialectic of distance — that is, a closeness to students marked by an awareness of who they are, their concerns, their interests, their experiences, their socio-economic background, their diverse forms of intelligence; but also a metaphorical distance which allows them to step back and watch from afar how their backgrounds affect their daily lives at school, their self-definitions, the perceptions of them held by other teachers, their educational success. (Bogdan and Biklen, 1983:209).

The qualitative question of appraising research value and credibility has been pondered by Elliot Eisner. Once we abandon quantitative empiricism, Eisner argues, we do not forfeit our right to make judgments about theoretical propositions and research processes. He then presents six qualitative criteria on which judgments can be made: 1) *Instrumental utility* — What does a particular perspective enable us to do?; 2) *Internal consistency* — Are the conclusions consistent with the theoretical premises on which they are based?; 3) *Validity of premises* — Do we accept the validity of the premises on which a view is based?; 4) *Economy of interpretation* — Are there more economical interpretations of data than those granted by a particular theoretical perspective?; 5) *Coherence* — Is the viewpoint logically sequential? Does it hang together?; and 6) *Aesthetic dimension* — Is the view elegantly stated? Does it evoke a strong reaction from us? (Eisner, 1983:14).

Eisner taps a wide range of mind functions and ways of knowing in his list of qualitative ways of appraising. A strong phenomenological current runs through both Eisner's list and qualitative thinking in general. Consciousness is an essential aspect of humanness, phenomenologists have argued, and should be studied if we are ever to gain significant insight into the affairs of human beings. However, the study of consciousness, phenomenologists warn, is limited by two important factors: 1) consciousness is not an object that is similar to the other objects of nature; and 2) there are aspects of consciousness which cannot be studied via traditional empirical methods of science. Ever fascinated with the content of elusive consciousness, therefore, phenomenologists cannot be concerned with the empirical question of what is or is not real. They simply begin with the nature of consciousness — whatever that nature might be — as significant data to be studied.

Phenomenology attempts to render problematic all presuppositions about the nature of its own activity, the object being investigated, and the method appropriate to this kind of inquiry (Husserl, 1970). The attempt to rid oneself of as many presuppositions as possible grants phenomenology the possibility of unmasking hidden assumptions about the nature of reality. Phenomenologists also attempt to view consciousness as intentional, meaning that it is directed toward a specific object. Another way of expressing this thought is that consciousness is consciousness of something. Thus, phenomenologists think that it is absurd to divide reality (or the research process) into subjects and objects. The two cannot be separated, and the attempt to do so distorts reality (Stewart and Mickunas, 1974:3–10).

As with *Verstehen* phenomenology involves an attempt to grasp a sense of the meaning that others ascribe to their own lived worlds. This form of understanding involves putting oneself in place of the other person and attempting to recreate his or her feelings in oneself. It is easy to see the impact of phenomenology on modes of research such as ethnography. When researchers ask not about the absolute meaning of a work of art but ask instead of its meaning for a certain individual or a group, they move research in new directions. The qualitative knowledge which emerges when researchers ask about and attempt to interpret the meanings that particular persons give to particular phenomena allows us new understandings and unique perspectives on social events and the human beings who participate in them. The human realm of intersubjective meaning becomes accessible in a way never imagined by empirical researchers, as scholars interrogate the conventions, forms, and codes of everyday social life (Smith, 1983:12; Donmoyer, 1985:17; Soltis, 1984:6).

Phenomenologically-produced understanding of the way individuals construe their world and their place in it is one way in which intersubjective knowledge leads us to new dimensions of seeing social experience. In educational inquiry such ways of seeing allow researchers to understand how teachers and students give meaning to their lived worlds in light of social and cultural forms they reflect and help produce. Indeed, such forms of inquiry facilitate our understanding of the often hidden and always ambiguous process by which education initiates us into our culture (Giroux, 1986:100; Soltis, 1984:6).

Phenomenology is a qualitative alternative to the epistemology of positivism. It presents in a sense a starting point for a teacher researcher in the attempt to move beyond the mind-set that too often runs the schools, perpetuates teacher deskilling, and makes schools bad workplaces. Having developed a critical system of meaning in Chapter 2, understanding phenomenology helps us begin our attempt to translate such a meaning system into a form of critical teaching practice. No longer do we see the role of teacher as an implementor of administrative policy, no longer do we see research as a part of a process of explaining, controlling, and predicting. Phenomenology teaches us that we cannot understand an educational act without understanding the framework, the context within which teachers, students, and administrators make sense of their thoughts, feelings, and actions. To become critical constructivist action researchers we must take at least one step *beyond* phenomenology; we must question the power relations, the ideological forces which shape that framework, that context which helps construct our thoughts, feelings, and actions (Fowler, 1984:7; Wilson, 1977:249).

Phenomenology teaches us to abandon positivistic deductive devices such as prior hypothesis formation which restricts researchers by directing their attention to often irrelevant variables. As with qualitative research in general the focus of our study in phenomenology emerges as the inquiry progresses. We focus on the perceptions of individuals, seeking the insiders' perspective. Of course, at the critical level we search for the various ways this perspective is constructed by larger social forces. To the critical phenomenologist the most influential and important reality is human perception. This reality is more important than any so-called objective reality because people act on what they perceive — perceptions have consequences, they move events, they shape lives. Consider how these ideas affect the research act in educational settings. While the positivistic researcher seeks objective, factual, verifiable portrayals of reality, phenomenologically-oriented action research will seek to understand the participants' comprehension of what is happening and how such perceptions affect their lives. Because they hold such different goals, research data derived via the two approaches will present quite different perspective on the world, the school (Fetterman, 1988:18).

This phenomenological concern with human perception of lived worlds cannot be separated from the growth of ethnography as a qualitative research method and its application to educational research over the past few decades. Ethnography is often described as the most basic form of social research. While ethnographers disagree over the relative importance of each purpose, ethnography attempts to gain knowledge about a particular culture, to identify patterns of social interaction, and to develop holistic interpretations of societies and social institutions. Thus, ethnography in education attempts to understand the nature of schools and other educational agencies in these ways, seeking to appreciate the social processes which move educational events. Phenomenology, ethnography, and historiography (which we will explore in more detail in Chapter 10) form a foundation for the qualitative challenge to positivism. Ethnography attempts to make explicit the assumptions one takes for granted as a culture member. The culture could be as broad as Japanese culture or as narrow as upper-middle class student culture of George Washington High School. The critical ethnographer of education seeks to describe the concrete experiences of everyday school/educational life and the social patterns, the deep structures which construct it. One of the most basic tools of the critical constructivist teacher researcher involves the research orientation derived from the phenomenological-ethnographic tradition (Hammersley and Atkinson, 1983:1–26).

Another basic tool of the qualitatively-oriented critical constructivist teacher researcher is semiotics. Semiotics involves the study of signs (it derives from a Greek word meaning sign) and codes. Semiotic researchers decode the systems of symbols and signs that enable human beings to derive meaning from their surroundings. Television wouldn't make sense to a Martian, for example, even if the alien could speak the language TV employed — too many signs and codes exist which could only be deciphered by an acquaintance with the lived world that TV represents. This is why individuals from one culture, even though they speak fluently the language of another culture, might completely fail to catch the humor of a situation — it is contextualized in the culture in which they are aliens.

Each language, each system of codes and signs is peculiar to a particular historically-grounded culture. Semiotics views everything in a culture as a form of communication arranged in ways similar to that of verbal language. Researchers who employ semiotics attempt to study culture as a communication phenomenon — they study it as a whole, always exploring interrelationships, never looking only at bits and pieces of it. They search for these relationships between phenomena in the context of an examination of the structures of institutions and individual consciousness. In the process they uncover previously unnoticed manifestations of how power is reproduced and how consciousness is constructed (Scholes, 1982:ix; Hodge and Kress, 1988:1).

In unexpected places semioticians uncover new insights into social and psychological processes — e.g., the forms of what people call courtesy, the packaging of fast food, the facial expressions of an employee while talking to his or her boss, the points at which movie-goers laugh during a film, etc. The school is a diamond mine for semiological study, for it abounds with codes and signs, in conventions which call for unique insight. The way teachers, students, and administrators dress, pupils' language when speaking to teachers as compared to conversations with classmates, graffiti in a middle school rest-room, systems of rewards and punishments for students, the use of bells in school, memos sent to parents, the nature of the local community's conversation about school athletics, are only a few of the many school topics which semioticians could study. Teacher researchers employing semiotics in their repertoire of qualitative research strategies might pay especially close attention to the ostensibly insignificant, off-hand comments of their students, for it is here in what is typically dismissed as noise that semiological significance is revealed. An adolescent's observation that 'You [the teacher] always pick on me', may be far more revealing when pursued than an expert's questionnaire. A pupil's excited attempt to interject a description of a RUN DMC rap into a class discussion of *Sister Carrie* may provide unique and multi-dimensional insight when analyzed semiotically. James Anthony Whitson provides excellent examples of techniques of semiotic analysis and how such techniques can be used to open new vistas on the meaning of schooling which can be adapted by critical constructivist teacher reseachers (Gibson, 1984:19; Whitson, 1986:418).

To the semiotician a text is not simply printed material. It is far more broadly defined, involving any aspect of culture which contains encoded meaning. For example, the text of a homecoming queen pageant holds multiple levels of meaning that can be read to reveal cultural insights and gender constructions. In the same way a child's lunch is a map to a child's home culture: e.g., a Mexican student in South Texas who packs a single tortilla in a paper bag; the 'lucky' suburban student whose single parent picks up lunch at McDonalds on the way to school. A basic characteristic of semiotics involves its assumption that the interpretation of a text is not tied to the author's conscious understanding of its meaning. It thus follows that the socio-educational importance of a school practice may have little to do with what those who devised and implemented it had in mind. Certain disciplinary practices may have been formulated in the minds of school leaders simply as mechanisms to keep order. The assumptions about the values, interests, and motivations of children, the purposes of schools, the meaning of democracy, the role of gender, definitions of good behavior, etc. embedded in such policies never entered into the consciousness of the school administrators as they conceived their discipline policy. The meaning of such practices is never static to the semiotician — meanings continue to reveal themselves as long as semioticians devise new questions of them. Thus, semiotics is a subversive form of research that teaches us to read the lived world in a new way. It is a form of reading that desocializes us from the official interpretations of the dominant codes; it frees us from the authorial interpretations of social texts that exploit those unequipped to question such impositions. What does the flag mean? What does school spirit mean? What does maturity mean? What does popularity in school mean? Semiotic researchers uncover their dominant meanings as well as a variety of subjugated, uncertified, oppositional meanings. As a result, semioticians cannot help but involve themselves in the study of ideology, how it expresses itself and shapes consciousness in a variety of ways in a number of different places (Whitson, 1986:419, 425; Scholes, 1982:x, 14).

Teacher researchers who employ semiotics begin to understand the school as a terrain of contestation, of competing power interests where rival groups struggle over the meaning of semiotic representations. Few forms of inquiry are better equipped to reveal the hidden divisions within the social fabric, the mystified and often unconscious struggle between the dominant and the dominated. To sustain their privilege the dominant must control representation — they must encode the world in forms that support their own interests, their own power. But such an attempt is not as easy as some analysts (e.g., traditional Marxists) have tried to portray it. V.N. Voloshinov writing in the first three decades of the twentieth century argued that we misconstruct reality when we assume that power groups simply impose their meanings on the symbols and codes of a culture. Voloshinov maintained that symbols and language systems were always 'multi-accentual,' meaning that lodged within cultural codes were oppositional interpretations. Therefore, while dominant groups certainly attempt to impose their meanings on, say, the signification of school symbols, they are not necessarily successful (Voloshinov, 1973:9; Whitson, 1986:417; Hodge and Kress, 1988:3, 19).

The study of this struggle to define cultural and educational codes and signs is one of the most important aspects of semiotic research. When the dominated are seen as merely the blind victims of the dominator's encoding of the world, a one-dimensional, deterministic view of the social world has been constructed. Hegemonized groups are not always ignorant of the attempts of the dominant to define social symbols. They resist — not all groups buy into the Bush administration's attempt to encode the American flag as a symbol of obedience to the dominant culture. Many Americans have resisted, offering a counter-hegemonic reading of the flag as a symbol of self-determination and freedom. Not all people accepted Ronald Reagan's attempt in the 1980s to appropriate the working class semiotic of Bruce Springsteen as a symbol for a restrictive, obedient form of patriotism. Many people resisted, offering a very different interpretation of the meaning of Springsteen's personal and musical imagery. Thus, the critical teacher researcher combines the insights of phenomenology and its concern with consciousness and perception, ethnography and its attention to cultural processes, historiography and its concern with the origins and intentions of educational practices, and semiotics and its identification of the variety of ways subliminal codes and signs help shape a student's and a society's educational/ideological consciousness.

The multiple readings of reality which semiotics uncovers provides an excellent starting point for our journey as qualitatively-oriented critical constructivist researchers into uncharted postmodern reality. We can no longer accept simple, linear, positivistic reality, for the complex reality of postmodernism demands recognition of multiple causations and the possibility of various vantage points in the web of the universe. The machine has functioned as the dominant metaphor of the linear positivist reality. The positivist researcher assumes that when machine-like social reality malfunctions a link in the cause-effect chain of parts has been broken. The job of the researcher is to identify the link and make the repair. But reality just doesn't work this way. For example, when the human body breaks down, doctors may identify a certain factor, but the 'cause' of the illness is always multiple. Living entities are always composed of a multitude of feedback loops — a cardinal concept in chaos theory. A home furnace is one of the most familiar forms of a simple feedback loop. We all know that when the room cools down below the temperature set on the thermostat, it responds by switching on the furnace. As the furnace heats up the room to a point above the second temperature set on the thermostat, the furnace automatically shuts off. The ear-splitting screeches produced when a microphone is placed close to a speaker, feedback, is another example of a feedback loop. Output from the amplifier is detected by the microphone and looped back into the amplifier. The chaotic sounds which result are the consequence of a feedback loop where the output of one stage turns into the input of another. Because human beings are composed of so many feedback loops — e.g., the transformation of food into energy, the increase in heart-rate in the presence of danger, etc., — the attempt to study them takes on far more complexity than traditional conceptions of cause-effect linearity could imagine (Lincoln and Guba, 1985:51; Briggs and Peat, 1989:25, 153–4).

In order to study such complex systems researchers have to move from hierarchic to heterarchic conceptions of order. Positivism saw an inherent order in the physical and social world, e.g., the divine right of kings to govern or Carl Brigham's hierarchy of the intelligence of ethnic groups. Postmodern researchers maintain that if orders exist, they exist side by side — if one order dominates, it is merely temporary and is subject to a variety of rapidly shifting forces. Because of this heterarchic conception of order any simplistic notion of determinism is destroyed. In a hierarchic universe positivists have maintained that if a researcher knows the location and velocity of all the bits and pieces of the world, the future can be predicted and controlled. But change is complex and qualitative researchers informed by a postmodern understanding have to accept the notion that change occurs dramatically and unpredictably. Operating in a closed system where variables are controlled, positivists have often promoted an orderly and predictable view of change. When the variables were controlled and protected from outside contamination, equations could be formulated and exact predictions devised. But even ostensibly very minor variables could have dramatic effects, sometimes not exhibiting themselves for long periods of time. When they did manifest themselves their effect seemed to the positivistic researcher as an aberration, probably a mistake in the construction of an equation. Not only does the critical researcher in a postmodern context lose the possibility of certainty, but he or she is faced with a need to find methods of exploring these multiple constructions of reality — thus the need for a critical constructivist view of the research act (Lincoln and Guba, 1985:51–5; Briggs and Peat, 1989:26–7).

Work in curriculum research over the last fifteen or so years has drawn upon these phenomenological, ethnographic, semiotic, and postmodern themes in an attempt to better understand the educational experience. Much of the focus of this work has been directed at apprehending the nature of the interior experience of the individual, especially within a broadly defined educational context. This interior experience is essential to social understanding in that: 1) it is affected by the external (social) world; and 2) it provides the basis for the understandings and actions which help shape the external (social) world. This reflexive purpose illustrates the importance of interior experience to educational research: it is the habitat of what we call human consciousness and the territory where meaning is produced; and it is the headquarters for a body of connections between human beings and their lived worlds. To understand the rich complexity of political and social forces, researchers must understand interior experience (Willis, 1978:68).

What we are talking about here involves the attempt to heighten individual awareness. Husserl delineated methodologies designed to facilitate understanding of the structure of consciousness and therefore the way meaning is attained. This method, which he called 'bracketing', involves consciously setting aside everyday, accepted assumptions about one's immediate apprehensions (Chamberlin, 1974:119–38). Once this bracketing of assumptions has taken place the individual examines and makes explicit all the meanings which were tacitly grounded within these immediate apprehensions. In this way individual awareness is heightened as previously hidden assumptions are revealed. The individual thus finds himself or herself more in touch with the values, fears, and associations which unconsciously direct his or her actions. Continued analysis of such factors may uncover their origins, thus contributing to greater self-understanding and self-knowledge. Admittedly, in explaining this conception of phenomenological understanding and bracketing, I have emphasized the idea of self-knowledge. This results not from a tendency toward self-absorption but from a practical necessity. The foundations of the phenomenological method must rest on a self-knowledge that once gained allows an individual or a researcher to turn his or her focus outward to more textured understanding of the interior experiences of others. Thus, the research approaches that new dimension of understanding which phenomenology claims to offer (Willis, 1978:68).

In his attempt to develop a practical method of analyzing the educational experience of the individual, William Pinar takes this phenomenological orientation and fuses it with psychoanalysis and aesthetics. He calls his analytical form, *currere* (the Latin root of the word, 'curriculum' meaning the investigation of the nature of the individual experience of the public). We are returned once again to the inner world, the *Lebenswelt*, and to its relationship with the educational experience. A traditional criticism of much of the theoretical work in education is that it is not connected with the everyday experiences of teachers and students. Pinar's use of the concept of *currere* helps bring about the synthesis of theorizing and *Lebenswelt* with all the benefits that are to be accrued from such a fusion (Pinar, 1975:384–95).

Pinar claims that in curriculum research meaning is typically derived from the analysis of the relationship between signs and experience. Taking his cue from Maxine Greene (Greene, 1975:299–317), Pinar contends that the quest for an understanding of experience impels researchers to tap their own subjectivity so that common sense may be transcended — i.e., we must go beyond what we take for granted. As researchers we must ask questions such as: What is involved in moving beyond the common sense world?; How does one initiate the process?; What possible benefits are to be derived?; Are there examples of other individuals who have accomplished such a transcendence and what did they gain?; and How do such attempts affect what we know in education? It is through such questions that we approach the *Lebenswelt* or, in Pinar's words, 'that realm of the *Lebenswelt* associated with *currere*' (Pinar, 1975:396–403).

As we engage in this phenomenological bracketing of experience in our own lives, Pinar argues that we are better prepared as researchers to apprehend the contents of consciousness as they appear to us in educational contexts. The liberation which results involves a freedom from modes of perception that reflect cultural conditioning and result in inauthentic behavior. We must loosen our identification with the contents of consciousness so that we gain some distance from them — a meta-perspective, if you will. From our new vantage point we may be able to see those psychic realms which are formed by conditioning and unconscious adherence to social convention. Critical theorists would identify the process as part of the attempt to demystify the ideological construction of consciousness (Pinar, 1975:406–7).

Once we have embarked on our quest to understand *currere*, Pinar tells us, we will uncover a great diversity of formats and sources. The educational *Lebenswelt* comes in a variety of packages — one package may contain historical information, another the insights of free association, another the contemplations of specific literary passages, and still another may hold ostensibly insignificant slices of school life. Both cognitive and intuitive insights (or a creative synthesis of the two) will inform our perception of *currere*.

At first, Pinar concludes, the information derived from our attempt to examine *currere* may be idiosyncratic. Eventually, however, our examinations will uncover 'aspects of a collective or transpersonal realm of educational experience'. In other words, once we transcend the unique details of an individual's biography, we may unlock the doors to a secret room where fundamental structures of human experience have been hidden from view. Such structures may, as phenomenologists have anticipated (Merleau-Ponty, 1962), appear very different when viewed at the stratum of individual personality but may be very similar when analyzed at the level of their roots. The understanding of these basic structures and their relationship to the socio-political world and thus their impact on the world of education may be one of the most important outcomes of phenomenological research applied to the educational *Lebenswelt* (Pinar, 1975:410–11).

In our search as critical action researchers for *currere* and the relationship between the basic structures of human experience and individual biography, we have once again run head-on into the complex dialectic of particularity and generalization. When *currere* is extended by insights from semiotics and critical constructivism, and an awareness of the dialectic of particularity and generalization is moved to the front of the researcher's consciousness, the possibility for interesting and dangerous insight emerges. In our theorizing on place, Pinar and I address this interplay of particularity and generalization. Our sense of place, our grounded particularity, loses nothing when exposed (by way of *currere's* connection of private sensation to the public space) to the anticipatory accommodation notion of generalization derived from critical constructivist research. This notion of generalization, of course, makes use of our knowledge of a variety of particular contexts, helping us to accommodate the uniqueness of each situation in a way that provides professional insight. This form of professional insight can be described as wisdom — wisdom which recognizes concurrently both similarity and difference in educational situations and allows us to anticipate what might happen and what we might do based on our recognitions (Kincheloe and Pinar, 1991:21–3).

Joel Kovel's concept of totality may extend our understanding of these issues. Totality implies a notion that is broader than either the particularity of private experience or the generalization of socio-economic pattern — yet it encompasses them both (Kovel, 1981:53). Human beings are entwined in countless ways in this totality which in the particularistic domain involves place and individual consciousness, and in the generalized realm includes psychological, social, political, and economic patterns: e.g., in psychology, patterns of learning styles; in socio-economics, patterns of school performance along the lines of class, race, and gender. Critical constructivist researchers must attend to both the particularistic and the general, especially the various levels of interaction between them — this is the totality, this is how we get to the *Lebenswelt*. The totality implies a radical reconceptualization of the research act as well as radical action. It not only directs our attention to the ways that socio-economic and ideological forces construct consciousness but also to how individual children, real life boys and girls, respond to such construction. This is why semiotics is so important to totality's extension of *currere* — it provides a method of uncovering the often hidden forces that construct consciousness at the level of everyday life, the mundane.

The totality connotes an understanding of individuals in relation to history in all its multi-dimensionality. Critical teacher researchers cannot view themselves outside of history, they need to understand the place in the web from which they see reality. History viewed from the perspective of Kovel's totality becomes a working concept inseparable from the act of critical constructivist educational research. History becomes, thus, not a simple linear story of social, economic, and political forces; neither is it a series of particularistic anecdotes. The critical teacher researcher sees history as an interplay between both the particularistic and the general that informs our understanding of our own consciousness, the forces which shape our professional lives, and the factors which help construct the world of our students. Our historical understanding sets up our move to Level 3 critical constructivist research cognition; such a move allows us entry to the private world of experience from which we were previously excluded. An ossified Marxism, for example, which disregarded the particularistic was unable to account for the conservatism of the proletariat — the working class support of Reagan-Bush militarism and trickle-down economics. It is by now a cliché to argue that control of the means of production is not a sufficient condition for emancipation — this recognition rests on Kovel's conception of totality which takes into account the ideological construction of individual consciousness (Kincheloe and Pinar, 1991:21–3). Critical teacher researchers operating in the qualitative context can make dramatic use of such a synthesis.

An example of research informed by this concern with totality, *currere*, and the *Lebenswelt* may be helpful. Feminist scholarship possibly serves as the best illustration of how researchers have tapped their own subjectivity to transcend socially-imposed, common sense definitions of reality. Feminist scholarship is almost by nature a phenomenologically-informed enterprise, finding its origin in the bracketing of everyday experiences as they relate to gender assumptions. It begins with a search for self-knowledge which eventuates in a broader knowledge of the interior experiences and the exterior social forces which shape the *Lebenswelt* of others. Feminism thus serves the critical function of liberating both men and women from a false consciousness which reflects cultural conditioning and grants humans a meta-perspective on the way gender expectations shape our inner selves.

Philosopher of science, Sandra Harding, offers an example of these phenomenological concerns in the context of biological research. Using her understanding of socially-constituted, gender-related influences on the *Lebenswelt* of biological researchers, Harding seeks to demystify androcentrism in biology. In her analysis of attempts to explain human evolution in terms of the strides made by men in hunting societies, Harding uncovers an interesting gender bias. Assuming that sex-role distinctions (hierarchical distinctions at that) exist across all cultures, biological researchers have traditionally argued that man-the-hunter developed tools as aids to hunting. This exclusive masculine use of tools contributed to bipedalism and upright posture. This led to more effective hunting techniques which were characterized by a division of labor among the hunters. This hunting behavior was viewed as the evolutionary origin of male bonding in modern society, and, as such, justifies the reason why males should want to bar women from their economic activities — the pursuit of science included. The traditional hypothesis portrays men as the agents who precipitated the evolutionary break from pre-human cultures and took the giant evolutionary leap into human culture.

The biological account of the activities of women in modern societies presents them as basically the same as feminine activities in pre-human groups. Feminist scholars aware of the unexamined androcentric *Lebenswelt* of traditional biological scholarship, have for the purposes of demystification posed an alternative 'woman-the-gatherer' hypothesis of human evolution. Where men had invented primarily stone tools, woman-the-gatherer invented tools made of sticks and reeds. Since women took care of the food gathering in the early societies, they also developed tools to defend against predators who interfered with their activities. Thus, it could be argued that woman-the-gatherer produced the tools which allowed the social organization which propelled humans into a new evolutionary epoch.

The point of the gynecentric story of the origins of human cultural evolution is not to prove its superiority over the androcentric interpretation. Harding specifically points out that it is equally impossible to prove one as it is to prove the other — and that is exactly the point. If one cannot be proved over the other then what is the basis of the androcentric theory? The origins of the interpretation come not from the data but from the assumptions of the researchers who formulated it. It was socially-construed, emerging from unexamined common sense assumptions of male superiority. The theory was epistemologically arbitrary, based on a restrictive understanding of human possibilities. In biology, undoubtedly, but in all sciences the value of intrapersonal and interpersonal knowledge has traditionally been seen as irrelevant. Harding alerts us to the value of such knowledge forms in a science as empirically-based as biology. We see androcentrism tacitly informing the research, as it dictates the selection of what might be considered a scientific problem, the important concepts and theories of the discipline, acceptable research methods, and interpretations of the result of research (Harding, 1986:95–100).

Harding's work alerts qualitatively-oriented critical constructivist researchers to the necessity of transcending surface appearances, of using the tools of phenomenology, ethnography, historiography, and semiotics to uncover the ideological constructions, the tacit assumptions which drive educational research. In the postmodern context we learn that little is as it appears to be. When critical action researchers search for deep structures which are there to be uncovered in any classroom, we discover a world of personal meaning which is socially constructed by a variety of forces and which often has little to do with the intended meaning of the official curriculum or the teacher presenting it. With this understanding the teacher researcher focuses on the world of the learner's consciousness, its uniqueness, the forces which have helped construct it, and the possible ways it may become aware of the ways it has been constructed. This realm of personal experience (Pinar's *currere*) is possibly the most unexplored aspect of school life. Testing and traditional assessment have no means of assessing it — it is not measurable in any positivistic sense.

To understand this hidden realm teacher researchers have to employ the phenomenological, ethnographic, semiotic synthesis, asking questions, making observations, and analyzing the codes which are contained in what they hear and see. Teacher research might begin with questions such as: What was going on in your mind during the lesson?; Do you see any relation between the lesson and your life out of school?; If you could have taught the lesson how would you have set it up?; What were some of the daydreams that ran through your mind during the lesson?; Can you imagine a way that you might ever use what you learned in your everyday life? The researcher might proceed with a semiotic reading of the codes embedded in the answers provided by the students. What signs and codes consistently turned up in the students' answers and what did they mean? What conspicuous silences were consistent in the student responses and what do they tell us? (Rogers, 1989:714–17).

Rosalie Wax provides insight into the way our qualitative research synthesis might be employed by educational action researchers. Examining education on an Indian reservation, Wax used her own personal experience as a foundation for analyzing the personal experiences and the perceptions of Native students and some of the forces which help shape them. As she and her research colleagues attempted to get to teacher meetings on time, they discovered at a very personal level, a level only perceivable by a 'human research instrument,' why reservation teachers and students experienced particular difficulties. Though they got out of bed at 6 a.m., washed, brushed, and groomed themselves vigorously, Wax and her research colleagues could never get themselves to look presentable in a middle-class way. The prairie dust was omnipresent, covering their clothes and toilet articles everyday. The researchers had no closets in which to protect their clothes, no irons, no clean water, no hot water for shaving, no mirrors, etc. Wax reported that the attempt to present a middle-class appearance exhausted the researchers. At this level of conscious empathy, not through questionnaires or even interviews, the ethnographers developed an emotional understanding of why people who lived and went to school on the reservation did not look middle class. It became apparent that teachers who had never lived without such conveniences, residing in homes off the reservation or in on-reservation teacher housing equipped with such middle-class accoutrements lacked an experiental background to understand why the Indian students and their parents looked the way they did. Teachers often say Indian students and parents are careless and dirty. Wax and her colleagues began to appreciate at a phenomenological level the anxiety of some of the Native mothers whose children insisted that they dress them in a way that would win the approval of their teachers (Wax, 1971:214).

Examples of qualitative research abound — examples which illustrate how the phenomenological, ethnographic, historiographic, semiotic tradition 'expands the research envelope' constructed by traditional researchers. One of the best examples of such research is Peter McLaren's critical ethnography of a Catholic school in downtown Toronto, *Schooling as a Ritual Performance: Toward a Political Economy of Educational Symbols and Gestures* (1986). McLaren employed phenomenology, ethnography, and semiotics to analyze schooling as a ritual system. In the course of his inquiry McLaren viewed school culture from an angle which uncovered new ways of seeing the race, class, and gender-based struggle to control school knowledge. For example, students resisted the school's attempt to marginalize their street culture and street knowledge. The visceral knowing, the bodily knowledge, and the rhythms and gestures of street culture were very different from the formal knowledge of the classroom with its fragmented data (factoids) and its suppression of the body, the visceral. McLaren watched students enlist their street semiotics in their attempt to counter the 'bland redundancy' of the school.

McLaren focused his attention on the class clown, analyzing the codes and symbols which the clown sought to subvert and the larger significance of the struggle between clown and school. The clown deconstructed the familiar, uncovering the boredom, the tenuousness and arbitrariness of school rules. The clown was not simply a buffoon — the 'fool' became a teacher, walking the thin line between street-corner and dominant cultures. The clown was an innocent semiotician, exposing the cultural codes on which the daily life of the classroom was built. The clown, McLaren found, illustrated through his actions that the codes of the school were tenuous, that they were not decreed from above. As a subversive agent, the clown undermined the authoritarian hold that the dominant codes had on the students. As an ethnographer, McLaren attempted to move beyond simply an emic perspective (the viewpoint of the native, in this case the students and the teachers). He attempted to attend to both an emic and an etic perspective (interpretations from the perspective of the outsider). Analyzing them separately and in relation to one another, McLaren examined actor subjectivity *vis-a-vis* structural conditions which help shape student and teacher consciousness. Thus McLaren, acting very much within the boundaries of our notion of critical constructivism, uses a critical system of meaning to ground his qualitative role as semiotician, ethnographer. In the process he reveals hidden relationships between formal classroom and student oppositional codes and the larger socio-economic structure.

A teacher researcher exploring classrooms from such angles can through his or her research develop strategies for resisting the tendency for classrooms to become repositories of dominant signifiers which anesthetize our souls, sever our connections to our *Lebenswelts*, and refuse to acknowledge the meaningfulness of the lived experience of students. Critical teacher researchers, drawing upon the qualitative example provided by McLaren, begin to act upon their research and the unique ways of seeing it provides. The one-dimensional view of the classroom provided to teachers in their pre-professional and in-service training is transformed by their acquaintance with critical constructivist action research. Once a black and white Kansas, the classroom becomes a colored Oz, an embattled symbolic arena in which the dominant culture, school administrators, teachers, and students struggle over how the classroom is to be read, which cultural meanings are to be legitimized (McLaren, 1986; McLaren, 1985). The application of these qualitative dimensions may grant us freedom from the pitfalls of positivism, but to reveal the deep structures of educational life we need more than an acquaintance with qualitative methodology. To achieve critical insight we must acquaint ourselves with research perspectives such as Pinar's *currere*, McLaren's critical ethnography, and our critical constructivism. Aided by such perspectives our qualitative insight becomes an entirely new way of perceiving and constructing our relationship to the world around us.

Chapter 9

Values, Objectivity and Ideology

If we adopt a critical constructivist epistemology, we reject the positivistic notion that facts and values are separate. From a critical constructivist perspective values are seen as a basic dimension of the research process from the selection of what is to be investigated, to the methods employed, to the definitions given to terms encountered during the investigation. This is quite a contrast to the traditional positivist belief that values play no role in the research process unless to undermine its validity.

A point which critical qualitative research has made repeatedly is that underlying all social research are specific assumptions about society — value-laden assumptions which refer to the way we view social control, order, and responsibility. Critical qualitative researchers have accepted the fact that inquiry is anything but a neutral activity, as it draws upon our values, our hopes, and the mysteries which come out of our social worlds. We are constantly confronted with value questions dealing with morality, critical constructivist researchers maintain, since the subjects and objects of social science are humans. Social and educational research finds it impossible to remove itself from value assumptions about social relationships. Indeed, many philosophers of research argue that educational research is meaningful only to the extent that it has a value orientation (Smith, 1983:11; Popkewitz, 1981a:298–307).

Critical constructivists, of course, reject the possibility of value-free research into social or educational phenomena and see attempts to argue the case for value freedom as a form of ideological mystification — i.e., an attempt to hide the political interests of educational practice and the research about it. If researchers fail to keep the normative or value dimension of educational research in mind, the research they produce and the ends to which it is applied will simply serve to reproduce hegemonic social relations. Thus, from the critical perspective an awareness of the value-orientation of research is essential, as it brings to awareness the fundamental embodiments of power which move social and educational events (Soltis, 1984:8–9).

Thomas Popkewitz maintains that social and educational research expresses the researcher's value orientation in at least two important ways: 1) The research we undertake reflects our view of socio-political values. Our research allows us to reconcile what we see as social contradiction and to ponder the consequences of the actions of institutions. For example, we may see a class-stratified society beset by problems resulting from the existence of a so-called permanent underclass. We want to know how the arrangement of educational institutions affects this situation. Our research questions and the manner in which we approach our study have been shaped by our value orientations; and 2) Since social research (especially empirical social research) holds such a high status in the society, many individuals promote the belief that educational problems can only be solved through the application of rigorous science. Thus, solutions that emerge from community participation and democratic negotiation are dismissed — society has come to rely on the cult of the expert, those social scientists with precise, dispassionate answers to technical problems (Popkewitz, 1981a:298–9).

When researchers fail to note the existence of this omnipresent value dimension, Kenneth Howe contends that unpleasant outcomes typically result: 1) The research will be useless as information which informs practical action. Value judgments are inseparable from educational descriptions because of the relationship between educational research and educational practice. If researchers do not allow values to serve as a link between research and practice, educational inquiry will be irrelevant to what teachers and administrators actually do. In other words, the relationship between what we know and how we act upon the knowledge is problematic. Values not only inform what we claim to know but the actions that we take as a result of the knowledge; 2) Value-free research will be inefficient. If research in the field is not grounded upon explicitly-stated values that are open to evaluation little benefit will ever be derived from such research. Thus, energy and resources will have been wasted; and 3) Value-free research holds the potential to produce harmful results (Howe, 1985:17). When research purports to be value-free but covertly promotes specific values, various groups and individuals are rendered quite vulnerable. Students who are culturally different may be labelled emotionally disturbed; young girls and boys who attempt to transcend gender restrictions may be seen as maladjusted; or thoughtful young people with intelligent questions about social convention may be labelled as troublemakers.

Obviously, values in research affect human beings in very concrete ways. If the values of research are typically hidden, then the justifications for the educational policies which are based on them are also concealed. When such restrictions are out of sight, teachers have only a restricted view of why they do the things that they do. An analysis of the historical forces which have structured values is an integral part of critical constructivist action research. As we know, research is never a neutral means to a particular end. Research and its methodology grow out of the values of a particular world view. This particular world view, this paradigm, determines what constitutes legitimate research or an acceptable way of thinking. Even though positivistic, instrumentally-rational research models have been challenged in some academic settings, they still dominate the mind-set of many elementary and secondary schools. Emerging from business and military (remember Alice Rivlin) sources, modern manifestations of positivistic research inject the values of business management and the military into the life of the school. Here is where the importance of our phenomenological, semiotic, and ethnographic forms of qualitative research become so important to the teacher researcher. They provide the tools with which we reveal the forces which make schools what they are, which tacitly construct the goals of education in an industrial society (Orteza, 1988:28; Cherryholmes, 1988:115)

Why do educational researchers use particular words, metaphors, and models when they design their inquiry, interpret it, and suggest policies based on it? Their research language reflects the effects of the influence of power in the larger society. Power, as Foucault has argued, has served to censor, exclude, block, and repress like a great superego; but, he continues, it also serves to produce knowledge, creating effects at the level of desire. As a censor in educational research, power serves to limit what constitutes a legitimate question, excluding 'dangerous' investigations such as explorations of how class factors affect student performances in school. As a producer in educational research, power serves to reward particular ways of seeing and particular activities. For example, educational researchers who desire success in the field learn and follow particular research norms which allow them the rewards of funded grants and promotions based on scholarly productivity. The way different research orientations draw boundaries between what is acceptable and what is not constitutes the ideological dimension of the act of inquiry (Cherryholmes, 1988:116–17). Here, power is at work, promoting particular views of educational excellence and educational failure.

As critical constructivist teacher researchers we make a mistake when we assume that this power is always consciously exercised by a cabal of conspirators seeking to control the educational world. Much of the time the ideological construction of consciousness emanating from sources of power does not take place at the level of conscious intention. For example, positivistic educational researchers do not seek to design research which results in the perpetuation of business and military values in school practices. School administrators do not seek to use educational research which represses ethical considerations and questions of justice in their efforts to run their schools. And teachers certainly do not consciously attempt to suppress their students' ability to think at a more critical level nor do they try to punish the underprivileged or reward the privileged. But all of these unfortunate things happen and most of the time we have no clue why. We don't catch on because we don't understand the subtle semiotic dimensions of power reproduction, i.e., how codes, symbols, and signs subtlety construct our world views. As critical constructivist action researchers we begin to see how educational research produced by such subtle forces legitimizes particular values and delegitimizes others

For example, in terms of concrete research practices who is legitimate to interview, to use as a reliable source, and who is not? As a high school social studies teacher I often watched social studies teachers bring experts to their say, economics classes to speak and to answer student questions. In my high school these experts were usually successful business*men* who delivered a remarkably standardized ideological package for student consumption. The idea of inviting individuals from other social classes or other ideological traditions (e.g., labor leaders, social workers, welfare rights leaders, etc.) was never considered. Dominant values and ideology were thus reproduced, not at a level of conscious intent on the part of the teachers, but at a tacit, unconscious stratum. On this same stratum the records of any historical era favor those who direct public events or produce the records; — the masses, the common voices of working people are excluded from the picture. Critical constructivist teacher researchers, aware of these hegemonic dimensions of power in inquiry, take special pains to collect testimonies of individuals outside of power (Reinharz, 1979:314).

Expert researchers from academic settings like to believe that the university, because it is called 'academic,' is removed from these historical realities, value dimensions, and ideological forces which shape the form their research takes. Our research, no matter who we are, is never as independent of outside influences as we would like to think — we are all caught at a particular point in the web of reality. Our project, of course, is to understand what our particular vantage point is and how it limits our vision. This process involves our awareness of our own historicity, or place in history. We become conscious of our own ideological inheritance and its relationship to our belief and value structures, our interests, our questions about our professional lives. In his studies of the eugenicists and their influence on the way educators came to view intelligence and school performance, Steven Selden traces how social visions shaped eugenicist research design. Ideological conceptions of what constituted civilization, human progress, and a good society could not be separated from the formulation of eugenicist research. What is ironic in this case, is that many of the instruments devised by eugenicist researchers to measure learning, intelligence, and ability are still employed in modern education. Thus, at an unseen level the value assumptions of the eugenicist movement are embedded in contemporary educational practices (Cherryholmes, 1988:115; Selden, 1984:282).

Mainstream researchers have ridiculed such claims, arguing that no one in modern educational research is an eugenicist. Indeed, they are correct in their assertion that eugenics is out of fashion and that educational researchers from almost any ideological perspective would vigorously reject association with the tradition; research, however derives its meaning and its importance from the purposes for which it was designed. Much of the time the purposes are not known by those educators who consume the research. Unfortunately, educators and political leaders too often only notice that research serves particular ideological intentions when those purposes confront some aspect of the status quo (Bogdan and Biklen, 1982:216–17). When an educational researcher, for example, contends that business sponsorship of excellence programs in particular schools serves to produce unquestioning attitudes toward the positive role of business in the local community and a one-dimensional perspective on the virtues of a Chamber of Commerce-view of unregulated free enterprise economics, the status quo is challenged. It is at this point that cries of bias and politicized research make their way into the popular media as well as teacher, parent, and community awareness. Power has its ways; research emerging from a system of meaning, like ours, that challenges dominant ideology will typically be viewed as politicized and biased. Research which does not will often be deemed neutral and value free.

It may sound trite on one level, but the analysis of values in educational inquiry must remind teacher researchers that they need to consider the desirability of what we do. Critical researchers have repeatedly broached this question in a variety of contexts. If self-direction and emancipation are possible, they remind us, we must become aware of hidden values in *how* and *what* we come to know. Human institutions and the various forms of work which go on within them must always be examined with these value questions in mind. Inquiry which fails to acknowledge this value dimension of educational research introduces, rather than eliminates, the possibility of bias. Once again let us use the example of intelligence testing in this society to illustrate the point. Such tests measure qualities that are tacitly valued as important or good. Many societies in different times and places would value abilities quite different from those that are often identified by this society as manifestations of intelligence. Thus, the emotions that are elicited by the attempts to generate standardized measurements of intelligence across ethnic, cultural, and racial lines are not surprising (Soltis, 1984:9; Howe, 1985:12). What is surprising is our inability to catch on to the value dimension (typically unstated) which must be understood to make sense of the intelligence debate. Let us extend our discussion of values and research with a more detailed example of the intelligence question.

David Owen, in his exposé of the Educational Testing Service (ETS), devotes much attention to uncovering the values which have contributed to the testing institution's definition and thus the society's definition of intelligence. Tracing the history of the ETS back to the days of Carl

Brigham and the College Board, Owen describes the value assumptions of those who developed the *SAT, LSAT, MCAT*, and many other instruments designed to measure aptitude, achievement, developed ability, higher-order reasoning abilities, or whatever term substituted for intelligence that had not yet developed pejorative connotations. If one wants to know the next synonym for intelligence employed by the ETS, Owen advises the reader to consult the thesaurus.

In 1961, Henry Chauncey inherited from Brigham the sceptre of leadership of the testing company. It is interesting to note that Brigham, the developer of the SAT, was an avowed eugenicist who believed that the 'dilution of the master race had been a direct consequence of the abolition of slavery'. Owen is quick to point out that Brigham did not create the SAT simply to promote his eugenicist views and keep blacks out of college. His purpose was to use the SAT as a basic tool in the creation of a new social order. He foresaw that a meritocratic society would reduce the potential for disappointment and frustration by quickly pointing out to those of inferior capabilities, aptitudes, or intelligence (often non-Anglo-Saxons) that their quest for high level, demanding positions was ill-advised. The efficient new society would appropriately place the less able in suitable slots.

Chauncey was a man very much after Brigham's heart, and as such carried on the traditions laid down by Brigham. Chauncey believed that intelligence was 'a hard, smooth nut' (i.e., discrete and easily measured) embedded deep in the brain. Standardized tests could measure the nut and in the process remake the society. Reflecting the spirit of Brigham, Chauncey believed in a meritocratic social order, where the intelligence-testing establishment served as the troll at the bridge who regulated access to schools, professions and jobs. Chauncey's political and social values shaped his view of the essential role of intelligence measurement in determining one's ultimate rung on the social ladder. Not only did one's values determine the definition of intelligence, they also determined one's view of the status quo. Intelligence tests, Owen argues, have bequeathed the nation's well-to-do with a conscience-soothing, scientifically-grounded rationalization for the benefits they have enjoyed. The wealthy lived well because they were smart; the poor lived in squalor because they were dumb. There was a just rationality to the status quo.

Chauncey believed that test scores were the equivalent of money in the pocket in the meritocratic marketplace. Since testing was based on value-free definitions of intelligence, the new society could be organized objectively and efficiently. Chauncey argued at length that the responsibility for ordering society rests with the test-makers, the scientifically trained experts. If the results of the test become the basis for the structuring of society, then the test becomes the schema for society. Under the banner of fairness and objectivity, Owen maintains, merit is defined as what the most powerful interests within a society value as meritorious. In a perverse way 'society's rewards become their own justification'. If the meritocratic society is supposed to honor the deserving by paying them lots of money, then the wealthy must be worthy. Thus, our values come to determine our strategies for determining aptitude, our definitions of merit, our educational objectives, and our socio-political policies. The claim of value freedom rings quite hollow, Owen maintains. Far from being value-free, the 'objective' system, Owen concludes, serves to perpetuate old injustices by portraying them as neutral workings of a system based upon the hard scientific research of dispassionate experts (Owen, 1985:178–99).

If value judgments in inquiry are deemed to have little to do with cognition, or if they are biased, of if they are viewed as beyond the realm which requires logical justification, then social and educational research will always be flawed. This outcome is not inevitable. If social and educational researchers approach value judgments as an essential thread in the fabric of their investigations, they will come to see that such judgments require defense and criticism just like any other form of assessment. Indeed, there are two kinds of value judgments: the well-supported and the poorly supported. To distinguish the two types of judgments, philosophers of research argue, researchers must transcend the conventional discourse which focuses exclusively on the reliability and validity of research procedures (Howe, 1985:12).

Analysis of reliability and validity procedures is important but it is unable to illuminate the social, cultural, and political values which may be embedded in the research procedures. If we accept the post-Kuhnian axiom that science is a socio-cultural activity, then scientific inquiry must be examined for its cultural definitions and its value assumptions. A routine portion of the research procedure should involve the consideration of questions which expose value orientations toward social and political affairs embedded in the various practices of the inquiry. Such value-appraising activities, many analysts argue, are especially important when educational researchers extend their work to the evaluation and the development of school programs.

Educational scholars who wish to incorporate the insights of value analysis into their work need to act upon three principles: 1) educational researchers must embrace a self-reflective and critical orientation; 2) the notion of research adequacy must be extended; and 3) the design of curriculum must be reconsidered in light of the knowledge we have gleaned from the analysis of the value dimension of research. Let us briefly explain each of these principles.

1 Educational researchers must embrace a self-reflective and critical orientation. Research methods and the theories derived from them are not neutral. As this survey of the debates in modern educational research attests, the traditions of objectivity, detachment,

and scientific disinterest have been reconceptualized by various philosophers of science. Unfortunately, very little of this intellectual activity has found its way into the everyday conversations of educational practice.

2   The notion of research adequacy must be extended. Scientific research is not adequate simply because it is valid and reliable. Adequacy must take into account moral considerations, purposes, and ethical premises. Educational research will succeed to the degree that it encourages a public conversation about the ways schools and educational agencies contribute to a just and ethical society. Educational research must expose the pretensions and deceptions which make unjust educational structures seem benevolent.

3   The design of curriculum must be reconsidered in light of the knowledge we have gleaned from the analysis of the value dimension of research. When formulating educational policy we are in essence applying research outcomes to practice. Without the benefits derived from understanding the value-dimension confusions about educational purpose are bound to arise. The inability of many educational leaders to discuss the social role of school or to have a clear view of the conflicts implicit in diverse plans for educational reform may be evidence of researchers' neglect of the value dimension (Popkewitz, 1981b:306, 312–13).

The debate over the value dimension in educational research has grown more intense in recent years as critical analysts have raised serious objections to what they describe as a misleading use of the term 'objectivity'. Henry Giroux asserts that the positivistic culture rationalizes its advocacy of value-free inquiry on the basis of an ill-conceived notion of objectivity. To produce worthwhile knowledge researchers must engage in value-free inquiry, far away from the messy world of beliefs and presuppositions. That this belief in pseudo-objectivity could last so long, science educator John Head contends, is amazing when we consider how scientific research actually takes place. The idea of a science patiently and objectively recording a series of observations and then arranging them in a logical pattern reflecting the nature of reality depicts a process much in conflict with the psychology of human perception. Human beings are quite selective about what they attend to and very subjective in ascribing meaning to their observations (Giroux, 1981:44; Head, 1979:23). This denial of the subjective nature of the process is frightening, for, as Robert N. Bellah reminds us, it is precisely a social science that sees itself uninvolved in the social world, that considers itself free from all ethical norms other than the dispassionate pursuit of knowledge, that will create engines of manipulation and human control for anyone who finds it possible to put them into practice (Bellah, 1983:40–1).

Giroux continues the argument claiming that when knowledge and research are separated from values more is hidden than uncovered. The notion of objectivity in any field reflects the values and assumptions of the scholars working in the field. In the name of objectivity these values and assumptions are hidden. It is impossible, he says, to separate values from facts and inquiry from ethics.

The effects, Giroux tells us, of a pseudo-objective, value-free research methodology are numerous. The most obvious effect is the inaccurate picture we get of social phenomena. Cursed with a distorted picture of reality, we find it difficult to recognize problems which exist in our political and educational lives. For all the assumptions that the pseudo-objective culture of positivism makes, it fails to base its view of the world on the pretext that humans should be free to direct their own lives. Filling the vacuum left by this failure to embrace human emancipation is an insidious form of social engineering. It is insidious in the sense that it does not admit its true nature. It is social engineering in the sense that it views humans as entities to be manipulated. The positivistic culture consistently denies the possibility that it begins with specific presuppositions. Examined thoughtfully, Giroux asserts, the failure to assume that the extension of human freedom is basic to any truly humane view of the world or any research question is a frightening assumption. The critical inquirer, he maintains, may begin his or her research with a set of assumptions; but at least they are openly-stated assumptions.

Worshipping the god of objectivity, Giroux claims that the culture of positivism succumbs to what has been called the 'fallacy of objectivism'. This fallacy occurs when a research methodology is self-limiting to the point it cannot reflect on its own presuppositions. It cannot reflect on presuppositions because it claims they do not exist. Trapped by its adulation of empirically-grounded fact, the culture of positivism fails to acknowledge the historical and social context which gave birth to it. Devoid of such context it fails to see itself clearly — it cannot perform self-analysis. Thus, it renews with a vengeance its focus on 'what is'. Typically, the result of the analysis of 'what is' is that the status quo is basically sound. Teaching that is based on this culture uncritically passes 'facts' along to students outside social or historical contexts.

Giroux argues that all human activity must be fragmented to meet the requirements of empirical investigation. Schools steeped in the culture of positivism teach the outcomes of such empirical fragmentation — isolated facts. The attempt to comprehend the world as a network of interconnections is lost. Students are taught to attack problems as if they emerged in isolation, detached from the dynamic social and political forces which bestow meaning.

Researchers and students of education in general can break the culture of positivism by exposing the pseudo-objectivity on which it is grounded. Such an unmasking, Giroux contends, will best be accomplished by a detailed analysis of the process which produces knowledge. In this way we will come to understand the logic behind the knowledge, its context and significance, and the implications of such understandings as we undertake new research. The process, critical researchers contend, will provide multi-dimensional educational benefits. By studying the process by which knowledge is produced students learn about the nature of learning. It is in this way that an individual student accomplishes that all important goal of education — learning to teach himself or herself. An individual who learns to teach himself or herself has engaged in one of the most basic acts of human emancipation. Because it is unconcerned with the attempt of men and women to control their own destiny, Giroux concludes that the culture of positivism is indifferent to learning which attempts to move beyond the acquisition of second-hand, authorized, ready made facts (Giroux, 1981:37–62).

One of the main points of the critical perspective as argued by Giroux, Habermas, Marcuse and many others is that this so-called culture of positivism is ideological. It is an ideology which induces us to focus our attention on technical questions — i.e., on the search for efficient means to educational ends that we take for granted. It is an ideology, critical analysts have argued, which accepts the common sense viewpoint that the social world is exactly as it appears. Such a viewpoint is a manifestation of a consciousness constructed by positivist ideology. As such beliefs dominate the minds of those who study and administer schools, educators fail to ask what kind of social and human life our schools produce and reproduce (Soltis, 1984:7; Smart, 1976:23).

Research, therefore, must be subjected to ideological analysis. Habermas writes of a dialogical process of ideological analysis where participants (the scholarly community) continuously take part in an examination of the social and psychological basis of one's attitudes. Thus, this continual dialogue allows researchers to frame their ideas in a manner where the effects of the ideological orientation, the milieu, and the historical period in which they have arisen are considered. Habermas is comfortable with the uncertainty of such a situation and admits that such a method provides no certainty for those in search of it (Holland and Mansell, 1983:105–7).

Peter McLaren picks up on Habermas's concern with ideological analysis and frames it in an educational context. Teachers as researchers have much to learn from McLaren's explanation of why an understanding of ideology, power, and consciousness construction is so important to teachers seeking to build democratic workplaces and to provide emancipatory experiences for students. In his preface to *Life in Schools* McLaren explains how as a teacher in the poverty stricken Jane-Finch Corridor of Toronto, he survived the classroom by drawing upon practical knowledge and untutored pedagogical instinct. But survival was not enough; McLaren was increasingly troubled by the feeling that he had not made a difference, that he had not helped his students in their pursuit of a hopeful future. Thwarted by a lack of acquaintance with social theory, with ideological analysis, McLaren could not see the connection between the schooling process and larger socio-economic realities. Without such understandings McLaren concluded that he missed an important opportunity to develop an educational perspective that would work to empower students and transform inequities in the local community (McLaren, 1989a:vii–viii).

To draw attention to the social conditions of the students he taught, the young McLaren published the journal he kept during his years in Jane-Finch. As the years passed, he grew increasingly dissatisfied with the journal's attempt to understand and communicate his classroom experiences. Advised by a prominent journalist to let the vignettes speak for themselves, McLaren's journal consisted basically of raw material, uninterpreted stories about schooling. Observations of events, McLaren learned, never speak for themselves — every story is ideologically loaded, full of signifiers and subtle reflections of power relations. No aspect of schooling is ideologically innocent; no thoughts, theories, or pedagogies are completely autonomous. Ideas, perspectives, research orientations and the teaching practices that come out of them are always connected to power and value interests. To 'know,' McLaren came to argue, is to deconstruct power/value/knowledge configurations. 'By failing to set my classroom journal within a critical theoretical context,' McLaren concluded, 'I could not reveal how power and knowledge work in the interests of certain groups over others' (McLaren, 1989a:ix).

McLaren's reconceptualization of his journal and his experience in Jane-Finch are very helpful in our attempt to understand the need for teacher researchers to grasp the value and ideological dimensions of action research. After teaching in Jane-Finch, McLaren worked to construct a system of meaning, a critical means of interpreting his experience. Like our efforts in this book, he turned to social theory to facilitate his ability to make sense of his teaching, his students, and the world they inhabited. To accomplish such a task we must transcend the traditional confines of action research both conceptually and geographically. We must move beyond the confines conceptually in the same sense that we have discussed throughout the book — we must construct a critical system of meaning which helps us ask new questions, to see from new angles. We must surpass traditional action research geographically in the sense that we do not allow our inquiry to be confined only to the school. If teacher researchers are to act on McLaren's ideological reconceptualization of teaching experience, we must analyze inter-institutional relationships and the ways that such connections shape school life.

Not only do critical teacher researchers need to study sites outside school to understand power and ideological relationships, but in the last three decades of the twentieth century schools have been replaced as the primary educational institutions within Western societies. If education is defined as consciousness construction and not simply as what occurs inside schools, then our attention as critical constructivist teacher researchers by necessity must focus not only on schools but on mass discourse and popular culture as well. Henry Giroux, Roger Simon, Phillip Wexler (Giroux and Simon, 1989; Wexler, 1987) and many other educational analysts have understood and acted on this notion. The forces of consciousness production involve the intersection of mass communications, youth culture, schooling, and countless other cultural entities. At this historical juncture the process of consciousness construction and the ideological production of self becomes more complex than ever before (Anderson, 1989:259; Wexler, 1987:55). Teacher researchers cannot allow themselves to be stuck in antiquated notions of theory implementation, validation, or invalidation; they must ask new questions of education in this age of mass discourse as pedagogical agent.

In Foucault's sense of the term 'geneology', critical constructivist teacher researchers must be self-critical geneologists who trace the formation of their own subjectivities. What are the ideological bases of our claims to truth in our research? By recognizing the many contradictions in the construction of our own consciousnesses, teacher researchers can understand not only the complexity of their students' *Lebenswelts* but also avoid the trap of the belief in the possibility of a transcendental view of the social world outside the web of reality. In other words, we come to recognize that there are no value-free, privileged knowers who ask ideologically unfettered questions about the methods they will employ in their studies. Drawing upon the early work of Alvin Gouldner, critical constructivist teacher researchers come to recognize that research methodology is not simply a logic but a morality in the sense that it represses or liberates particular moral questions about social and educational reality. Teachers, researchers, and teacher researchers are moral agents, rejecting or accepting the moral obligations of moral imperatives (McLaren, forthcoming:27; Goodlad, 1988:109).

As we engage in our self-critical geneology, draw on our critical system of meaning, employ our phenomenological, semiological, ethnographic, and historiographical techniques, our action research becomes 'immoral' from the perspective of those positivists who wag their fingers at our lack of research piety, i.e., rigor. Our self-critical geneology and the critical action research which grows out of it, constitutes an emancipatory right of passage as we leave behind our research 'adolescence'. Exercising our new maturity we come to formulate more penetrating questions about our professional practice, see new levels of activity and meaning in our classrooms, decipher connections between socio-cultural meanings and the everyday life of school, and reconceptualize what we already 'know'. As we grow to understand the race, class, and gender locations of the students and others that we study, we come to appreciate our own location and the social relationships such locations produce (Reinharz, 1982:165; McLaren, forthcoming:27).

Without this ideological self-criticism we cannot find the path to the *Lebenswelt*. As Hans-Georg Gadamer argued, the critique of both the prevalent notions of objectivity and the way these ideas have shaped us, allows us to get behind the objectivity of inquiry so that we might discover the life-world (Gadamer, 1975:225). Standing at the intersection of his or her own subjectivity and that which is being observed, the researcher discovers a crack in time and space through which he or she might crawl. From the other side of this temporal and spatial fissure, the world can be seen afresh — the trivial becomes the profound, comfortable assumptions are turned inside-out. This geneological self-criticism has become an epic reconstruction of consciousness; indeed, we have stumbled on the process of not only how researchers make new discoveries but how fields of inquiry are transformed. Major advances in how we see social and educational phenomena do not emerge from a linear accumulation or extension within the matrix of previous discoveries. Major reconceptualizations come out of a meta-analysis of the ideological assumptions on which the framework underlying the accumulation of extant knowledge is grounded. Critical knowledge is produced not as much by asking questions *within* the framework as it is by asking questions *about* the framework (Reinharz, 1979:123–4, 355).

The very notion of critical constructivist action research is an example of how fields advance. Its existence is predicated on a set of inquiries about the framework of traditional educational research — about the ideological assumptions on which it rests. Advocates of critical action research have questioned the viability of propositional knowledge in a particular field, the ethics of employing educational research in the attempt to predict and thus control the effects of technical process-product reasoning on how teachers conduct their professional lives, and the trustworthiness of linear cause–effect research designs in socio-educational settings. Such questions are value-laden in that they promote action research in education as a form of ethical reflection within the domain of practice. Action research would never have existed if consciousness of the ideological malformations of the workplace had not existed. Advocates of action research based their ideas on the assumption that the established way of doing research did not benefit practitioners as it produced a series of top-down rules for directing the professional lives of teachers. In the name of scientific objectivity, very specific ideological assumptions about knowledge, and the organization of the workplace, the role of teachers *vis-à-vis* administrators were being promoted (Elliott, 1989a:7).

Critical constructivist teacher researchers see objectivity from another angle — a vantage point which advances our understanding of practitioner knowledge. Let us use some non-schooling examples to illustrate the critical constructivist attempt to demystify uncritical notions of objectivity. Until the Vietnam War journalists (with significant exceptions) conceived of objectivity as 'official-source journalism'. Tom Wicker writes that journalists who did not rely on governmental and corporate official sources were considered subjective, if not subversive. But their front line experience in the South-east Asian jungles changed the minds of many in the profession as they began to uncover the lack of truth in the information provided by official governmental sources. As reporters spent time with Vietnamese people, low ranking U.S. officials in the hinterland, and soldiers and nurses, they began to uncover a very different picture of how the war was going. These reporters surrendered their official source objectivity, and in the manner of action researchers began seeing for themselves and analyzing for themselves, often at the risk of physical harm and governmental wrath. From the perspective of those who fought the war and cared for its victims, the claims of the Pentagon spokespeople, the generals, and the ambassadors began to appear fatuous and hollow. The reporters had taken a dangerous and subversive step: they had abandoned their official source objectivity for a phenomenological first-hand engagement with the lived world of the war. It was at this very point that they were accused of bias; the dominant view of proper reporter behavior was able to persuade a large portion of the American public of their 'misguided, pro-Communist' motives (Bogdan and Biklen, 1982:218).

The critical constructivist action research attempt to demystify objectivity can be informed by an acquaintance with Edward Herman's and Noam Chomsky's analysis of how dominant ideology insidiously works to construct consciousness in the late twentieth century. Their analysis of what they call 'manufactured consent' can be applied to any institution, education in particular, and can help us transcend positivistic notions of objectivity. Herman's and Chomsky's analysis forces action researchers to rethink our notions of source evaluation, how we designate a source as credible. Typically, perspectives, such as critical constructivism, which focus our attention on domination are dismissed by mainstream researchers as conspiracy theories. Herman's and Chomsky's analysis of manufactured consent or the process of domination is *not*, they zealously contend, a conspiracy theory. In the modern media, for example, most ideological domination comes from the pre-selection of innocent people, internalized perceptions, and the influences of ownership, organization, market, and political power on reporters and editors. Censorship is usually self-censorship, by researchers and commentators who have internalized the constraints imposed by sources, media organization, market considerations, and governmental power.

Herman and Chomsky direct their attention to how money and power work to filter out news unfavorable to their interests, marginalize dissent, and grant access to government and dominant private interests to get their messages across to the public. These so-called news filters include four headings with important implications for action researchers attempting to analyze consciousness construction. The first filter involves the size, ownership, and profit orientation of the mass media. Since the industrial revolution ownership of media has been limited to the required large investment — in the modern era only twenty-nine media systems account for more than half of the output of newspapers and most of the magazines, broadcasting, books, and movies. These media systems are large profit-seeking organizations which have been fully integrated into the culture of the economic marketplace. Thus, they face pressures of stockholders, directors, and bankers to direct their attention to the bottom line. Because of their profitability media systems constantly face the threat of takeovers prompting their managers to focus even more exclusively on profitability. Thus, content and coverage decisions fall increasingly in the hands of finance directors, bankers, and investors. Market objectives thus take precedence over traditional journalistic goals.

The second filter involves advertising as the primary income source for the mass media. An examination of the history of newspapers seems to indicate the power of advertisers to influence content and perspective. Papers that could attract ads could sell copies well below production costs. Papers which could not by necessity had to keep copy prices high and price of packaging (format, features, promotion) low. Thus, advertising-supported papers drove out of existence or marginalized papers that depended on sales alone. In the newspaper business papers which were typically driven out of business or marginalized were those with perspectives critical of business and other potential advertisers. Modern broadcast media are affected by similar forces but take the process one step farther: TV networks labor to assure their stockholders that they are not interested in appealing to audiences *per se* but to audiences with buying power. When combined with TV network competition for advertisers' patronage — networks hire and train special staffs to assure advertisers how their programs serve advertisers' needs — the effect on the content of TV programs becomes clear. Examples abound: when public station WNET aired 'Hungry for Profit', a documentary containing material critical of multinational corporate activities in the Third World, Gulf and Western withdrew its funding. The message to other broadcasters was clear.

The third filter involves the reliance of media on information supplied by government, business, and experts (educational and otherwise) funded or approved by these power sources. To survive, to meet their news schedules, mass media need a steady flow of raw material of news. Practical economics dictates that they concentrate their resources where pre-packaged news emanates in the form of carefully planned leaks and formal press conferences: the White House, the Pentagon, the State Department, the Department of Education are all such venues. On the local level, city hall, the police department, business corporations, trade organizations, and the central office of a local school district provide analogous settings. These bureaucracies can be trusted consistently to turn out the volume necessary to media needs. Such bureaucracies also have the merit of credibility granted by status and prestige. Falling prey to the cult of the expert, newsworkers treat bureaucratic accounts as factual because they refuse to question the order of authorized knowers in the society. In this context a bureaucracy's claim to knowledge is viewed not as a claim but as a validated piece of knowledge. When one examines the resources allocated by these bureaucracies to get the word out the scope of their control over information is staggering.

The forth filter involves 'flak' as a means of disciplining the media. Flak refers to negative reactions to a media statement or media programming often taking the form of letters, telegrams, phone calls, petitions, lawsuits, boycotts, etc. If flak is large scale it can prove to be very costly to the media, as positions have to be defended and advertisers withdraw patronage. During the McCarthy period TV and radio stations were routinely subdued by flak from determined 'Red hunters'. In the 1990s advertisers and media systems are very careful not to offend certain constituencies that are potential flak producers. Certain topics or types of programming are consistently avoided in hopes of avoiding flak. The ability of an interest group to produce flak which is effective is related to power. In the 1970s and 1980s numerous organizations were funded by business and industrial groups for the expressed purpose of producing flak. Such efforts have proved very successful in filtering what topics are covered and how they are covered in newspapers and on TV. Herman and Chomsky grant action researchers insight into the alleged innocence of the information which shapes the consciousness of students, teacher, administrators, and community members. As they destroy the myth of an ideology-free consciousness, they teach a lesson on the insidious, unintended process by which consciousness is shaped (Herman and Chomsky, 1988:2–28). No longer can action researchers explore the educational world outside of a cultural frame; no longer can they fail to see the impact of power relationships on everyday life in school and society. Such awarenesses set the stage for critical constructivist teacher research as a form of political action.

But before action research can become a form of praxis (i.e., action informed by reflection with an emancipatory intent), teacher inquirers must understand that many aspects of the research process inhibit political actions. The relationship, for example, between researcher and researched is shaped, of course, by dominant ideological perspectives on the goals and methods of inquiry. Dominant research orientations preclude researchers from pointing out forms of domination to the researched; such orientations obstruct attempts to encourage emancipatory social change for the betterment of the individuals, groups, and communities being studied. An understanding of the hierarchical relationships between researcher–researched alerts teacher researchers to the dynamics of the emancipatory relationships they hope to establish with the students, other teachers, administrators, and community members they research. Drawing upon our understanding of subjugated knowledge, we examine the hierarchical relations between qualititative researchers and minority groups, e.g., Blacks, Hispanics, and Native Americans. Because they intuitively understand the researchers' hierarchical view of them (listen to Floyd Westerman's insightful song, 'Here Come the Anthros', as an example of the perspective of the researched), the subjugated objects of research view inquirers with distrust and often refuse to let them into their lives. As researchers fail to understand many of the unique and subtle characteristics of the informants' world, their research distorts the lived conditions and the potentials of the researched. Such misrepresentations limit the possibility of the inquiry to serve as a basis for improving the life chances of the people being studied. The researchers just report what they see; and what they see may be severely limited by the ideological construction of their own psyche (McLaren, *forthcoming*:27–8; Gordon, Miller, and Rollock, 1990:14).

There is a lot more to the act of research, critical constructivist researchers argue, if it is to be praxiological, if it is to make a difference in the lives of the researchers and the researched. Since the social perceptions of the researched are ideologically constructed either by way of traditional forces such as religion in pre-industrial cultures or by Herman's and Chomsky's media filters in late industrial societies, then an important aspect of the research act involves unmasking these social constructions. In late industrial societies the praxiological unmasking of informant constructions of reality is important because such constructions perpetuate powerlessness. Beginning with a phenomenological understanding of the consciousness of the researched, critical constructivist researchers interrogate the forces which contribute to the shaping of that consciousness. Thus, critical constructivist action researchers unmask the consciousness of educational actors, deconstructing the ways that ideology constructs concepts such as giftedness, intelligence, success, effective schools, quality education, etc. Questioning such concepts in the context of their critical system of meaning, critical teachers as researchers are able to identify the sources of power which define the concepts and the interests that benefit from the perpetuation of prevailing definitions. Having identified power sources and privileged interests, critical researchers and their informants can move to the praxiological dimension; they can transform the distorted situation, emancipating the informants and themselves from the repression, the hegemony. Patti Lather argues that educational research is valid only if it moves to this level of praxis. Eschewing traditional notions of the term, Lather contends that research has achieved 'catalytic validity' if it enlightens and energizes the researcher and researched and moves them in the direction of self-determination of their own consciousness construction (Anderson, 1989:253–4).

The subjugated, critical researchers such as Patti Lather, Peter McLaren, and Gary Anderson would argue, they have the right to name their reality. Critical action researchers have much to learn from this principle, as they take seriously the experiences of our students and the others we might research. Not only do we attend closely to the way our informants construe their realities, but we assist by encouraging them to break out of the culture of silence and apply their constructions to the shaping of their own lives. For example, empowered students and parents from a subjugated class or racial culture who were able to reconstruct a view of intelligence which was more sensitive to the talents that they already possessed, could help reshape both curricula and modes of evaluation which typically valued only dominant forms of intelligence. In a sense, critical action research becomes pedagogical, as it teaches researcher and informant empowerment. Teachers as researchers through their understandings empower both themselves as professional agents in schools and their students and other informants as they expose ideological restrictions on their own lives and the lived experience of others (Besag, 1986b:21). Thus, action research as praxis involves three basic steps: 1) phenomenological empathy — researchers develop an interpretive appreciation of the intersubjectivities, the values, and the motives held by participants in a particular venue; 2) geneological disclosure — researchers employ historical research to reveal the origins and present forms of the ideologies, the social conditions, and the linguistic, political, and economic structures that limit the aspirations of informants and construct their world views and self-images; and 3) transformative self-production — researchers in close consultation with the researched formulate strategies of resistance to those impediments to self-direction which were identified in the previous steps of the research. Aware of ideological malformations such as definitions of intelligence and success that favor privileged groups, critical researchers challenge such hegemonic constructions by helping to form networks of resistance composed of victims of the constructions and individuals who are willing to act on their recognitions of the injustices which result from them.

As critical constructivist teacher researchers move through these three steps, they can employ a variety of research techniques to move their inquiry to the praxiological dimension. Oral history and informant narratives from ethnography can be used to reveal ideological consciousness construction and to lay the foundation for emancipatory action. Most research interviews tend to examine the responses of the researched as if they existed in isolation from the social contexts that produced them. Critical action researchers listen carefully to an informant's construction of his or her own life history, the stories, the anecdotes, the digressions which are important to the researched. The teacher researcher as semiotician views these stories and the ways that they were told as texts full of signs and codes. He or she then helps the respondent restructure them in a narrative form — a form comfortable to the respondent, a form which encourages the respondent to discover and then speak in his or her own voices (Anderson, 1989:260–2). Embedded in this non-hierarchical collaboration between researcher and researched rests the essence of teachers as researchers; not only does critical teacher research serve to expose ideological malformations existing in the school and the community that surrounds it, but the act of collaboration itself is counter-hegemonic as it redefines the way knowledge about schooling is produced. No longer can educational researchers view the objects of their inquiry as characters on television. Critical constructivist action researchers are more than voyeurs — they are agents, participants in the praxis of the research act.

Chapter 10

An Example:
Historiographical Research for Teachers

Throughout this book I have attempted to acquaint teachers with various qualitative research methods and with how they might be incorporated by teacher researchers into studies which would help sophisticate their professional practice. A basic form of qualitative research often overlooked by qualitative researchers is historiography — the research method employed by historians. When viewed in a critical constructivist action research context, historiography has much to offer the teacher as researcher. Not only does historiography provide insight into an understanding of the relationships between the past and the present, but it serves as a research orientation which provides insight into established notions of educational research. A critical constructivist historiography can establish a starting place for our exploration of consciousness construction and the forces which have helped shape the lived world of our students and ourselves. With a few adjustments to traditional approaches to historiography, educational researchers from a critical constructivist background can make historiography another form of action research.

Those who engage in historical research should be aware of the consequences of the historical ignorances which afflict late industrial societies and handcuffs their institutions, education included, to past malformations. Russell Jacoby labelled this atrophy of memory 'social amnesia'. Few institutions suffer from social amnesia more than education. Education suffers, in the same manner as do consumer goods, from planned obsolescence in that education avoids substantive change by creating the illusion that it is perpetually new. Planned obsolescence is ubiquitous in late industrial societies, from education, to cars, to sexuality, to thinking. Because the past is forgotten, it directs without resistance — everything which exists is natural, it could not have come to exist in any other form (reification) (Jacoby, 1975:xviii, 4–5). Thus, our modern unconsciousness of history does not free us from the past, but, to the contrary, traps us in the snare of an unconscious destiny (Lucas, 1985:25). Contrary to what many 'objective' historians might argue, history will be judged by the contributions it makes to the attempt to understand the present and to shape the future. The point is so obvious that it might not be worth stressing, except for the fact that many historians have worked so diligently to deny it.

Thus, the attempt to avoid social amnesia forces us to ask ourselves as critical teacher researchers: how might we employ historical research in our attempt to grow professionally? On a micro-level we can employ historical research methodology to help us trace the life histories of our students and the historical forces which have shaped the school. It is at the macro-level that we begin to focus our attention on the concept of memory and on how it relates to the connections between past and present (Popular Memory Group, 1982:211). Memory, unlike history, has a verb form — to remember. Because the past lives in the present — and certainly in the minds of people who inhabit the present — memory becomes a focus of the struggle for self-production, for consciousness construction. How memory is approached by professional historians or teacher researchers is by nature a political act. How we remember matters because it informs our existence in the present, our view of the purpose of schooling, our vision of what constitutes good teaching, our vision of the future (Frisch, 1981:11).

What does it mean for a teacher researcher to remember student life histories, school history, or more general educational histories? What can we as educational action researchers do to such historical memories to make them active and alive rather than quaint curiosities that are 'interesting'? Memory is a vital resource in political life, in social action, or in education. Memory counters the oppressive presentism of late twentieth-century life as it helps us make sense of the nature and changeability of our current conditions. Memory is the means that teachers, educational leaders, community members, and students use to gain self-consciousness about the genesis of our own common sense beliefs, derived as they are from our ideological, social and cultural milieu. This self-consciousness applies not only to individuals but to institutions as well. The collective memory of educators, for example, aids understanding of a shared social reality that underlies our perception of purpose. In other words, it matters if teachers forget John Dewey or the origins of public schooling in industrial societies or the historical justifications for vocational education. As Jacoby and Giroux argue, memory matters so much because the relationship between memory and history is so fractured in the late twentieth century (Popular Memory Group, 1982:214; Giroux, 1981:37–62). How and why were curricula originally developed? How and why have schools assumed their present forms? Teachers, administrators, and the public often have no idea.

Our system of emancipatory meaning from Chapter 2 once again guides us as we theorize how we might employ historical methodology in teacher research. Critical educators are bearers of 'dangerous memory', transformative agents who preserve the memory of human suffering and the forms of knowledge which work to reveal its cover-up. If we are to be emancipatory agents, we must begin our pedagogy with a recognition of who has suffered and how such a disclosure illuminates present forms of oppression in our schools and our classrooms (Giroux, 1988:99). We do not seek to uncover memory for its own sake, i.e., for the purpose of collecting historical data. We pursue memory because we recognize that the past 'is' — i.e., it continues to live undetected in present social relations. In history people have been killed or have experienced serious trouble because they have attempted to name the suffering which surrounds them (Harrison, 1985:250; Welch, 1985:36–7). Critical constructivism revolves around such dangerous memories.

Critical constructivist accounts of historical oppression are both descriptions and critiques. There are two forms of dangerous memories as critiques: 1) Critiques which undermine the inegalitarian structure of society and schools by exposing their unfounded claim of universality; that is, dangerous memories discredit the society's or the schools' claim that they represent the interests of all individuals. When we remember suffering it reminds us that political and educational systems all too often benefit the few at the expense of the many; 2) Critiques emanating from dangerous memories subvert the authority of Western education by revealing its failure to account for the grave problems of racism, sexism, and class bias. As critical constructivist researchers uncover the suffering unaddressed and thus insidiously tolerated by Western education, its universalist facade is exposed and it is revealed as schooling for the benefit of the middle and upper-middle class. When exploited groups have revealed their memory of suffering, they have derived power to resist the dominant culture's threat to their identity. Minority groups, the poor, workers, women, and teachers have begun to discover that official history (that included within adopted textbooks) is often silent about their suffering. This official story is controlled by privileged groups within the society and contains little evidence of resistance and dissent against the status quo. The past is viewed as an inevitability, a triumph of the deserving. Critical constructivist teacher researchers and oppressed groups use dangerous memory to make the connection between emancipatory action and the dominant consciousness of the school — adversarial though it may be. They see the oppressiveness of the belief that education is neutral or ideologically innocent. Hope rests on such recognitions; it is a hope grounded on solidarity between the teacher and the oppressed groups, a hope that uses the consciousness of the oppressed to disrupt the constructions of history devised by dominant groups (Metz, 1980:66–7, 89; Giroux, 1988:98).

Traditional professional historians have often experienced difficulty with the concept of memory because of their research orientation with its particular notions of objectivity and its methods of verification. Thus, in mainstream historical circles popular memory is viewed as relatively un-important; it is a source that might be used to corroborate historical research when employed in conjunction with objective scholarly inquiry. Critical teacher researchers move beyond this restricted perception of the value of memory, viewing it as one of the most valuable sites to study consciousness formation. At this site we learn how the past figures in the lives of our students, our administrators, educational policy makers. In addition we learn how the past figures in our own lives as teachers — we learn how to define ourselves, to place ourselves historically.

The past figures in our professional lives in a powerful way. Employing historical methodology teacher researchers reveal the non-necessity of the dominant technologies of a social or an educational system, hold up to view the thin ice on which the system rests, and uncover the tendency for such systems to attain and maintain power by exclusion and repression. The schools can perpetuate particular definitions of success, for example, by locking out challenges to such constrictions from non-dominant groups. Emancipatory use of dangerous memory will reveal the fact that dominance is usually seized rather than earned, and that domination by particular ideologies is rarely beneficial to non-whites, women, or poor people (Frisch, 1981:16–17). Critical teacher researchers make themselves and their students active shapers of history when they confront the official story by exposing it as based on a world view supportive of dominant power relations (Metz, 1980:66). To examine, for example, the history of vocational education in Western societies and the way it has served to hamper the economic mobility of working people is to expose a power struggle in education which was resolved without a concern for the best interests of the oppressed.

Understanding these historical dimensions of domination, critical constructivist teacher researchers can envision a new form of solidarity and community which is dedicated to a confrontation with domination in educational settings. Drawing upon an understanding and appreciation of dangerous memory and subjugated knowledge, teacher researchers are empowered to delineate specific effects on the ways in which conscious-ness is constructed and school works. Dangerous memory and subjugated knowledge make the relationship between emancipation and the lived world of the school accessible to teachers, students, and the community. Critical constructivist teacher researchers derive insight into modes of resistance — based on a recognition of the alienation embedded in the dominant ideology, the devaluation of human life revealed by historical understanding. Such revelations form the foundation on which hope is built; they focus our attention on the search for historical instances of resistance and liberation. Critical teacher researchers uncover memories of past emancipation which serve as the catalyst for future emancipation. The struggle against education which suppresses human dignity, which condones bad work, and which allows for unexamined and repressive definitions of intelligence, success, and excellence is ignited (Giroux, 1988:99; Metz, 1989:89; Welch, 1985:39–41).

Before ethnography, phenomenology, semiotics, and hermeneutics, history resides. It is history that paints the setting which gives meaning to the details of ethnography, phenomenology, semiotics, and hermeneutics. In critical constructivist research none of the qualitative methods stand alone — they are all employed in relation to one another. The methods of emancipatory pedagogy are always historical, as memories of the struggles of our ancestors are recovered and put to use in the present. Any attempt at social or educational theorizing must be historically grounded. Uncritical practitioners of action research fail to recognize this reality; they fail to understand that educational problems whether small or large are generated by the historical processes of which they are a part (Semmes, 1981:6; Giroux, 1988:94; Harrison, 1985:250). This is why historiography is such an important dimension of the action research process. Critical history can break open the past revealing a web of connections which, once comprehended, help represent history as an epic depicting men and women struggling against domination. Even if the struggle is unsuccessful, it still implies a degree of emancipation. The failed resistance grants us a powerful example of courage that informs our present concerns as critical teachers. As long as there is rage, resistance, and insurrection, there is hope (Welch, 1985:39).

Foucault finds the grounding of his historical work in these insurrections, these resistances of the hegemonized (the oppressed). Critical constructivist researchers derive from Foucault a pre-theoretical commitment that the voices of the oppressed, subjugated knowledges, are valuable and should be heard. Drawing upon this commitment the researcher thus brings the methods of his or her own inquiry to the analysis of the power relations in a particular institution. It is at this point that an educational action researcher uncovers the concrete mechanisms of exclusion and domination in the schools. Returning to our discussion of subjugated knowledges in Chapter 2, Foucault looks at such knowledges in relation to the dynamics of power relations in two ways: 1) the history, the dangerous ideas, that have been suppressed; and 2) knowledges, ways of knowing that have been disqualified or insufficiently elaborated. Foucault maintains that it is through the re-emergence of these low-ranking knowledges that alternate, emancipatory visions of education are possible. Through the disqualified knowledges of working class people, blacks, ethnic minorities, along with the knowledge constructed by critical theorists, critical constructivist action researchers formulate their questions, re-interpret the social and education history which shapes them and their students, develop modes of critique of educational practice, and reveal the silences and omissions which insidiously contribute to domination in school settings (Foucault, 1980:82; Welch, 1985:42–3).

Redefining historical work along the lines of this genealogy of

Foucault, critical constructivist teacher researchers view their role as the vehicles for dangerous memory, as agents who draw upon and promote the resurgence of subjugated knowledges suppressed by dominant culture and schools. Such teachers can become transformative agents who alert the community to its genealogy and in the process help individuals name their oppression. Such a naming process allows students, other teachers, and community members the ability to reflect on the structural construction of their lived worlds. With, as Freire put it, such conscientization individuals develop the ability to become the subjects of their own lives. Thus, critical constructivist action researchers grounding their inquiry in history uncover a form of dangerous memory which involves the remembrance of how various groups and individuals have gained awareness of their place in the web of reality. Such awareness frees students, teachers, and community members to claim an identity apart from the one that was forced on them. Johann Baptist Metz claims that identity is constructed when memories are aroused — in other words, confrontation with dangerous memory changes our perception of the forces which shape us, which in turn moves us to redefine our world views, our ways of seeing (Welch, 1985:35–6, 42; Metz, 1980:66). The oppressive forces which shape us have formed the identities of both the powerful and the exploited. Without historical analysis of this process it will never be clear to teacher researchers why students succeed or fail in schools. They will forever be blind to the tacit ideological forces which construct student perceptions of school and the impact such perceptions have made on their school experiences. Such blindness restricts our view of our own and our student's view of their place in history. Historical decontextualization renders us vulnerable to ideologies and myths employed to perpetuate social domination (Harrison, 1985:250–1).

Teacher researchers need to be aware of a tension embedded in the articulation of dangerous memories. As analysts who help formulate modes of resistance, critical constructivist action researchers must be sensitive to their own potential oppressive role. This possible oppressiveness rests in what Foucault labels the indignity of speaking for the oppressed. Critical constructivist researchers walk a tightrope — they cannot avoid issuing their historical analyses, their educational critiques, but they must refrain from speaking for the victims of hegemonic forces. Critical teacher researchers, thus, set the stage for the resistance of oppressed community members, their students, and their fellow teachers; they expose the ideological malformations, the injustices, the forced silences, but they don't speak for the oppressed. Emancipatory resistance will emerge only when the victims of history are empowered — through their understandings — to make history. When victims speak for themselves in educational contexts, they propose new interpretations of the codes and texts of the school, new analyses of school hierarchies, criticisms of the institutional structures of the school, and new perspectives on how they might stand beside, be in solidarity with other historical victims in the larger society (Welch, 1985:43–5).

Armed with their genealogical understanding of history, critical constructivist researchers can seek out the connections between the everyday life of students (both academic and social) and their historical moment. Mundane classroom activity becomes a valuable source of insight when subjected to genealogical analysis. Student language is seen in a new light as a manifestation of history. Reading, for example, is a process which occurs within a historical context — it is a social construction open to critical analysis. As a social construction it designates the reader as the locus of integration in the sense that students synthesize their own cultural meanings with the meanings of the author to produce a reading of texts. Teacher researchers can use their historical understandings as a starting place for analyzing their student's readings, in the process gaining valuable insight into the consciousness of their students — their cultural histories, their fears, their dreams, and the forces which shape them. Such understandings provide critical teacher researchers with a special vantage point on how students from, say, dominated cultures bring their own experiences, desires, voices, and ghosts to the reading act.

Thus, the teacher researcher's historical grounding allows him or her a revolutionary perspective on what happens in classrooms. Traditionally, school personnel and researchers have looked only at how students receive knowledge: how much did they retain?; how good is their memory?; did they master European history? Armed with their historically-grounded critical constructivist perspective, teacher researchers begin to look at how students produce knowledge. They examine how students bring their own socially-constructed meanings into the learning situation; they explore the dialectic between student life histories and school knowledge. Thus, critical constructivist action researchers take seriously the historical experiences of their students. When such history is appreciated then education can no longer serve as a tool of cultural conquest, a form of intellectual colonialism — it becomes an agency which rescues the valuable insights, the cultural uniqueness, the subjugated knowledges of subordinate groups. Liberal attempts to free people outside their own histories and cultures will always turn into just another form, albeit unintentional, of opposition. When freedom is defined by the privileged, the oppressed are victimized not only by traditional modes of labor exploitation, racism, or patriarchy but by liberal arrogance (Giroux, 1988:192–3; Welch, 1985:82–3).

Once teacher researchers begin to focus on knowledge production and student emancipation based on student histories and subjugated knowledges, then their pedagogy is forever transformed. Teacher researchers begin to construct their curricula around student experience, encouraging student understanding of the social, economic, and cultural forms that shape their lived worlds. Student learn to deconstruct the ideology that is embedded in their everyday lives — their place in the social hierarchy of their peer group, their romantic relationships, their vocational aspirations, their relationships with teachers. Michelle Gibbs Russell concretizes our understanding of the use of memory and student histories as a basis for grasping the ways in which ideology shapes student (and teacher) lived worlds. Teacher researchers start with student memory, she writes, exchanging stories of everyday life, e.g., how a student got a funny name, how a student's clothes were ripped, why some students are always late. Teacher researchers as life historians elicit descriptions of the dreams students hold for the future and the specific factors which have worked to interfere with those dreams. Russell encourages critical teachers to make lists on the board of these dreams as well as the impediments which thwart their realization. Once the lists are completed the teacher then encourages students to generalize from these concrete specifics. The histories don't speak for themselves; they are manifestations of ideological forces which covertly shape history and our own lives. This is the critical aspect of action research, interpreting for oneself and one's students the information collected about their lives. In the process of constructing these interpretations, historically-grounded teacher researchers employ their understanding of the community to connect students, especially students from subjugated cultures, to the traditions of the community (Russell, 1983:273).

In our examination of the role of history and the use of historical methods in teacher research we draw upon the people's history movement which has developed over the past twenty-five years. People's history, like critical action research, is grounded on Antonio Gramsci's notion that non-intellectuals do not exist (Gramsci, 1988:320–1). Nobody is incapable, advocates of people's history argue, of playing a role in the construction of their own history or the history of the community. People's history when applied to education focuses the attention of action researchers on: 1) the subjective historical experience of consciousness construction of the student, other teachers, and the action researchers themselves; 2) the student's understanding of his or her own school experience and the forces which have shaped it; 3) the effort to blur the boundaries of professional and amateur educational history (to subvert the cult of the expert), as action researchers construct their own educational histories of groups, communities, schools, and individuals; and 4) the attempt to understand the role of schooling and informal agencies of education such as media, religion, advertising, *ad infinitum* in consciousness formation, i.e., popular memory.

This type of useful history is similar in many ways to Paulo Freire's literacy work in that it holds the potential for intellectual and political empowerment. People's history, like Freire's emancipatory pedagogy, lets people know that they can make their own history in both meanings of the phrase (Green, 1984:181–3). In a Deweyan and Freirean sense the

'doing' of people's history may have as much empowering, political significance as the findings it produces. Critical teacher researchers can ex-
trapolate pedagogies from people's history which teach their students to
teach themselves, to view themselves as participants in the social, political,
and educational world of which they are a part. Such historical work can
teach individuals that the social, political, economic, and educational institutions that help construct their lives are not above history but have
been formed by historical forces and human choices (Benson, Brier, and
Rosenzweig, 1986:xxiv). The purposes which modern schools serve are
not the purposes of schooling in any place or time. The values which
modern media promote are not supra-historical, i.e., values constant at
any time or place. The definition of a good student commonly accepted in
contemporary schools does not close the book on what constitutes a good
student. Through the application of people's history the tyranny of the
present can be overthrown.

   With the commitments of people's history in mind, action researchers
must become good listeners — they must listen to the voice of the public
as it speaks of education, the voice of their students as they express their
concerns about their own education, the voice of their educational leaders
as they make policies which affect the profession. What they hear may be
inspirational but it may also be disturbing with its prejudices, miscon-
ceptions, and manufactured consciousness. These subjectivities, however,
are the raw materials of people's history, of popular memory, of critical
constructivist action research. A praxiological history, a critical action
research interrogates how these memories, these subjectivities were constructed and their effects on social and educational policy and the lives of
the people who hold them. Critical constructivist teacher researchers can
learn from Gerda Lerner's challenge to historians to redefine professionalism in the historical craft in a way that values the relationship of the
public to the past and that seeks to communicate with lay people on a
level that is meaningful to their experience (Kaye, 1987:357).

   Historically-informed teacher researchers extend the possibility of
transformative action as they operate on the basis of Lerner's challenge.
Action research transcends the boundaries of the classroom and investigations of instructional technique — it connects the school and community
via the identification of common historical forces which have helped shape
individuals and institutions. As an example, historically-grounded action
researchers might inform community members of the original justification
for vocational programs within the local school district, who promoted
them, and whose interests were served or not served by their adoption.
Such a historical investigation could be used to spark contemporary community interrogations of the effects of vocational programs — interrogations which could lead to political action on the part of those adversely
affected by such programs. Such a form of teacher research takes seriously
Harvey Kaye's contention that history must be made ever more public; it

must become a part of the popular media, the everyday life of citizens in democratic societies (Kaye, 1987:357).

Lerner's and Kaye's calls have been ignored. History and historical methodology have been sequestered — those certified by the culture to 'do history' have turned away from the concerns of the public. Critical constructivist teacher researchers have much to learn from an understanding of the professionalization of history marked by its esoteric concerns. Teacher researchers will come to see that the self-absorption of the profession does not represent the traditional orientation of historical scholarship. For most of its existence history has been regarded as an art and a science conducted *outside* the walls of academia. Non-professionals wrote much of the best history, proving that academicians had no franchise on the historical craft. The genesis of the modern dismissal of history as irrelevant — a dismissal which exacerbates social amnesia — can be traced to the professionalization of history in the late nineteenth century. This professionalization accompanied the more general rise of the cult of the expert and attempted to exalt the status of the historian often at the expense of the social value or his or her (mainly his) work. Incarcerated in the prison of the academy, the historian's view of contemporary society was shielded — he came to see only his shadow on the cell block wall. The historian's view of the world was furthered restricted by the competition, narcissism, and one-up*man*ship so characteristic of the professionalized craft.

Teacher researchers have much to learn from the mistakes made by advocates of people's history and the difficulties they have encountered in their attempt to redefine historical professionalism. Too often the public history conducted to date has focused on the chronicling of memory and anecdote while neglecting serious analysis. Like uncritical action research, people's history has been limited by a persistent parochialism — it has often ignored the hidden realities and relationships which move the social world. The most common methodology employed by people's historians so far is oral history. Such a method has constituted a direct challenge to traditional historiography as it confronts the traditional reliance on written documents. Embedded within the use of oral history are a host of ideological assumptions about what constitutes a valid source — exclusive reliance on written documents almost by necessity excludes the voices of the poor and hegemonized because they rarely leave written records. As people's history makes use of oral history in its inquiry into popular memory and historical consciousness formation, it must overcome the tendency of much of the oral history undertaken to date to base its interpretation on personal experience (Green, 1984:175–7). In the same manner that we theorized the interpretive strategies of critical constructivist action research, people's history must seek its voice in oral history but frame its analysis in an emancipatory system of meaning.

The theoretical grounding which emerges from our emancipatory system of meaning will dispel the naive idea that once people are put in touch with their history the hegemonic dominant culture will be subverted and critical consciousness will be established. Oral history has often been presented simply for consumption; its significance and meaning were assumed to be self-evident. In researching a history of a group of teachers, for example, the action researcher may simply lapse into collecting recollections and cute stories of the participants. Without an emancipatory system of meaning the teacher researcher may employ no mechanism to encourage participant discussion about different ways of seeing the past, the reasons for these different visions, and their effect on views of schooling and its purposes. Indeed, a more critical teacher researcher might induce the participants to discuss how different views of the purpose of schooling might have shaped the nature of their vision of the past. In the discussion that would follow the posing of such questions everyone might benefit: the teacher researcher would gain deeper insights into the consciousness of the teachers and the historical forces which formed it; the teachers would ask questions of their own life histories and their profession that they may never have asked before. For example: What did they perceive as the historic purposes of schooling in general and how do such purposes affect their teaching in particular? How did historical constructions of gender role affect the direction of their career and their social position within the school? What differences have reform movements made on their everyday life in the classroom?

When action research is historically grounded and approached in this critical manner not only are democratic dialogues and participatory processes established, but a new form of educational life history is created. This new form of educational people's history is not simply anecdotal nor is it traditionally academic. It invades a new territory, juxtaposing subjective historical memory and popular perceptions of the past with an emancipatory system of meaning. History, viewed in this context, does not merely become a form of public discussion — it merges with public discourse. No longer is history seen as a discrete scholarly practice and public discourse viewed as a democratic practice (Kaye, 1987:336). Such a bifurcation smacks of positivism: the separation of fact from value, of scholarship from civics. The teacher researcher utilizes this reconceptualized notion of people's history to expand the scope of what may be considered an important historical topic, to reconsider the complex relationships between past and present, and to reformulate what might pass as proper methods of historical research and use them to extend the range of qualitative strategies he or she can employ in his or her inquiry. Such a reconceptualization does not allow history or action research in general to become the servant of the vocal and the powerful.

A couple of examples of historically-grounded teacher research may help us understand in a more concrete manner the aims of critical constructivist research. Historically-grounded action research will find few more appropriate venues than black communities and the black students who came of age in them. Teacher inquirers may make use of students and community members as co-researchers in their attempt to generate understandings of their black students and the communities in which they have lived. Dominic Candeloro describes a black people's history project which holds important implications for the methodological strategies employed by critical constructivist teacher researchers. Candeloro began his research with a two-hour interview of a local black leader who provided a general historical overview of the black community in Lima, Ohio, and a list of themes which could be pursued to gain additional insight. From the interview Candeloro constructed a battery of questions which sought to elicit data on black participation in politics, religion, the union movements, and education. He then assembled a list of resource persons who contributed special insights into particular aspects of Lima's black history. The resource people not only contributed valuable oral historical accounts but alerted researchers to numerous forgotten documents and other sources of information. Candeloro reported that the project heightened awareness of the origins of the problems in the black community and how the past influenced present realities in Lima. Not only did Candeloro gain significant insight into the research process, but his students were introduced to the methods and purposes of inquiry and the ways research contributes to cognitive development. Research became for Candeloro and his students a form of critical pedagogy, a method of sophisticating cognitive processes (Candeloro, 1973:24–7).

Thad Sitton also writes of methods of incorporating black people's history in public school settings. The school, he contends, is an ideal place to locate public history projects. Teachers have access to the school's technical resources (typewriters, computers, tape recorders, VCRs, photographic equipment, etc.) which are invaluable in historically-oriented action research. Sitton modeled his Lockhart, Texas, black history project after the student oral history/folklore work of Foxfire. Drawing power from ethnic pride and sense of place, Foxfire projects have developed unique insights into the techniques of people's history and have initiated hundreds of school research/publishing projects around North America since the early 1970s. Operating originally in the rural South, Foxfire exposed the consequences of Anglo-domination of socio-economic life — consequences which involved the non-existence of documentary raw materials which could be used to construct an understanding of the historical context from which black students emerge. But when granted access to a microphone or a video recorder, black adults and students begin to tell their valuable stories — historical sources are instantly created (Sitton, 1981:173–4). The act of creation of this oral history can be the beginning step of an emancipatory journey. As many social studies teachers and Black Studies scholars have argued for almost thirty years, and as Dewey maintained before that, the community is a laboratory from which students can study data, draw conclusions, make decisions, and think about the future of their neighborhood, school, and city (Hayden, 1986: 186). Hopefully teacher researchers drawing upon an emancipatory system of meaning can extend such notions.

How exactly does a critical constructivist researcher orientation extend such notions? Aren't they sufficient? Drawing on feminist theory, phenomenology and semiotics, critical constructivism moves historical examination to a new level. Let us trace that process carefully by extending our examination of race in a historically-grounded critical constructivist context. Race identification and historical racial oppression, like other forms of oppression, are experienced at the subjective level. If teacher researchers are to understand oppression in a way which informs their practice, they must gain access to this level, the *Lebenswelt*. Feminist theory has taught us that the personal (the subjective) and the political cannot be separated — one cannot be understood outside the context of the other. Consider, for example, the way lawyers, politicians, and social scientists have discussed rape — the victim's account, her emotions, her range of subjectivities are pushed to the background. Her feelings of humiliation and disgust are treated as secondary issues. The most important element in rape involves the emotions and feelings of the victim. The failure to place importance on the feelings of the victim illustrates the failure of traditional forms of research — especially research involving oppressed groups. The notions of *currere* and the *Lebenswelt* once again emerge as central concepts in critical constructivism — action research as we conceive it must penetrate the realm of surface appearances and give voice to the perceptions, the feelings of the researched.

Once such subjectivities are exposed they must be viewed in conjunction with the historic structural (the economic and social) context in which they occur. In South Carolina, for example, individuals learn that they are Black or White not simply in terms of the historical expectations of racial culture but in terms of their relative power and status. A black child growing up in Charleston learns quickly that he or she is not treated the same way as a non-black child. Children are socialized by way of a set of socio-economic relationships as well as by cultures of race. Race identity and racism, thus, are manifestations of the way particular individuals and groups are status-located in a community, i.e., subjectivity cannot be separated from socio-economic structure. Thus, oppression, racism, discrimination have profound consequences, but we miss an essential point if we assume that black culture, black consciousness is simply constructed by such forces. Black people do not always respond to oppression, to historical structural contexts in a passive way. It is at this juncture that critical constructivist teacher researchers can move beyond the researchers of the past. Traditional researchers have often seen oppression only through the eyes of the oppressors, focusing their attention on the actions of the dominant group. Many modern historians have pointed out that even slaves resisted and overcame various forms of the system's dehumanization. While many forces in modern society and modern schools work to devalue the culture and subjectivity of the oppressed, it would be wrong for us to assume that these forces achieve what many assume they achieve (Brittan and Maynard, 1984:22–3, 31, 99–106).

Consciousness formation, thus, is not the result of simple cause–effect relationships. Historically-grounded critical constructivist researchers understand that is a far more complex *process*, ever changing, ever mutating, ever evolving. Indeed, contrary to traditional accounts, racial consciousness, the subjectivity of the oppressed, are never fixed, never established once and for all — self-definitions change as historical conditions evolve, and historical conditions change precipitously in the late twentieth century. Essential definitions of black men or black women or Hispanics or Native Americans do not exist; that is, what it means to be Black or Hispanic or Native American or White is constantly mutating as identities intersect with forces of gender, class, religion, and the terrain of popular culture. Thus, individuals resist oppression, 'rewrite' themselves in relation to shifting historical, interpersonal, intra-personal, and political contexts (de Lauretis, 1986:8). For example, a black female student raised in a poor southern rural setting who is interested in academic work, mathematics in particular, has contradictory forces at work in the construction of her consciousness. Her self-definitions are heterogeneous and often self-contradictory in that she identifies with a Pan-Africanism, rejects the ruralness of her parents with its attendant passivity, is uncomfortable with feminism and its interference with her heterosexual concern with her popularity with the males at school, is motivated by her desire for success in mathematics yet fears how such success may estrange her from her peer group. To argue that the young woman's consciousness is simply shaped by her blackness or her class position is to miss the way consciousness construction works, it is to be guilty of a crass reductionism. The forces of consciousness construction, like the forces of oppression, are interconnected and inseparable. Historically-grounded critical constructivist teacher researchers must grasp this insight, if their research is to hold any pedagogical value.

Drawing upon critical theory Stanley Aronwitz and Henry Giroux sophisticate our understanding of what a historically-grounded critical constructivist action research might involve. Consciousness construction, they agree, is contradictory and the result of the collision of a variety of ideologically oppositional forces. If teacher researchers are to understand historical oppression, how it affects students in educational settings, and how they might incorporate these understandings into their teaching, they have to appreciate the interconnectedness of hegemonic forces. Racism, sexism, and class bias do not stand alone, they work together in concert with the domination of nature. The historical view that supports androcentric social structures, that stereotypes blacks as being moved by a forbidden and irrepressible sexuality, that reifies unequal distribution of wealth as the result of the inferiority of the poor, that connects women with an illogical emotionalism and an intimidating sexuality, is grounded in an instrumental rationality, a dehumanizing separation of ethics from everyday life.

At the basis of this rationality is the logic of domination which revolves around a positivism with its emphasis on prediction and control and the *mastery* of nature. As a teacher researcher understands how these hegemonic forces emanate from a common 'logic', they understand that a failure to recognize the interconnectedness of the forces can lead to serious consequences. If an emancipatory teacher researcher attempts to explore domination in a way which focuses only on economic forms of hegemony, he or she sees a distorted, one-dimensional picture of how oppression operates. The consequences of such a distorted view may blind the teacher to the ways that hegemony pits different oppressed groups against one another: poor whites against blacks (think of the struggle in the 1890s in the southern United States between the poor white Populists and Blacks); lower socio-economic class men against women; or Blacks against recently immigrated Asians. The teacher researcher who fails to understand the insidious damage which results from a one-dimensional economic view of hegemony will consistently fail in his or her attempt to construct democratic classrooms, emancipatory communities, and good workplaces for teachers (Aronowitz and Giroux, 1985:129–30).

Thus, critical constructivist teacher researchers drawing upon their historical understandings seek the multiple ways that identities are established, that consciousness is constructed, that resistance is expressed. They do not see oppressed groups as perpetual victims always reacting to the oppressive structures of the larger society; they do not focus on only the material taught in school but also on the historical experiences, the lived experiences students bring to school; they move beyond the study of the cultural artifacts produced by oppressed groups at particular sites in previous historical eras with another set of social relations, e.g., art, music, religion, dress, shelter, food, etc. Critical constructivist teacher researchers seek to explore oppressed cultures in a way which connects historical struggle with contemporary lived experience and the multitude of contradictions resulting from this intersection. When teachers teach about an oppressed culture's traditional religion, food, dress, and music such information may have little to do with the way students from the culture being studied live their lives. Consider the way North Americans teach about Native Americans in light of the nature of contemporary reservation life. British teacher researchers operating in urban settings, for example, might want to explore the cultural meaning of reggae music. Reggae can be read as a form of resistance of urban black youth in London, but it can also be viewed as dance music produced and marketed for the consumption of white audiences (Carby, 1980:67–8). How is it read by students in the teacher researcher's classroom? What do the multiple readings tell us about the intersection of historical struggle with the contemporary lived experiences of our student? Teacher researchers begin to see the lived worlds of their students in a far more textured way. Their experiences are sites of struggle over cultural meanings. When viewed from this perspective, students who are labelled as insolent by mainstream educators can be better understood — often they are rejecting the official meanings, the linguistic codes, the 'correct' submissive attitudes required by the school.

Thus, critical constructivist action research seeks to uncover what we might label the phenomenological life history of actors in education settings. Just as a way of connecting our analysis of such a research orientation, let us focus our attention on what is involved in the teacher researcher's attempt to piece together phenomenological life histories of students. In the attempt to understand consciousness as it is subjectively experienced by individuals, we need to ask them how they feel, what they remember about their experiences, the reasons they act as they do. Our familiarity with critical theory and the ideological construction of consciousness extends the insight we gain from our understanding of how experiences appeared to students, what the students thought they had to deal with, and what alternatives they perceived to be available. In this manner the action researcher as life historian makes use of the interaction of: 1) the phenomenology of life history (the nature of the student's experience as a discrete phenomenon, i.e., lived events just as they exist); and 2) critical hermeneutics involving the *interpretation* of life history. Starting with Hans Georg Gadamer's explanation of hermeneutics, we recognize the importance of bridging the gap that separates our consciousness as researchers from the phenomenon being researched (Gadamer, 1975:256–90). Thus, a critical hermeneutics would force us to use our ideological understandings to interrogate our initial perceptions of the phenomenon under study, i.e., how do we feel about students we are investigating? The interaction of phenomenology and critical hermeneutics produces a familiarity of students' 'lives as they are' coupled with interpretive strategies which would help us understand how their lives came to be that way, how they could change for the better. Employing a critical hermeneutics we enter into an authentic dialogue with our students, taking pains to avoid the all too common kitsch of teacher-student conversations. Indeed, the critical constructivist action researcher as life historian always sees the student both as he or she is and in a larger context — never as simply one or the other (Watson-Franke and Watson, 1975:247–62).

As part of the investigative process a teacher exploring student life histories would have to take into account the conditions under which information was obtained. A student-teacher relationship is never innocent, never free of ideological dimensions, and unequal power relations. The teacher researcher must have the savvy to assure the students that there is no need for him or her to tell the teacher researcher only what might be acceptable in the culture of the school. Because of the unequal power relations students will tend to tell teacher researchers what they think they want to hear. With such concerns in mind teacher researchers need to consider the physical setting in which the life history is related. Is the teacher sitting behind his or her desk asking questions to a student sitting in a classroom seat? Might a more intimate, non-hierarchical, neutral setting be more conducive to authentic communication? Removing the student from the hierarchical setting of school may break down role assignments which always work to restrict authentic communication. When the teacher can engage the student as a fellow human being, authentic revelations of the student's life history begin to emerge (Lincoln and Guba, 1985:268–73).

As this authentic life history is revealed, the teacher researcher begins the difficult task of discerning the way the student makes sense of the information, how the life history helps construct the student's consciousness. The action researcher uncovers the student's perceptual organization of the information and gains insight into who the student really is by asking a series of questions of the student *and* of the information obtained: 1) What aspects of the student's life does he or she choose to remember and how does ideology affect the choices?; 2) How do the narrative forms chosen to relate and categorize events reflect ideological formulas that unconsciously construct memory?; 3) What are the competing forces that are structuring consciousness and what are the psychological 'fault lines' formed by the clash of such forces?; 4) How does the student's perceptual organization of his or her life history with the accompanying fault lines of ideology-conflict help construct the student's relationship with the school, the learning process in general?; 5) How might the teacher researcher relate to school and to teachers if he or she had a similar life history? Such research promises to grant teachers a degree of empathy with students rarely achieved in educational settings.

Herbert Marcuse argued that emancipation required the recognition of past as present. Such a recognition keeps possibility alive by subverting a closed, fixed socio-educational universe (Giroux, 1981: 46), Historically-grounded critical constructivist teacher researchers have much to learn from such pronouncements as they examine historical dimensions of their schools and communities and, of course, the life histories of their students. Students do not come to our classes already frozen in history, incapable of escape from the structural forces which work to limit them. Only when we develop our capacity as teacher researchers to understand the way unconfronted ideology works to constrain our students, to keep the poor in their place, to limit women's options, to perpetuate racial oppression, and to foster passive uncritical thinking, will history be overcome. Only when we as teachers are able to rescue wisdom from the cult of the expert will we control our own professional destinies and release our students from the burden of history.

Bibliography

ADORNO, T. et al. (1950) *The Authoritarian Personality*. New York, Harper and Row.

ALTRICHTER, H. and POSCH, P. (1989) 'Does the "grounded theory" approach offer a guiding paradigm for teacher research?', *Cambridge Journal of Education*, **19**, 1, pp. 21–31.

ANDERSON, G. (1989) 'Critical ethnography in education: Origins, current status, and new directions', *Review of Educational Research*, **59**, 3, pp. 249–70.

ARLIN, P. (1975) 'Cognitive development in adulthood: A fifth stage?', *Developmental Psychology*, **11**, 5, pp. 602–6.

ARMSTRONG, M. (1981) 'The case of Louise and the painting of land-scapes', in NIXON, J. (Ed.) *A Teachers' Guide to Action Research*, London, Grant McIntyre.

ARONOWITZ, S. (1973) *False Promises*, New York, Mcgraw-Hill.

ARONOWITZ, S. (1983) 'The relativity of theory' in *The Village Voice*, 27 December, p. 60.

ASTMAN, J. (1984) 'Special education as a moral enterprise', *Learning Disability Quarterly*, **7**, 4, pp. 299–308.

BALDWIN, E. (1987) 'Theory vs. ideology in the practice of teacher education', *Journal of Teacher Education*, **38**, pp. 16–19.

BARROW, R. (1984) *Giving Teaching Back to Teachers*, Totowa, New Jersey, Barnes and Noble Books.

BELENKY, M., CLINCHY, B., GOLDBERGER, N. and TARULE, J. (1986) *Women's Ways of Knowing: The Development of Self, Voice, and Mind*, New York, Basic Books.

BELLAH, R. (1983) 'Social science as practical reason', in CALLAHAN, D. and JENNINGS, B. (Eds) *Ethics, the Social Sciences, and Policy Analysis*, New York, Plenum Press.

BENSON, S., BRIER, S. and ROSENZWEIG, R. (1986) 'Introduction', in BENSON, S., BRIER, S. and ROSENZWEIG, R. *Presenting the Past: Essays on History and the Public*, Philadelphia, Temple University Press.

Bibliography

BESAG, F. (1986) 'Reality and research', *American Behavioral Scientist*, 30, 1, pp. 6–14.

BESAG, F. (1986b) 'Striving after the wind', *American Behavioral Scientist*, 30, 1, pp. 15–22.

BODNER, G. (1986) 'Constructivism: A theory of knowledge', *Journal of Chemical Education*, 63, 10, pp. 873–8.

BOGDAN, R. and BIKLEN, S. (1982) *Qualitative Research for Education: An Introduction to Theory and Methods*, Boston, Allyn and Bacon.

BOURRICAUD, F. (1979) 'Individualistic mobilization and the crisis of professional authority', *Daedalus*, 108, 2, pp. 1–20.

BOWLES, G. (1982) 'Is women's studies an academic discipline?', in BOWLES, G. and KLEIN, R. *Theories of Women's Studies*, Boston, Routledge and Kegan Paul.

BRACY, G. (1987) 'Measurement-driven instruction: Catchy phrase, dangerous practice', *Phi Delta Kappan*, 68, 9, pp. 683–6.

BRIGGS, J. and PEAT, F. (1989) *Turbulent Mirror*, New York, Harper and Row.

BRITTON, A. and MAYNARD, M. (1984) *Sexism, Racism, and Oppression*, New York, Basil Blackwell.

CALLAHAN, R. (1962) *Education and the Cult of Efficiency*, Chicago, University of Chicago Press.

CARBY, H. (1980) 'Multi-Culture', *Screen Education*, 34, pp. 62–70.

CARR, W. and KEMMIS, S. (1986) *Becoming Critical*, Basingstoke, The Falmer Press.

CHAMBERLIN, G. (1974) 'Phenomenological methodology and understanding education', in DENTON, D. (Ed.) *Existentialism and Phenomenology in Education*, New York, Teachers College Press.

CHATTIN-McNICHOLS, J. and LOEFFLER, M. (1989) 'Teachers as researchers: The first cycle of the teachers' research network', *Young Children*, 44, 5, pp. 20–7.

CHERRYHOLMES, C. (1988) *Power and Criticism: Poststructural Investigations in Education*, New York, Teachers College Press.

CHILD, D. and SMITHERS, A. (1971) 'Some cognitive and affective factors in subject choice', *Research in Education*, 5, pp. 1–9.

CHURCH, R. and SEDLAK, M. (1976) *Education in the United States*, New York, Macmillan.

CANDELORO, D. (1973) 'Undergraduates as historians: Recovering the history of a black community', *The History Teacher*, 7, 1, pp. 24–9.

CONNELL, R. (1989) 'Curriculum politics, hegemony, and strategies of social change', in GIROUX, H. and SIMON, R. *Popular Culture: Schooling and Everyday Life*, Granby, Massachusetts, Bergin and Garvey Publishers.

CONNELLY, F. and BEN-PERETZ, M. (1980) 'Teachers' roles in the using and doing of research and 'curriculum development?', *Journal of Curriculum Studies*, 12, 2, pp. 95–107.

CULBERTSON, J. (1981) 'Antecedents of the theory movement', *Educational Administration Quarterly*, **17**, pp. 25–47.

DAVID, J. (1988) 'The use of indicators by school districts: Aid or threat to improvement' *Phi Delta Kappan*, **69**, 7, pp. 499–503.

DE LAURETIS, T. (1986) 'Feminist studies/critical studies: Issues, terms, and contexts' in DE LAURETIS, T. (Ed.) *Feminist Studies/Critical Studies*, Bloomington, Indiana, Indiana University Press.

DEWEY, J. (1916) *Democracy and Education*, New York, The Free Press.

DEWEY, J. (1908) *Ethics*, New York, Henry Holt and Company.

DEWEY, D. (1929) *The Sources of a Science of Education*, New York, Horace Liveright.

DOBSON, R., DOBSON, J. and KOETTING, R. (1987) 'Problematic aspects of school reform', *Capstone Journal of Education*, 7, 2, pp. 3–13.

DOLL, W. (1989) 'Foundations for a post-modern curriculum', *Journal of Curriculum Studies*, 21, 3, pp. 243–53.

DONMOYER, R. (1987) 'Beyond Thorndike/beyond melodrama', *Curriculum Inquiry*, **17**, 4, pp. 353–63.

DONMOYER, R. (1985) 'The rescue from relativism: Two failed attempts and an alternative strategy', *Educational Researcher*, **14**, pp..

DONMOYER, R. (forthcoming a) 'Curriculum evaluation and the negotiation of meaning', *Language Arts*.

DONMOYER, R. (forthcoming b) 'Generalizability and the single case study', in PESHKIN, A. and EISNER, E. (Eds) *Qualitative Research in Education*, New York, Teachers College Press.

DOYLE, W. (1977) 'Paradigms for research on teacher effectiveness', *Review of Research in Education*, **5**, pp. 163–198.

DUBOIS, B. (1982) 'Passionate scholarship: Notes on values, knowing, and method in feminist social science', in BOWLES, G. and KLEIN, R. *Theories of Women's Studies*, Boston, Routledge and Kegan Paul.

DUCKWORTH, E. (1987) *'The Having of Wonderful Ideas' and Other Essays on Teaching and Learning*, New York, Teachers College Press.

DUKE, D. (1977) 'Debriefing: A tool for curriculum research and course improvement', *Journal of Currulum Studies*, 9, 2, pp. 157–63.

DUKE, D. (1985) 'What is the nature of educational excellence and should we try to measure it?' *Phi Delta Kappan*, **66**, 10, pp. 671–4.

EISNER, E. (1983) 'Anastasia might still be alive, but the monarchy is dead', *Educational Researcher*, **12**, pp. 13–14, 23–4.

EISNER, E. (1984) 'Can educational research inform educational practice?', *Phi Delta Kappan*, **65**, 7, pp. 447–52.

ELLIOTT, J. (1981) 'Introduction', in NIXON, J. (Ed.) *A Teachers' Guide to Action Research*, London, Grant McIntyre.

ELLIOTT, J. (1989a) 'Studying the school curriculum through insider research', Paper presented to the International Conference on School-Based Innovations: Looking Foward to the 1990s, Hong Kong.

Bibliography

ELLIOTT, J. (1989b) 'Action-research and the emergence of teacher appraisal in the United Kingdom', Paper presented to the American Educational Research Association, San Francisco.

EMERY, F. and THORSRUD, E. (1976) *Democracy at Work*, Leiden, Martinus Nijhoff.

FAY, B. (1975) *Social Theory and Political Practice*, London, George Allen and Unwin.

FEE, E. (1982) 'Is Feminism a threat to scientific objectivity?', *International Journal of Women's Studies*, 4, 4, pp. 378–92.

FETTERMAN, D. (1988) 'Qualitative approaches to evaluating education', *Educational Researcher*, 17, 8, pp. 17–23.

FINN, C. (1982) 'A call for quality education', *American Education*, 108, pp. 28–34.

FISKE, D. (1986) 'Specificity of method and knowledge in social science', in FISKE, D. and SHWEDER, R. *Metatheory in Social Science: Pluralisms and Subjectivities*, Chicago, University of Chicago Press.

FLAVELL, J. (1977) *Cognitive Development*, Englewood Cliffs, New Jersey, Prentice-Hall.

FOUCAULT, M. (1980) *Power/Knowledge: Selected Interviews and Other Writings*, Ed. GORDON, C., New York, Pantheon.

FOWLER, G. (1984) 'Philosophical assumptions and contemporary research perspectives', Paper Presented to the Speech Communication Association, Chicago.

FRANKEL, B. (1986) 'Two extremes on the commitment continuum', in FISKE, D. and SHWEDER, R. *Metatheory in Social Science: Pluralisms and Subjectivities*, Chicago, University of Chicago Press.

FREIRE, P. (1972) 'Research methods', Paper presented to a seminar entitled Studies in Adult Education, Dar-es-Salaam, Tanzania.

FRISCH, M. (1981) 'The memory of history', *Radical History Review*, 25, pp. 9–23.

GADAMER, H. (1975) *Truth and Method*, BARDEN, G. and CUMMING, J. (Eds) New York, Seabury Press.

GARMAN, N. and HAZI, H. (1988) 'Teachers ask: Is there life after Madeline Hunter?' *Phi Delta Kappan*, 69, pp. 670–2.

GIARELLI, J. and CHAMBLISS, J. (1984) 'Philosophy of education as qualitative inquiry', *Journal of Thought*, 19, pp. 34–46.

GIBSON, R. (1984) *Structuralism and Education*, London, Hodder and Stoughton.

GIBSON, R. (1986) *Critical Theory and Education*, London, Hodder and Stoughton.

GIROUX, H. (1981) *Ideology, Culture, and the Process of Schooling*, Philadelphia, Temple University Press.

GIROUX, H. (1983) *Theory and Resistance in Education*, South Hadley, Massachusetts, Bergin and Garvey.

GIROUX, H. (1986) 'Critical theory and the politics of culture and voice:

Rethinking the discourse of educational research', *Journal of Thought*, **21**, pp. 84–105.

GIROUX, H. (1988) *Schooling and the Struggle for Public Life*, Minneapolis, University of Minnesota Press.

GIROUX, H. and ARONOWITZ, S. (1985) *Education Under Siege*, South Hadley, Massachusetts, Bergin and Garvey.

GIROUX, H. and SIMON, R. (1989) 'Popular culture as a pedagogy of pleasure and meaning', in GIROUX, H. and SIMON, R. (Eds) *Popular Culture: Schooling and Everyday Life*, Granby, Massachusetts, Bergin and Garvey.

GIROUX, H. and SIMON, R. (Eds) (1989) *Popular Culture: Schooling and Everyday Life*, Granby, Massachusetts, Bergin and Garvey.

GOODLAD, J. (1988) 'Studying the education of educators: Values-driven inquiry', *Phi Delta Kappan*, **70**, 2, pp. 105–111.

GORDON, E., MILLER, F. and ROLLOCK, D. (1990) 'Coping with communicentric bias in knowledge production in the social sciences', *Educational Researcher*, **19**, 3, pp. 14–19.

GRADY, H. and WELLS, S. (1985–1986) 'Toward a rhetoric of intersubjectivity: Introducing Jürgen Habermas', *Journal of Advanced Composition*, **6**, pp. 33–47.

GRAMSCI, A. (1988) *An Antonio Gramsci Reader*, edited by FORGACS, D., New York, Schocken Books.

GREEN, J. (1984) 'People's history and Socialist theory: A review essay', *Radical History Review*, **28**, pp. 169–86.

GREEN, M. (1985) 'A philosophic look at merit and mastery in teaching', *The Elementary School Journal*, **86**, pp. 17–23.

GREENE, M. (1975) Curriculum and consciousness', in PINAR, W. *Curriculum Theorizing; The Reconceptualist*, Berkeley, McCutchan Publishing Company.

GRUMET, M. (1988) *Bitter Milk: Women and Teaching*, Amherst, Massachusetts, University of Massachusetts Press.

HABERMAS, J. (1971) *Knowledge and Human Interests*, trans. J. Shapiro, Boston, Beacon Press.

HABERMAS, J. (1973) *Theory and Practice*, trans. VIERTEL, J. Boston, Beacon Press.

HAMMERSLEY, M. and ATKINSON, P. (1983) *Ethnography: Principle in Practice*, New York, Tavistock Publications.

HANEY, W. and MADAUS, G. (1989) 'Searching for alternatives to standardized tests: Whys, whats, and whithers', *Phi Delta Kappan*, **70**, 9, pp. 683–7.

HARDING, S. (1986) *The Science Question in Feminism*, Ithaca, New York, Cornell University Press.

HARRIS, M. (1981) *America Now*, New York, Simon and Schuster.

HARRISON, B. (1985) *Making the Connections: Essays in Feminist Social Ethics*, Boston, Beacon Press.

HAYDEN, R. (1986) 'Comment', in HINE, D. *The State of Afro-American History: Past, Present, and Future*, Baton Rouge, Louisiana, Louisiana State University Press.

HEAD, J. (1979) 'Personality and pursuit of science', *Studies in Science Education*, 6, pp. 35–45.

HELD, D. (1980) *Introduction to Critical Theory: Horkheimer to Habermas*, Berkeley, California, University of California Press.

HERMAN, E. and CHOMSKY, N. (1988) *Manufacturing Consent: The Political Economy of the Mass Media*, New York, Pantheon Books.

HODGE, R. and KRESS, G. (1988) *Social Semiotics*, Ithaca, New York, Cornell University Press.

HOLLAND, R. and MANSELL, T. (1983) 'Meanings and their interpretations in science education research', *Studies in Science Education*, 10, pp. 100–107.

HORKHEIMER, M. (1974) *Critique of Instrumental Reason*, New York, Seabury Press.

HOUSE, E. (1978) 'Evaluation as scientific management in U.S. School reform', *Comparative Education Review*, 22, 3, pp. 388–401.

HOWE, K. (1985) 'Two dogmas of educational research', *Educational Researcher*, 14, pp. 10–18.

HUSSERL, E. (1970) *The Crisis of European Sciences and Transcendental Phenomenology: An Introduction to Phenomenology*, Evanston, Illinois, Northwestern University Press.

JACOBY, R. (1975) *Social Amnesia*, Boston, Beacon Press.

JAGGAR, A. (1983) *Feminist Politics and Human Nature*, Totowa, New Jersey, Rowman and Allanheld.

JAMES, M. and EBBUTT, D. (1981) 'Problems and potential' in NIXON, J. (Ed.) *A Teachers' Guide to Action Research*, London, Grant McIntyre.

JAMES, W. (1956) *The Will to Believe and Other Popular Essays in Popular Philosophy*, New York, Dover Publications.

JAYARATNE, T. (1982) 'The value of quantitative methodology for feminist research', in BOWLES, G. and KLEIN, R. (Eds) *Theories of Women's Studies*, Boston, Routledge and Kegan Paul.

JAYNES, J. (1976) *The Origin of Consciousness in the Breakdown of the Bicameral Mind*, Boston, Houghton Mifflin Company.

KAYE, H. (1987) 'The use and abuse of the past: The New Right and the crisis of history', *Socialist Register*, ref.? pp. 332–65.

KEAT, R. (1981) *Politics of Social Theory: Habermas, Freud, and the Critique of Positivism*, Chicago, The University of Chicago Press.

KEGAN, R. (1982) *The Evolving Self: Problem and Process in Human Development*, Cambridge, Massachusetts, Harvard University Press.

KEMMIS, S. *et al.* (Eds) (1982) *The Action Research Reader*, Geelong, Victoria, Deakin University Press.

KERLINGER, F. (1973) *Foundations of Behavioral Research*, New York, Holt, Rinehart and Winston, Inc.

KICKBUSCH, K. (1985) 'Ideological innocence and dialogue: A critical perspective on discourse in the social studies', *Theory and Research in the Social Studies*, 13, 3, pp. 45–56.

KINCHELOE, J. et al. (1987) 'From Jaynesian consciousness to critical consciousness', Paper presented to the Louisiana Philosophy of Education Society, New Orleans, Louisiana.

KINCHELOE, J. and PINAR, W. (1991) 'Introduction', in KINCHELOE, J. and PINAR, W. (Eds) *Curriculum as Social Psychoanalysis: Essays on the Significance of Place*, Albany, New York, SUNY Press.

KITCHNER, K. (1983) 'Cognition, metacognition, and epistemic cognition', *Human Development*, 26, pp. 222–32.

KLEIN, R. (1982) 'How to do what we want to do: Thoughts about feminist methodology', in BOWLES, G. and KLEIN, R. (Eds) *Theories of Women's Studies*, Boston, Routledge and Kegan Paul.

KNELLER, G. (1984) *Movements of Thought in Modern Education*, 2nd ed., New York, John Wiley and Sons.

KOLLER, A. (1981) *An Unknown Woman: A Journey to Self-Discovery*, New York, Bantam Books.

KOVEL, J. (1981) *The Age of Desire*, New York, Pantheon Books.

KRAMER, D. (1983) 'Post-formal operations? A need for further conceptualization', *Human Development*, 26, pp. 91–105.

KROATH, F. (1989) 'How do teachers change their practical theories?' *Cambridge Journal of Education*, 19, 1, pp. 59–69.

LASCH, C. (1979) *The Culture of Narcissism*, New York, W. W. Norton and Company.

LATHER, PATTI (1986) 'Research as praxis', *Harvard Educational Review*, 56, pp. 257–77.

LAVINE, T. (1984) *From Socrates to Sartre: The Philosophic Quest*, New York, Bantam Books.

LEWIN, K. (1946) 'Action research and minority problems', *Journal of Social Issues*, 2, pp. 34–6.

LINCOLN, Y. and GUBA, E. (1985) *Naturalistic Inquiry*, Beverly Hills, California, Sage Publications.

LONGSTREET, W. (1982) 'Action research: A paradigm', *The Educational Forum*, 46, 2, pp. 136–49.

LOWE, D. (1982) *History of Bourgeois Perception*, Chicago, University of Chicago Press.

LUCAS, C. (1985) 'Toward a pedagogy of the useful past for teacher preparation', *Journal of Thought*, 20, pp. 19–33.

LYND, S. (1987) 'Foreword', in WELLS, D. (Ed.) *Empty Promises*, New York, Monthly Review Press.

McCUTCHEON, G. (1981) 'The impact of the insider', in NIXON, J. (Ed.) *A Teachers' Guide to Action Research*, London, Grant McIntyre.

MacDonald, J. (1975) 'Curriculum and human interests', in Pinar, W. *Curriculum Theorizing: The Reconceptualists*, Berkeley, McCutchan Publishing Company.

McKernan, J. (1988) 'The countenance of curriculum action research: Traditional, collaborative, and emancipatory-critical conceptions', *Journal of Curriculum and Supervision*, 3, 3, pp. 173–200.

McLaren, P. (forthcoming) 'Field relations and the discourse of the other: Collaboration in our own ruin', unpublished paper.

McLaren, P. (1989a) *Life in Schools*, New York, Longman.

McLaren, P. (1989b) 'On ideology and education: Critical pedagogy and the cultural politics of resistance', in Giroux, H. and McLaren, P. (Eds) *Critical Pedagogy, The State, and Cultural Struggles*, Albany, New York, SUNY Press.

McLaren, P. (1985) 'The ritual dimensions of resistance: Clowning and symbolic inversion', *Journal of Education*, 168, 2, pp. 84–97.

McLaren, P. (1986) *Schooling as Ritual Performance: Toward a Political Economy of Educational Symbols and Gestures*, London, Routledge and Kegan Paul.

Macmillan, C. and Garrison, J. (1984) 'Using the "new philosophy of science" in criticizing current research traditions in education', *Educational Researcher*, 13, pp. 15–21.

McKernan, J. (1988) 'Teacher as researcher: Paradigm and praxis', *Contemporary Education*, 59, 3, pp. 154–8.

McMahon, M. (1970) 'Positivism and the public schools', *Phi Delta Kappan*, 51, pp. 515–17.

McNay, M. (1988) 'Educational research and the nature of science', *The Educational Forum*, 52, 4, pp. 353–62.

McNeil, L. (1988) 'Contradictions of reform', *Phi Delta Kappan*, 69, 7, pp. 478–86.

Madaus, G. (1985) 'Test scores as administrative mechanisms in educational policy', *Phi Delta Kappan*, 66, 9, pp. 611–17.

Maeroff, G. (1988) 'A blueprint for empowering teachers', *Phi Delta Kappan*, 69, 7, pp. 472–7.

Mahoney, M. and Lyddon, W. (1988) 'Recent developments in cognitive approaches to counseling and psychotherapy', *The Counseling Psychologist*, 16, 2, pp. 190–234.

Marcuse, H. (1955) *Eros and Civilization*, Boston, Beacon Press.

Marcuse, H. (1964) *One Dimensional Man*, Boston, Beacon Press.

Meehl, P. (1986) 'What social scientists don't understand', in Fiske, D. and R. Shweder (Eds) *Metatheory in Social Science: Pluralisms and Subjectivities*, Chicage, University of Chicago Press.

Merleau-Ponty, M. (1962) *Phenomenology of Perception*, London, Routledge and Kegan Paul.

Metz, J. (1980) *Faith in History and Society*, trans. by Smith, D. New York, The Seabury Press.

MIES, M. (1982) 'Toward a methodology for feminist research', in BOWLES, G. and KLEIN, R., *Theories of Women's Studies*, Boston, Routledge and Kegan Paul.

MUNDAY, L. and DAVIS, J. (1974) *Varieties of Accomplishment After College: Perspectives on the Meaning of Academeic Talent*, Iowa City, Iowa, ACT Publications.

MYERS, L. (1987) 'The deep structure of culture: Relevance of traditional African culture in contemporary Life', *Journal of Black Studies*, **18**, 1, pp. 72–85.

NIXON, J. (1981) 'Postscript', in NIXON, J. (Ed.) *A Teachers' Guide to Action Research*, London, Grant McIntyre.

NOBLIT, G. (1984) 'The prospects of an applied ethnography for education: A sociology of knowledge interpretation', *Educational Evaluation and Policy Analysis*, **6**, 1, pp. 95–101

NOBLIT, G. and EAKER, D. (1987) 'Evaluation designs as political strategies', Paper presented to the American Educational Research Association, Washington, D.C.

NYANG, S. and VANDI, A. (1980) 'Pan Africanism in world history' in ASANTE, M. and VANDI, A., *Contemporary Black Thought: Alternative Analyses in Social and Behavioral Science*, Beverly Hills, California, Sag Publications.

NYBERG, D. and FARBER, P. (1986) 'Authority in education', *Teachers College Record*, **88**, 1, pp. 4–14.

ODI, A. (1981) 'The process of theory construction', *Journal of Research and Development in Education*. **15**, 2, pp. 53–8.

OJA, S. and HAM, M. (1984) 'A cognitive developmental approach to collaborative action research with teachers', *Teachers College Record*, **86**, 1, pp. 171–92.

OLDROYD, D. (1985) 'Indigenous action research for individual and system development', *Educational Management and Administration*, **13**, pp. 113–18.

OLDROYD, D. and TILLER, T. (1987) 'Change from within: An account of school-based collaborative action research in an English secondary school', *Journal of Education for Teaching*, **12**, 3, pp. 13–27.

ORTEZA Y MIRANDA, (1988) 'Broadening the focus of research in education', *Journal of Research and Development in Education*, **22**, 1, pp. 23–8.

OWEN, D. (1985) *None of the Above: Behind the Myth of Scholastic Aptitude*, Boston, Houghton Mifflin Company.

OXTOBY, M. and SMITH, B. (1970) 'Students entering Sussex and Essex Universities in 1966: Some similarities and differences', *Research in Education*, **3**, pp. 87–100.

PALEY, V. (1986) 'On listening to what the children say', *Harvard Educational Review*, **56**, 2, pp. 122–31.

PHILLIPS, D. (1983) 'After the wake: Postpositivistic educational thought',

Educational Researcher, **12**, pp. 4–12.
PIAGET, J. (1973) *To Understand is to Invent: The Furture of Education*, New York, Grossman.
PINAR, W. (1975) 'Currere: Toward Reconceptualization', in PINAR, W. (Ed.), *Curriculum Theorizing: The Reconceptualists*, Berkeley, McCutchan Publishing Company.
PINAR, W. (1975) 'The analysis of educational experience', in PINAR, W. (Ed.) *Curriculum Theorizing; The Reconceptualists*, Berkeley, McCutchan Publishing Company.
PINAR, W. and GRUMET, M. (1988) 'Socratic *Caesura* and the theory-practice relationship', in PINAR, W. (Ed.) *Contemporary Curriculum Discourses*, Scottsdale, Arizona, Gorsuch Scarisbrick.
PONZIO, R. (1985) 'Can we change content without changing context?' *Teacher Education Quarterly*, **12**, 3, pp. 39–43.
POPKEWITZ, T. (1981a) 'The study of schooling: Paradigms and field-based methodologies in education research and evaluation', in POPKEWITZ, T. and TABACHNICK, B. (Eds) *The Study of Schooling*, New York, Praeger Publisher.
POPKEWITZ, T. (1981b) 'Education research: Values and visions of social order', in GIROUX, H., PENNA, A. and PINAR, W. (Eds) *Curriculum and Instruction*, Berkeley, McCutchan Publishing Company.
POPULAR MEMORY GROUP (1982) 'Popular memory: Theory, politics, and method', in Centre for Contemporary Studies, *Making Histories: Studies in History-Writing and Politics*, Minneapolis, University of Minnesota Press.
PORTER, A. (1988) 'Indicators: Objective data or political tool?' *Phi Delta Kappan*, **69**, 7, pp. 503–8.
POSNER, G. (1982) 'Cognitive science and a conceptual change epistemology: A new approach to curricular research', *Journal of Curriculum Theorizing*, **4**, pp. 106–26.
POSTER, M. (1989) *Critical Theory and Poststructuralism: In Search of a Context*, Ithaca, New York, Cornell University Press.
PRIGOGINE, I. and STENGERS, I. (1984) *Order Out of Chaos*, New York, Basic Books.
REINHARZ, S. (1982) 'Experimental analysis: A contribution to feminist research', in BOWLES, G. and KLEIN, R. (Eds) *Theories of Women's Studies*, Boston, Routledge and Kegan Paul.
REINHARZ, S. (1979) *On Becoming a Social Scientist*, San Francisco, Jossey-Bass.
RICHARDS, C. (1988) 'Indicators and three types of educational monitoring systems: Implications for design', *Phi Delta Kappan*, **69**, 7, pp. 495–9.
RIVLIN, A. (1971) *Systematic Thinking for Social Action*, Washington, D.C., The Brookings Institution.

ROGERS, V. (1989) 'Assessing the curriculum experienced by children', *Phi Delta Kappan*, 70, 9, pp. 715–17.

ROMANISH, B. (1986) 'Critical thinking and the curriculum: A critique', *The Educational Forum*, 51, 1, pp. 45–56.

ROSENHOLTZ, S. (1987) 'Education reform strategies: Will they increase teacher commitment?', 37, pp. 534–62.

ROSS, D. (1984) 'A practical model for conducting action research in public school settings', *Contemporary Education*, 55, 2, pp. 113–17.

RUDDICK, J. (1989) 'Critical thinking and practitioner research: Have they a place in initial teacher training?' Paper presented to the American Educational Research Association, San Francisco.

RUDDICK, S. (1980) 'Material thinking', *Feminist Studies*, 6, 2, pp. 342–67.

RUSSELL, M. (1983) 'Black eyed blues connections: From the inside out', in BUNCH, C. and POLLACK, S. (Eds) *Learning Our Way: Essays in Feminist Education*. New York, The Crossing Press.

SALGANIK, L. (1985) 'Why testing reforms are so popular and how they are changing education', *Phi Delta Kappan*, 66, 9, pp. 607–10.

SCHOLES, R. (1982) *Semiotics and Interpretation*, New Haven, Yale University Press.

SCHON, D. (1987) *Educating the Reflective Practitioner*, San Francisco, Jossey-Bass.

SELDEN, S. (1984) 'Objectivity and ideology in educational research', *Phi Delta Kappan*, 66, 4, pp. 281–3.

SEMMES, C. (1981) 'Foundations of an Afrocentric social science', *Journal of Black Studies*, 12, 1, pp. 3–17.

SHERMAN, R. (1985) 'The trial and error of merit pay', Paper presented to the Southeast Philosophy of Education Society, Tuscaloosa, Alabama.

SHERMAN, R., WEBB, R. and ANDREWS, S. (1984) 'Qualitative Inquiry: An introduction', *Journal of Thought*, 19, pp. 22–33.

SHOR, I. (1987) *Critical Teaching and Everyday Life*, Chicago, University of Chicago Press.

SHOR, I. and FREIRE, P. (1987) *A Pedagogy for Liberation*, South Hadley, Massachusetts, Bergin and Garvey.

SHWEDER, R. and FISKE, D. (1986) 'Introduction: Uneasy social science', in FISKE, D. and SHWEDER, R. *Metatheory in Social Science: Pluralisms and Subjectivities*, Chicago, University of Chicago Press.

SITTON, T. (1981) 'Black history from the community: The strategies of fieldwork', *Journal of Negro Education*, 50, 2, pp. 171–81.

SLAUGHTER, R. (1989) 'Cultural reconstruction in the postmodern world', *Journal of Curriculum Studies*, 3, pp. 255–70.

SLEETER, C. and GRANT, C. (1988) *Making Choices for Multicultural Education*, Columbus, Merrill Publishing Company.

SMART, B. (1976) *Sociology, Phenomenology, and Marxian Analysis*, London, Routledge and Kegan Paul.

SMITH, D. (1974) 'Women's perspective as a radical critique of sociology', *Sociological Inquiry*, **44**, 1, pp. 7–13.

SMITH, J. (1983) 'Quantitative versus qualitative research: An attempt to clarify the issue', *Educational Researcher*, **12**, pp. 6–13.

SOLTIS, J. (1984) 'On the nature of educational research', *Educational Researcher*, **13**, pp. 5–10.

STANLEY, L. and WISE, S. (1982) ' "Back to the personal" or: Our attempt to construct "feminist research" ', in BOWLES, G. and KLEIN, R. (Eds) *Theories of Women's Studies*, Boston, Routledge and Kegan Paul.

STERNBERG, R. (1985) *Beyond I.Q.*, New York, Cambridge University Press.

STEWART, D. and MICKUNAS, A. (1974) *Exploring Phenomenology*, Chicago, American Library Association.

STRICKLAND, D. (1988) 'The teacher as researcher: Toward the extended professional', *Language Arts*, **65**, 8, pp. 754–64.

TOLSTOY, L. (1981) *Anna Karenina*, in BLY, C. *Letters from the Country*, New York, Penguin Books.

TORNEY-PURTA, J. (1985) 'Linking faculties of education with classroom teachers through collaborative research', *The Journal of Educational Thought*, **19**, 1, pp. 71–7.

TRIPP, D. (1988) 'Teacher journals in collaborative classroom research', Paper presented at the American Educational Research Association, New Orleans.

TUTHILL, D. and ASHTON, P. (1983) 'Improving educational research through the development of educational paradigms', *Educational Researcher*, **12**, pp. 6–14.

VAN DEN BERG, O. and NICHOLSON, S. (1989) 'Teacher transformation in the South African context: An action research approach', Paper presented to the International Conference on School Based Innovations: Looking Forward to the 1990s, Hong Kong.

VAN HESTERAN, F. (1986) 'Counselling research in a different key: The promise of human science perspective', *Canadian Journal of Counselling*, **20**, 4, pp. 200–34.

VAN MANEN, M. (1978) 'Objective inquiry into structures of subjectivity, *Journal of Curriculum Theorizing*, **1**, pp. 44–64.

VOLOSHINOV, V. (1973) *Marxism and the Philosophy of Language* New York, Seminar Press.

VON GLASERSFELD, E. (forthcoming) 'An exposition of constructivism: Why some like it radical', in DAVIS, R., MAHER, C. and NODDINGS, N. (Eds) *Constructivist Views on the Teaching and Learning of Mathematics*.

WALLACE, M. (1987) 'A historical review of action research: Some implications for the education of teachers in the managerial role', *Journal of Education for Teaching*, **13**, 2, pp. 97–115.

WAX, R. (1971) *Doing Fieldwork: Warnings and Advice*, Chicago, University of Chicago Press.

WELCH, S. (1985) *Communities of Resistance and Solidarity*, Maryknoll, New York, Orbis Books.

WELLS, D. (1987) *Empty Promises*, New York, Monthly Review Press.

WESTKOFF, M. (1982) 'Women's studies as a strategy for change: Between criticism and vision', in BOWLES, G. and KLEIN, R. (Eds) *Theories of Women's Studies*, Boston, Routledge and Kegan Paul.

WEXLER, P. (1987) *Social Analysis of Education: After the New Sociology*, London, Routledge and Kegan Paul.

WHITE, H. (1978) *Topics of Discourse*, Baltimore, John Hopkins University Press.

WHITSON, J. (1986) 'Interpreting "the freedom of speech"': Some first amendment education cases', in DEELY, J. (Ed.) *Semiotics: 1985*, New York, University Press of America.

WIGGINS, G. (1989) 'A true test: toward a more authentic and equitable assessment', *Phi Delta Kappan*, 70, 9, pp. 703–13.

WILLERS, J. (1987) 'Interpretive social inquiry as future educational history', Paper presented to the Southern History of Education Society, Knoxville, Tennessee.

WILLIS, G. (1978) 'Phenomenological methodologies in curriculum', *Journal of Curriculum Theorizing*, 1, pp. 65–79.

WILSON, S. (1977) 'The use of ethnographic techniques in educational research', *Review of Educational Research*, 47, 1, pp. 245–65.

WIRTH, A. (1983) *Productive Work — In Industry and Schools*, Lanham, Maryland, University Press of America.

WOOD, P. (1988) 'Action research: A field perspective', *Journal of Education for Teaching*, 14, 2, pp. 135–50.

YEAKEY, C. (1987) 'Critical thought and administrative theory: Conceptual approaches to the study of decision-making', *Planning and Changing*, 18, 1, pp. 23–32.

YOUNG, M. (1971) *Knowledge and Control: New Directions for the Sociology of Education*, London, Macmillan.

YOUNG, S. (1986) 'Guba as a vanguard of naturalistic inquiry: A harbinger of the future?' Paper presented to the Bergamo Conference on Curriculum Theory and Practice, Dayton, Ohio.

Author Index

Adorno, T. 51–52, 112, 114
Altrichter, H., 13, 54, 101–102, 117, 124–125
Anderson, G., 173, 179–180
Andrews, S., 144–145
Archimedes, 26
Aristotle, 145
Arlin, P., 44
Armstrong, M., 61–62, 107–108
Aronowitz, S., 6, 23, 24, 53, 58, 61, 64, 78–80, 194–195
Astman, J., 54, 56
Atkinson, P. 149
Ayer, A.J., 49–50

Baldwin, E., 71, 89
Barrow, R., 131–133
Belenky, M., 30, 41
Bellah, R.N., 169
Bennett, W., 65
Ben-Peretz, M., 83
Benson, S., 189
Besag, F., 56, 122, 140, 179
Biklen, S., 56, 108–110, 146–147, 166, 175
Bogdan, R., 56, 108–110, 146–147, 166, 175
Bourricaud, F., 65
Bracy, G. 86
Brier, S., 189
Briggs, J., 153
Brighan, C., 166–168
Brittan, A., 193–194
Bush, G., 65, 152, 156

Callahan, R., 92, 94–95
Candeloro, D., 192

Carby, H., 195–196
Carnegie, D., 38
Carr, W., 18, 19–20, 21–22, 23
Carter, J., 77–78
Chamberlin, G., 153–154
Chambliss, J., 88
Chattin-McNichols, J., 14, 15
Chauncey, H., 167–168
Cherryholmes, C., 116–117, 118, 164–165
Chomsky, N., 175–179
Church, R., 91
Clinchy, B., 30–41
Comte, A., 48–49, 62
Connell, R., 39
Connelly, F., 83
Corey, S., 19
Culbertson, J., 57

Darwin, C., 111–112
David, J., 97, 101
Davis, J., 96–97
de Lauretis, T., 194
Derrida, J., 116–117
Descartes, R., 27, 28, 30, 32, 38, 41–42, 43–45, 46
Dewey, J., 3–4, 7, 16, 20–21, 33, 79–81, 120, 182, 188–189, 192–193
Dobson, J., 62–63
Dobson, R., 62–63
Doll, W., 119
Donmoyer, R., 88, 117–118, 121–122, 127, 130, 137–138, 141–142, 145–146, 147–148
Doyle, W., 57–58, 59, 101
Duckworth, E., 16
Duke, D., 96–97, 103, 105

Eaker, D., 62–63
Ebbutt, D., 104
Einstein, A., 35–36, 46, 118, 122
Eisner, E., 59, 64, 71, 86, 113–115, 116, 127–129, 134–135, 147
Elliot, J., 13, 14, 17, 19, 61, 81, 82, 96, 103, 140, 174
Emery, F., 5

Fay, B., 90
Fee, E., 30, 31, 38, 40
Fetterman, D., 148–149
Finn, C., 78–79, 81
Fiske, D., 49–50, 68, 71–72, 115–117, 131
Flavell, J., 141
Foucault, M., 15, 164, 173, 185
Fowler, G., 148
Frankel, B., 50, 71, 115, 116, 133
Freire, P., 12, 21, 22–23, 33–34, 105–106, 186, 188–189
Freud, S., 6
Frisch, M., 182–184

Gadamer, H., 174, 196
Gardner, H., 141
Garman, N., 92–93
Garrison, J., 88, 127
Giarelli, J., 88
Gibson, R., 1, 150
Giroux, H., 23, 24, 33–35, 49, 51–53, 55, 65, 78–80, 112, 127–129, 148, 169–171, 173, 182–183, 185, 187, 194–195, 197
Goldberger, N., 30, 41
Goodlad, J., 54, 173
Gordon, E., 26, 45, 116, 178
Gorhan, W., 73–74
Gouldner, A., 28, 173
Grady, H., 60, 106
Gramsci, A., 42–43, 188
Green, J., 188, 190
Greene, M., 89–90, 154
Grosse, R., 74–74
Grumet, M., 37, 41, 82–83
Guba, E., 30, 35, 54, 60, 61–62, 63, 81, 118, 120–121, 135, 138–142, 153, 197

Habermas, J., 2, 60, 68–71, 72–73, 76, 78, 88, 106, 112, 171
Hall, G.S., 94
Ham, M., 125
Hammersley, M., 149
Haney, W., 98

Harding, S., 157–158
Harris, M., 11, 94
Harrison, B., 182–183, 185–186
Hayden, R., 192–193
Hazi, H., 92–93
Head, J., 114, 169
Hegel, G., 80, 94
Heisenberg, W., 60, 122
Held, D., 7, 20, 48, 70, 71
Herbart, J.F., 94
Herman, E., 175–179
Hodge, R., 149–150, 151
Holland, R., 142, 171
Horkheimer, M., 20, 51–52, 112
House, E., 8, 73, 74–75, 76, 77
Howe, K.R., 71, 129–130, 143–160, 163, 166–168
Hunter, M., 92–93
Husserl, E., 147, 153–154

Jacoby, R., 181–182
Jaggar, A., 40
James, M., 88, 104
James, W., 87
Jayarante, T., 58, 63–64
Jaynes, J., 111, 112–113, 114
Johnson, L., 73

Kaye, H., 189–191
Keat, R., 50–51, 69
Kegan, R., 46
Kemmis, S., 18, 19–20, 21–22, 23
Kennedy, R., 73
Kerlinger, F., 50, 127, 130–31
Kickbusch, K., 95–96
Kierkegaard, S., 41–42
Kincheloe, J., 112, 133–134, 140, 155–157
Kitchner, K., 124–125
Klein, R.D., 33
Knoller, C., 18
Koetting, R., 62–63
Koller, A., 64
Kovel, J., 156–157
Kramer, D., 44–45
Kress, G., 149–150, 151
Kroath, F., 87, 108–110
Kuhn, T., 168

Lasch, C., 2
Lather, P., 3, 19, 179
Lavine, T., 27
Lerner, G., 189–190
Lewin, K., 18–19

Lincoln, Y., 30, 35, 54, 60, 63, 81, 118, 120–21, 135, 138–142, 153, 197
Loeffler, M., 14, 15
Longstreet, W., 61, 81, 100, 108–110
Lowe, D., 26, 27, 28–29
Lucas, C., 181
Lyddon, W., 27, 28, 40–41, 61–62
Lynd, S., 11

MacDonald, J., 69
Macmillan, C., 88, 127
Madaus, G., 98, 101–102
Maeroff, G., 15
Mahoney, M., 27, 28, 40–41
Mansell, T., 143, 171
Marcuse, H., 5, 6, 51–52, 88, 112
Marx, K., 45, 84, 151, 156
Maynard, M., 193–194
McCarthy, J., 177
McCutcheon, G., 14, 16
McKernan, J., 14, 19, 83
McLaren, P., 35, 37, 43, 159–161, 171–174, 178–180
McMahon, M., 65
McNay, M., 54, 97, 100–101
McNeil, L., 97, 98–99
Merleau-Ponty, M., 155
Metz, J., 183–186
Mickunas, A., 147
Mies, M., 30, 32–33, 39–40, 59
Mill, J., 85
Miller, F., 26, 45, 116, 178
Munday, L., 96–97
Mussolini, B., 42
Myers, L., 42

Newton, I., 27, 44–45, 121–122, 129
Nicholson, J., 139
Nicholson, S., 59, 62–63, 65–66
Nixon, J., 120
Noblit, G., 15, 35–36, 62–63, 120–121
Nyang, S., 42

O'Connor, F., 31
Odi, A., 60
Oja, S., 125
Oldroyd, D., 12, 14, 15, 100, 106–108, 108–110
Orteza Y Miranda, E., 83, 100–101, 134, 138, 164
Orwell, G., 139
Owen, D., 166–168
Oxtoby, M., 114

Peat, F., 153
Phillips, D., 49, 52, 127–128
Piaget, J., 17, 40–41, 44, 46, 117, 136–137
Pinar, W., 82–83, 133–134, 140, 154–157, 158, 161
Plato, 4
Polanyi, M., 41, 77
Ponzio, R., 46, 83–84, 101
Popkewitz, T., 1, 3, 71, 89, 113–114, 127, 143, 162–163, 168–169
Porter, A., 13, 62–63, 99
Posch, P., 13, 54, 101–102, 117, 124–125
Poster, M., 43
Prigogine, I., 118–120

Reagan, R., 65, 152, 156
Reinharz, S., 26, 28, 30–31, 32, 40, 41–42, 55, 58–59, 63–64, 104–105, 118, 120–121, 135, 141, 146, 165, 173–174
Richards, C., 96
Rivlin, A., 73–81, 164
Rockwell, N., 119
Rogers, V., 158–159
Rollock, D., 26, 45, 116, 178
Romanish, B., 125–126
Rosenholtz, S., 99–100
Rosenzweig, R., 189
Ross, D., 18
Ruddick, J., 15, 58, 83–84, 108
Russell, M.G., 188

Salganik, L., 99
Scholes, R., 52, 149–151
Schon, D., 15, 46, 60, 87, 100, 121, 125–126
Schultz, C., 77–78
Sedlak, M., 91
Selden, S., 165
Semmes, C., 185
Sherman, R., 90, 144–145
Shor, I., 21, 22–23
Schulman, L., 101
Shweder, R., 49–50, 71–72, 115, 131
Simon, R., 173
Sitton, T., 192
Slaughter, R., 45, 118, 119, 121, 124–125
Smart, B., 171
Smith, D., 30, 48, 113–115, 128, 147–148, 162

Soltis, J., 71, 130–131, 147–148, 162, 166, 171
Spaulding, F., 94
Springsteen, B., 152
Stengers, I., 118–119
Sternberg, R., 44
Stewart, D., 147
Strickland, D., 60
Sullivan, E., 12

Tarvle, J., 30, 41
Taylor, F., 3–4, 90–94, 97, 98
Thatcher, M., 65
Thorndike, E., 95
Thorsrud, E., 5
Tichener, E., 85
Tiller, T., 14, 15, 108–110
Tolstoy, L., 6–7
Torney-Purta, J., 17, 82, 104, 108–110
Tripp, D., 13, 15, 59, 65–66

Van den Berg, O., 59, 62–63
Vandi, A., 42
Van Hesteren, F., 18, 44–45, 65–66
van Manen, M., 72–73

Vico, G., 27–28
Voloshinov, V.N., 151

Wallace, M., 14
Watson, T., 196
Watson-Franke, R., 196
Wax, R., 158
Webb, R., 144–145
Welch, S., 37, 182–183, 184–187
Wells, D., 11, 60, 106
Westerman, F., 178
Westkott, M., 31, 35
Wexler, P., 173
White, H., 28
Whitson, J.A., 150–151
Wicker, T., 175
Wiggins, G., 87
Wigner, E.P., 116
Willers, J., 143
Willis, P., 102, 153–154
Wilson, S., 133–135, 148
Wirth, A., 7, 8, 9, 78, 90–91
Wood, P., 17, 104, 107–108

Yeakey, C., 35–36, 54, 63
Young, M., 36

Subject Index

Ability grouping, 122
Anticipation
  the imaginative construction
    of the possible, 121
  Replaces certainty and
    prediction, 121
Accomodation (Piaget), 40, 41
  Anticipatory accomodation as an
    alternative to positivist external
    validity, 136–138, 140–141, 146,
    155–156
  and novelty of settings, 140
  and particularity, 139, 155–156
Accountability, 73, 102, 110
  Focused on outputs, 77
Action research
  as act of teaching, 105–160, 179,
    187–190
  Capture by positivism, 83, 103
  Criteria of critical form, 19–25, 34–35,
    36, 46–47, 188
  and dialectic of distance, 146–147
  Discerning patterns in observations,
    104, 108–109
  Examples of historically-grounded
    action research, 191–192
  and the exposure of hidden
    assumptions, 122, 158, 171–172
  and the generation of new knowledge,
    125, 187–188
  as heuristic, 138
  and historiography, 181–182, 185, 186,
    188–192, 196–197
  History of, 18–19, 81
  Incompatibility with bad work, 23
  and instrumental rationality, 102–103

Interviews of students by teachers,
    104–105, 197
  and listening, 189
  Motivated by rejection of positivism,
    81
  and multiplicity of research methods,
    104, 109, 124–125
  as praxis, 20, 32–33, 146, 177, 178, 179,
    180
  as problem-solving, 117
  and the redefinition of educational
    research, 18, 46–47, 137, 172
  as self-reflection, 19, 23, 44–45
  Set of tentative guidelines for
    incorporating action research into
    teaching, 108–110
  Teachers as researchers of the
    construction of their own
    consciousness, 34–35, 121, 146
  Ungrounded by a system of meaning is
    just another fad, 108
  Use of journals, 107
  Used to meet national standardized
    curriculum targets, 14
  and variety of topics open to inquiry,
    104
  as vehicle for empowerment, 34, 37,
    100, 109–110
Aesthetics, 154
Anti-Cartesian tradition, 32, 38
  Affirmation of spatio-temporal
    location of knower in the world, 28
  Critique of alienation, 28
  Indigenous knowledge/ways of
    knowing, 42
Authoritarian personality, 114

Autobiography, 41
Assessment of Performance in Teaching
     (APT), 98

Basics education, 72–73
     Attempts to ensure teaching of, 102
     Denial of the future reference of
          knowledge, 80–81
     Dewey's rejection of, 79–80
     and testing, 85
Behaviorism
     Behavioral management, 63
     and positivism, 127
Bureaucracy, 10, 42
     and instrumental rationality, 86, 99
     and labor unions, 10
     and quality of production, 10
     Under attack by critical teachers as
          researchers, 24

Cartesian-Newtonian paradigm,
     Bifurcation of mind and matter/body,
          27, 40–41, 45
     Cartesian knowledge and everyday
          experience, 43
     and certainty, 40
     Conflict with indigenous ways of
          knowing, 42
     and critical constructivism, 121
     and formal thinking, 44–45
     and logic of domination, 38
     and patriarchy, 40
     and postformalism, 44–45
     and postmodernism, 43
     Reductionism, 27
Certainty, 40, 75, 111–126
     and alternative ways of knowing, 126
     and basics education, 72
     and common frames of reference,
          116–117, 119
     and the delimiting of what science
          wants to know, 115–116
     and the denial of particularity, 139
     and determinism, 118, 153
     and empirical data, 122
     and history, 111–112, 114
     and human incapability of final
          perceptions, 118
     Impossibility of, 114, 135–136
     and instrumental rationality, 86
     and logocentrism, 116
     and measurability, 112, 129–130
     Obscures more than it uncovers, 116

and positivism, 112–113, 121, 171
and post-formal thinking, 125
Quest for certainty focuses attention
     on the trivial, 112
Researchers as infallible measuring
     instruments, 115
Results of abandonment of quest for,
     115
Sacrificed by the recognition of
     descrepancies between surface
     appearances and inner reality, 125
Search for social laws, 115–116
and textual meaning, 116–117
Universal knowledge applicable in all
     situations, 118, 123
Chaos theory, 119
     Extraneous perturbations, 119
     and feedback loops, 152
Citizenship, 37, 86, 103, 108
Class, 26, 38, 39, 40, 61, 95, 96, 122,
     123–124, 125, 146, 159, 163, 173, 183,
     185, 194, 195, 198
Community, 9
     grounded upon an identification of
          domination, 184
     History links school and community,
          189
Compensatory education, 73
Consciousness
     Construction of consciousness not the
          result of simple cause-effect
          relationships, 194–195
     Extension of, 2, 46, 65, 104, 106, 125,
          155, 174
     and geneology, 173–174
     History and, 2, 31, 34–35, 111–112,
          119, 156, 181, 189, 196–197
     Interior experience of the individual,
          153–156, 197
     Phenomenological, 145, 147–149,
          153–156
     Semiological contribution to
          understanding of, 151–153, 164–165
Conservative theory of authority, 34
Constructivism
     and feminist theory, 41
     and generalizations, 136
     Grounded on anti-Cartesian tradition,
          27
     and postmodernism, 44
     Rejection of Cartesian dualism, 27
     and teaching, 117
Covariation of research findings, 68

Critical constructivism, 26–47
  and the advancement of fields of study,
    174
  and anti-determinism, 45
  Attempt to uncover consciousness
    construction, 35, 45, 121, 194
  Commitment to perspective of the
    oppressed, 39
  and dangerous memory, 183, 186
  Democratic social theory as foundation
    of, 26, 146
  Exposure of sources of educational
    advantage and disadvantage, 39, 195
  Exposure of pseudo-objectivity,
    37–38, 162, 165
  as highest level of research cognition,
    122–126
  and historiography, 193
  and ideological demystification, 121,
    148, 162, 174–177
  and the interpretation of knowledge,
    126
  Knower-known inseparability, 26–47
  and *Lebenswelt*, 156, 193
  Oppressive potential of, 186
  and origins of problems, 117, 123
  Passionate scholarship, 41
  and place, 134, 156
  and popular culture, 172–173, 194
  and post-formal thinking, 42, 46,
    124–125
  and postmodernism, 44, 121, 123,
    135–136, 152
  and "primitive" ways of knowing, 42
  and qualitative research, 148–149
  Research as world making, 121
  and the revelation of allegiances, 38,
    168
  School problems are not generic or
    innate but constructed by social
    forces, 46
  and uncertainty, 126, 135–136
  Use of human as instrument of
    research, 31, 125
  Use of voice of subjugated as basis of
    educational reform, 39, 185
  Values study of inter-institutional
    relationships and sites outside
    school, 172–173
Critical literacy, 33–34
Critical pedagogy, 38, 192
Critical theory
  as basis for emancipatory system of
    meaning, 35

and critical social science, 2, 3, 36
and critique of positivism, 52, 66,
  112
and instrumental rationality, 85
Intersubjectivity and the rejection of
  scientist methods of understanding
  human behavior, 106, 148
and principles for action, 3
and social research, 1, 61, 66
Cult of the Expert, 1–2, 30
  and centralization of educational
    decision-making, 75–77
  and democracy, 163
  and historical profession, 190
  and liberalism, 65
  Negation of, 20–21, 23, 78, 83, 106,
    188–190, 198
  Negates uncertainty and ambiguity of
    teaching situations, 126
  and people's history movement,
    188–190
  and positivism, 63
  Right-wing attack on, 65
  and systems analysis, 76–78
  Teachers as passive recipients of expert
    knowledge, 43, 76, 82, 140
Cultural Literacy, 78
Currere, 154–156, 157, 158–159, 161,
  193
Curriculum theory, 33, 36, 39, 89
  and bureaucracy, 99
  and instrumental rationality, 97, 99
  and values, 169

Deconstruction, 33, 54, 172, 187–188
Democratic social theory
  and community building, 20
  as ethical base on which social
    institutions are constructed, 4, 34,
    103
  and good work, 4–6, 7, 12
  and inclusive conception of authority,
    34, 121
  and positivism, 64
  and postmodernism, 44, 121
  and voice, 20
Department of Defense, 73
Department of Education, 176
Department of Health, Education, and
  Welfare, 73, 75
Deskilling of Teachers
  and bad work, 12–13, 15
  and educational reform, 13
  In the name of professionalism, 62

overcoming by use of critical
constructivist research, 125, 148
and phenomenology, 148
and pre-packaged materials, 12
and scientific management, 91
Discursive practices
and disconfirmation of student culture,
37
and power, 36

Educational administration, 94
Education of administrators, 94–95
Educational purpose
and critical research, 82–83, 85
Failure of educational research to
focus on, 90, 96
and measurability, 74
and outcome research, 96
and positivism, 62
and postmodernism, 120
and power of business, 94
Educational Testing Service (ETS),
166–168
Efficiency and Education, 8, 9, 28, 65, 72,
75, 90, 94, 98, 167
Emancipation
and action, 35, 109–110, 179
and dangerous memory, 184
Forces which thwart, 83, 102
and the insufficiency of the control of
the means of production, 156–157
and knowledge, 70
learning to teach oneself, 25
and measurability, 65
and qualitative research, 146
and self-critical geneology, 173
and system of meaning, 33–34, 37, 103
Via ideological disembedding, 46
Empowerment of teachers
and critical constructivism, 46–47
and critical system of meaning, 34
and subjugated perspectives, 39
Role of critical research in, 20–21, 66,
107–108
Role of theory in, 15
The Enlightenment, 48, 111
Esperanto of inquiry, 115
Ethnography, 144, 145, 148, 149, 152,
153, 158, 159, 160, 161, 164, 173, 185
informant narratives, 179
Eugenics, 165–166
Euro-centrism, 36
Evaluation, 39
and cost-benefit analysis, 73

Determines goals of education, 74–75
Devoid of questions of justice or
humanity, 90
and Great Society education programs,
73–76
and National Commission on
Excellence, 89
Outside of larger context, 97
Self-evaluation by teachers, 62, 82, 100
and systems analysis, 73–74
Traditional methods undermined by
teachers as researchers, 82
Used to control teachers and teaching,
97–100
Ways our textual meaning shape
evaluation, 117–118
Excellence movement, 36, 103

Feminist theory, 30–33, 42
the body, 41
and critical constructivist research, 193
as a critical theory, 35, 157
and the dismystification of
androcentric bias in research,
157–158
and the devaluation of emotion, 31,
40–42
and the effort to expose ideological
malformations, 84
Grounded on the assumption of
historical location of knower, 30, 58,
84
and identification with organic life and
its preservation, 40
and indigenous ways of knowing, 42
Inseparability of knowledge and
judgment, 31
Kierkegaard and, 42
Logocentrism, 40–41
Making the private public, 32
and phenomenology, 157
and positivism, 58
and the purpose of research, 32
Reconnection of knower and known,
30, 41–42, 120
and self-knowledge, 157
as subjugated knowledge, 40, 42
Truth as a process of construction, 41
Five Easy Pieces, 139
Florida Master Teacher Plan, 90
Formal thinking, 35
and the Cartesian-Newtonian
paradigm, 44–45
Definition of, 44

Focus on problem-solving, 46, 117
Insufficient for critical teacher research, 117
and standardized tests, 44
Foundations of Behavioral Research (Kerlinger), 50
Foxfire, 106, 192
Frankfurt School, 35, 60
Fundamentalism, 68, 112
    Compared to positivism, 128

Gender, 26, 38, 40, 61, 68, 96, 104, 124, 125, 151, 159, 173, 183, 191, 194, 195, 198
Generalization, 13, 30, 56, 77
    and critical constructivism, 121–122, 135–137
    and delegitimization of the experience of teachers, 82
    Dialectic of particularity and generalization, 141, 155–156
    and ethical precepts, 121–122
    external validity, 135–136
    and human way of learning from experience, 140
    Positivist truth involves ability to generalize a proposition, 60, 135, 136–139
    Relationship to the teaching act, 81, 101
    and totality, 156
    and verifiability, 128, 132–133, 134–139
Giftedness, 178
Great Society education programs, 73–78

Harvard Business Review, 9
Hermeneutics, 185
    Critical hermeneutics as interpretation of life history, 196–197
Historiography, 149, 152, 158, 159, 173, 181–198
    Critical constructivist conception of, 181, 183, 193
    and emancipatory system of meaning, 182–183
    as foundation for other qualitative research strategies, 185
    People's history movement, 188–191
History, 181–198
    Burden of history, 198
    and the certification of knowledge, 61

and connections between the past and the present, 182, 192, 197
and consciousness of self-production, 2–3, 32–33, 34, 35, 42, 119, 156, 173, 182, 185–186, 189–190, 194, 197
and contextualization of teacher education, 18
esoteric concerns of, 190
and feminist theory, 30, 41, 193
and the genesis of educational institutions, 3, 182
and geneology, 173, 185–187
and ideological inheritance, 165
and insurrection, 185
and life history, 180, 181–182, 187, 188, 191, 196–197
and memory, 24, 34, 37, 181–184, 188, 189, 190
Oral, 179, 190–192
Planned obsolescence of education ideas, 181
Professionalization of historical craft, 190, 191
as a search for new forms of authority, 111–112
and social amnesia, 181–182, 190
and subjugated knowledges, 183, 185, 187
System analysts' denial of historial context of knowledge, 74
and truth, 37
and the tyranny of the present, 189
and universality, 183
Human agency
    and the assignment of meaning to data, 143
    and the creation of the social world, 63
    and cult of the expert, 21
    Enables cultural reconstruction, 125
    Forces which preclude, 1–2, 32–33, 95–96
    and industrialization, 2
    and qualitative research, 146
Humility of researcher, 58
    and postmodernism, 58, 121

Ideology, 34, 38, 162–180
    and action research, 83–84
    and choice of problems for teachers to explore, 83, 117
    and the determination of the professional lives of teachers, 121

and the generation of facts, 61, 178
Ideological innocence supports the
    status quo, 95, 116–117, 171–172,
    183
and instrumental rationality, 86, 95
and logocentric designs, 116, 117
and manufactured consent, 175–177,
    178
and power relations, 148
and positivism, 52, 60–61, 95, 171
and reproduction of power, 142, 198
and the shaping of inquiry, 36, 83
and structure of classrooms, 83
and the transcendence of surface
    appearances, 158, 171
Unknown to the researcher himself/
    herself, 60, 95, 136, 151, 155, 164
The Individual
and dominant notions of individualism,
    24
as puppet of wider forces, 1
and the production of knowledge, 2
Industrialization, 2
and bad work, 6–11
and the demand for submission to
    authority, 23
and instrumental rationality, 6, 90–93,
    99–100
and separation of workers from one
    another, 5
Social impact, 90
and worker control, 3, 80–93, 99–100
and worker productivity, 36
Instability of objects of educational
    research, 56
Instrumental rationality, 6–7, 85–110
and administrative surveillance
    procedures, 108
Critique of, 87
Defined, 85
Deification of "technique," 6–7,
    85–87
and erosion of teacher autonomy, 60,
    86, 96–99
and learning in isolation, 85–86
Logocentrism, 87
and measurability, 86–87
and outcome measurement, 96–99
and purpose of research, 85, 96, 139
and purposes of education, 90, 95
and the reward of conventionality, 96
and research outside of context, 97
Teacher resistance to, 97–100

and values, 86, 90, 195
and teacher voice, 99–100
and the well-formed problem, 87
Integration (Piaget), 40–41
Intelligence
and certainty, 120, 123
and class, 124
and critical constructivism, 140–141,
    146, 178, 179
Defined by dominant culture, 39, 123
and dominant conceptions of science,
    72, 96, 166–168
and operational definitions, 127
and positivism, 61, 64, 127
Testing for, 68, 86, 166
Theory of multiple intelligences
    (Gardner), 141

The Knower, 26–47
as a part of a socio-historical world, 26,
    28
as a participant in all acts of
    understanding, 26
Role in Cartesian-Newtonian
    paradigm, 27–28
Knowledge, 67–84
Action research and teachers as
    generators of new, 125, 180
Based on connections, 80, 171
and Cartesian-Newtonian paradigm,
    27–28, 30, 43
Certified, 1, 82, 126
Critical theory of knowing, 21, 36,
    172, 174
and the democratization of the research
    act, 2, 20–21, 108–110
Epistemological crisis, 67, 70, 114–115
as external body of information, 53, 79,
    85
Historical context, 61, 74, 78
and judgment, 31, 122
Knowledge-constitutive interests,
    68–71
Knowledge Industry, 2
Must always be interpreted, 122
Need for constant redefinition, 78, 110
Personal knowledge, 41, 45, 79,
    159–160
and positivism, 52–55, 79, 83–84, 110,
    120, 125, 128, 170–171
and power, 1, 15, 172, 182
Practical knowledge of teachers, 15, 59,
    174

as preparation for tests, 96
Relationship/connection to other
    information, 80
and role of student, 23–24, 65, 88, 187
Sacred role of science, 64
Science as "fact" provider, 7, 78
Social construction of, 67–68, 117,
    170–171
Student knowledge vis-a-vis classroom
    knowledge, 43, 159–160
and systems analysis, 73–81
and Taylorism, 97
Verified knowledge as basis for the
    school curriculum, 113
Zeitgeist and, 68

Lebenswelt, 120, 154–157, 160, 173, 174,
    193
Liberalism, 39
and the absence of criticism of
    positivism, 65–66
and the attempt to free people outside
    their own histories and cultures,
    187
and blindness to subtle forces of
    dominations, 65, 187
Liberation theology, 33
and the development of an
    emancipatory system of meaning, 37,
    43
Roots of, 37
Life history, 32–33, 180–182, 187, 188,
    191, 196–197
Life in Schools (McLaren), 171
Logic of capital, 38

Manufacturing metaphor, 75, 79, 93–94,
    152
Marxism
Denigration of importance of the
    subject (the knower), 84
and determinism, 45, 84
and the particularistic, 156
and representation, 151
Mind as a research tool, 29, 31, 113

National Commission on Excellence in
    Education, 89
Native Americans, 131, 159, 194, 195
Neo-Taylorism, 14
Hunter supervision as example of,
    192–193
Neutrality, Objectivity, 162–180
and androcentrism, 30

and certainty, 113, 115, 171
Dominant definitions of, 23
Example of the way values shape
    inquiry, 163
Fallacy of objectivism, 170
and history, 181
and instrumental rationality, 99
and *Lebenswelt*, 174
as method of social control, 62, 93, 169
Myth of Archimedes, 26–27
Myth of political neutrality of school,
    95
and positivism, 52–66, 99, 110, 113,
    149, 169–170
Politicization of research, 37–38, 166
and reification, 38, 95, 168, 181
Shields managers/administrators from
    interrogation, 93
and the silencing of divergent voices,
    36, 93
Teachers as researchers always have an
    agenda, 101–102, 110
and value dimension of research, 162,
    168–169, 174
Noise of research, 54–55, 104, 115

*Origin of Consciousness in the
    Breakdown of the Bicameral Mind*
    (Jaynes), 111

Patriotism, 152
Particularity, 13, 30, 56
as a basic aspect of teacher knowledge,
    59, 153
Different meaning for teacher
    researcher than empirical researcher,
    81
Importance denied when entities are
    treated as a sample or a type,
    139–140
and the nature of understanding, 79–80
and reconceptualization of
    generalization, 137–138, 141
and totality, 136
Unencountered problems, 79
The Pentagon, 75
Phenomenology, 41, 185
and bracketing, 153–155
and consciousness, 145, 147–149, 152,
    196
as epistemological alternative to
    positivism, 148–149, 164
and historical research, 193, 196
and perception, 145, 146–149, 152, 159

and qualitative ways of appraising, 147,
153, 158, 173
and significance, 148
Philosophy of science, 26–47
and crisis in social inquiry, 114–115
Place, 134
and anticipatory accomodation, 155
and critical constructivism's attempt to
reconceptualize the notion of
generalization, 155–156
and notion of particularity, 140,
155–156
and the rejection of positivist
reductionism, 140
and totality, 156
Positive thinking, 38
Positivism, 48–66,
and accountability, 73
Alleged death of positivism, 49–50
and the attempt to improve teaching,
101
Avoidance of ambiguity of educational
situations, 58–59, 61, 83, 101,
108–110, 115
and basics education, 72–79
and Cartesian-Newtonian foundations,
28, 48
and common, universal language of
research, 115
Culture of positivism, 52–54, 55, 101,
102, 112, 120, 169–170, 171
Decontextualization, 61, 80–81, 84, 86,
101, 134
and educational voyeurism, 63, 64
Examples of positivistic research, 55,
57–58
Generalizations as *raison d'etre* of
research, 138
Historical development of, 48–50, 69
and ideology, 52, 60–61, 85
Inseparability of research methods of
physical and social sciences, 48,
56–57, 73, 78, 112
and linearity, 118–119, 152, 174
Main themes, 50, 85
Misrepresentation of, 127–128
Neo-positivism, 50, 51
and obsession with measurement, 85,
143
and power, 107
and prediction, 57, 58, 62, 76, 100, 119,
121, 139, 153, 174, 195
and questionaires, 58–59
as religion, 112

Rejection of traditional role of theory,
52
Silencing of natural language, 64
Society as a body of neutral facts, 48,
58–62, 119, 169
Suppression of political discussion,
53–54
and teacher as technician, 60, 81,
85–86
Unobservable variables, 60, 87,
134–135
and the Vienna Circle, 49, 127
Post-formal thinking, 42, 44
and the ability to ask questions never
before asked, 46, 117
and dialogue with self, 46
and the escape from modernity, 44–45
and loss of certainty, 125
and multiple realities, 125
and nature of genius, 46
and non-linearity, 45
and the perception of the educational
world, 44, 124–125
and postmodernity, 45–46, 125
and problem posing, 46, 117, 124–125
and purpose, 124
Rejection of privileged vantage points,
45, 125
and self-knowledge, 45–46
thinking about one's own thinking,
45–46
Postmodernism
and exposure of traditional science's
construction of an imaginary world,
43–44
and feminism, 43, 120, 158
Heterarchic vs. hierarchic conceptions
of order, 153
Little is as it appears to be, 158
and multiple frames of reference, 120,
135–136, 152–153
postmodern science of becoming, 121
and the reconceptualization of
educational research, 119, 152–153,
158
and the rejection of cause-effect
relationships, 135–136, 152–153
and researcher humility, 58
and uncertainty, 43–44, 116, 120, 153
and the world as a web-like
configuration of interacting forces,
119–120, 152, 165, 172
Praxis, 20, 146, 177, 178, 179, 180
and history, 189

Process-product research, 57
Psychoanalysis, 154

Qualitative research, 143–161
  Artistic framing of, 135
  Basic characteristics of, 144
  Challenge of knowledge base, 60
  and critical constructivism, 146,
    148–149, 152, 156, 160
  and culture, 149, 150
  Data cannot escape meaning placed on
    them by human agents, 143, 148
  Distinguished from quantitative
    research, 143–146
  Diversity of research methods,
    145–161
  Failure to transcend positivist criteria,
    135
  and judgments, 145–147
  and positivism, 143, 160
  Problems positivists find with, 129
  and relativism, 128
  and representation, 151–152
  as a response to positivistic context-
    stripping, 101, 144–145
  and significance, 145, 147, 148
  and the sophistication of professional
    practice, 181
  Usefulness of data that is not absolute,
    121
  and verifiability, 129–130, 135,
    145–147
Quality of Working Life (QWL)
  programs, 11
  and power over employees, 11
  and similarity to educational
    management/administration, 14
Questions and research, 31, 39
  and action, 106
  Assumptions which shape, 37, 100, 117
  Critical constructivist
    reconceptualization of, 35–36, 121,
    124, 125, 138, 146, 172
  and mass discourse as a pedagogical
    agent, 173
  and power, 164
  Question formulation, 46, 109, 122,
    125, 138, 146, 172, 185
  Questions determine what we see, 60,
    100
  Questions within research framework
    vis-a-vis questions about research
    framework, 174

and significance of dats, 124
and subjugated knowledges, 103, 185

Race, 26, 38, 39, 40, 61, 68, 96, 124, 131,
  159, 166, 173, 179, 183, 185, 192–194,
  198
Rationalism, 27, 35, 43
Realism, 27
  as foundation for basics education, 72
Reductionism, 27, 62
  and attempts to explain student
    performance, 101
  and cause-effect relationships, 81, 194
  and measurability, 65
  and verifiability
Reform of education
  Based on elite research, 13, 64, 74, 89
  and centralization of educational
    control, 13, 14
  and deskilling, 13
  and power, 36
  and requirement of the teaching of
    low-level thinking skills, 98
  Results in disenfranchisement and
    alienation of teachers, 13
  and systems analysis, 74–75
  Top-down variety of, 63–64, 102
Reggae, 195–196
Relativism, 78, 128
Replication, 72
  Critical reconceptualization of, 81
  In laboratory settings, 62
  and systems analysis, 76
Representation
  Multi-accentual nature of, 151–152
  and power to control, 151, 160,
    164–165
  and semiotics, 151–152, 160
Research on humans,
  Ambiguity, 81, 83, 101, 108–110, 115
  Special complexity of humans as
    objects of research, 71, 81
Research on teaching and education
  Disregard of the atypical, 30
  as form of social engineering, 71, 113
  and generalization, 13, 30, 56, 60, 81,
    135–137, 138, 139–141, 155–156
  and improvement of student
    performance/test scores, 87, 104
  Involves moral considerations at almost
    every level, 57, 173
  and justification of over-management
    of teachers, 14, 74, 88, 89

as logic in use, 130
Methodological pluralism, 114, 128
Methodological unitarianism, 71,
100–101
as outcome measurement, 96–99
Outside of natural setting, 61–62, 101
Pre-defined problems, 125
Presupposes an epistemological stance,
67
as production of a body of causal laws,
89, 113, 116
and separation of fact from value, 14,
31, 38, 42, 52–53, 62, 86, 130, 144,
162–174
So-called "research base" and its
tendency to invalidate teacher
knowledge, 13–14, 17–18, 31,
59–60, 74, 81, 99–100, 113
as research undertaken for other
researchers, 12
Researcher as client of school
administrators, 63, 139
Use of data collected to control
teachers, 13, 36, 62, 74, 89, 139
and the view of teacher as aborigine,
12–13
Ways human and educational research
differ from physical science inquiry,
57, 72, 75–76
Research as problem solving
Problems do not unambiguously
present themselves, 117
Right-wing movements
Nature of success based on cooption
of anti-authority rhetoric of
counterculture, 65
Rigor of research, 72, 76, 87, 113
and critical constructivism, 173
as means of avoiding mistakes, 129
and significance, 131
Rote memorization, 53

Schooling and the Struggle for Public Life
(Giroux), 33
*Schooling as a Ritual Performance:
Toward a Political Economy of
Educational Symbols and Gestures*
(McLaren), 159–160
Science as a cultural artifact, 72
Scientific Management, 14
Applied to education, 91–93
and the denigration of workers, 3,
90–93

as form of social control, 2
and instrumental rationality, 91
and positivism, 63
Taylorism, 90–93
Time-and-motion studies, 90
Self-production
Awareness of self-production as basis
of research act, 29
and history, 2–3, 32–33, 34, 35, 42,
119, 156, 182, 186–190, 194,
196–197
and popular culture, 173
Rewriting oneself in relation to shifting
ideological contexts, 194
Self-definitions change as historical
conditions evolve, 194
Semiotics, 33, 149–153, 156, 158–159,
164, 173, 180, 193
Social Darwinism
and bad work, 7
Social justice, 35, 62, 103, 124, 164
Students as researchers, 106
Subjugated knowledge,
Afro-centric ways of knowing, 42
and the disruption of dominant
conceptions of history, 183
Dominant schooling's repression of,
37, 118
Double consciousness, 39–40
Education defined as the eradication of,
103
and emancipation, 184
Failure of liberalism to recognize value
of, 39
and incompatibility with quest for
certainty, 118
and the insurrection of the dominated,
185
Native American ways of knowing, 42
and power dynamics, 185
and semiotics, 151
Street knowledge as form of, 43
and understanding of oppressed
people's distrust of researchers, 39,
178
Use in critical constructivist research,
38–39, 184–187
as a way of seeing the socio-
educational whole, 39
Women's ways of knowing as form of,
40
Suffering, 40, 183
Supervision of teachers, 92–93

System of meaning, 28–47
Absence in mainstream research, 36
and action research, 108, 121
and historiography, 182–183, 190–191
Inseparable from various ways of
knowing, 40, 42, 43, 84
and justice, 124
Nature of immature, 36
and Newtonian-like generalizations,
121
and phenomenology, 148
Philosophical foundations, 33–34, 42,
43
and post-formal thinking, 46
and postmodern humility, 44
and purpose of research, 141
and redefinition of validation, 142
and the selection of a set of
assumptions to base research, 37,
103, 104
and the separation of the significant
from the insignificant, 84
Systematic Thinking for Social Action
(Rivlin), 74
Systems analysis
and bad work, 8
and evaluation, 73–77

Tacit knowledge, 29
Taylorism, 90–93, 97, 98
Teacher education
Absence of reflection, 12, 15
and critical constructivism, 126
Designed to enhance supervision
efficiency, 12
Emphasis on technique, 12, 60
and positivism, 126
and postmodernity's multiple frames of
reference, 120
Results of absence of education on
research, 15, 18
as a study of the formation of
professional consciousness, 15, 120
and systems analysis, 76
Transformation of, 18
Teacher knowledge, 15, 59, 62, 77
of the complexity of classrooms, 138
Does not meet the demands of external
validity, 140
Incompatibility with abstract
generalizations of positivism, 81
Uncertain nature of, 126, 138
Undermined by expert-produced
theory, 82

Unexamined, 102
Value of, 102
Teachers
and control of the workplace, 12–13,
126
and critical constructivist research, 125
and discursive practices, 36–37, 101
as executors of their profession, 13, 83,
86, 92–93, 98
as information delivers, 84, 110
Low status of, 12–14, 36–37, 43, 64,
65, 75, 84
as members of a "Third World"
culture, 12
as passive consumers of top-down,
expert knowledge, 43, 64, 76, 82, 89
Perceived as incapable of conducting
research, 13, 83
Public perception of teacher
incompetence, 12, 102
Resistance to demeaning control
strategies, 98–99, 102–103, 106
Teachers as researchers
as active producers of knowledge and
meaning, 34, 59, 62, 71, 106, 121, 184
Critical conception of, 14, 21–23, 35,
66, 82, 84, 103,
105, 110
Do not fit with positivist
authoritarianism, 63, 100, 140, 173
Examples of: 21–23, 32–33, 107
and good work, 4, 25, 83
and meta-theoretical thinking, 18,
108–109
Need for awareness of assumptions of
positivistic research, 56, 65–66,
108–110
Negation of critical dimension, 83
and networks with other social groups,
24
as partners with those researched,
105–106, 180
as a political act, 22–25
in a postmodern context, 121
and rejection of traditional empirical
educational science, 81, 100, 173
as a response to failure of technocratic,
teacher-proof reform, 14, 22–23
Study of students, 22, 104–107, 159,
179, 182, 187–188,
195–197
Teachers as researchers of themselves,
34, 42, 45–46, 71, 82, 103, 146, 156,
168–169, 191

and translation of values into practice, 81–82, 108–110
and use of private experience, 32
and verifiability, 134–135, 140
Technicalization, 1
  of action research, 83
  and basics education, 72
  and deskilling, 12
  and educational reform, 14
  and objectivity, 37
  and positivism, 51, 62, 85
  and quality of workmanship, 10
  and theory, 82
  Teaching as "how-to", 60, 62, 82
  and values, 88, 146
Tennessee Master Teacher Plan, 100
Textbooks, 22–23
Theory
  Classical perspective on, 52
  and the connection of schooling to
    larger socio-economic realities,
    172
  as expression of human regularities,
    113
  Metatheory in social science,
    67–68
  and power of researchers, 82
  Reconceptualized notion of theorizing,
    82–83
  Teacher rejection of force-feeding of,
    82
  Theoretical pre-assumptions of
    researchers, 54, 61, 108–110,
    137
Theory of cognitive interests (Habermas),
  68–71
Title I, 74, 76
Totality, 156–157
  Extension of *currere*, 156
Tracking, 63
Transformative intellectual, 24
The Unobservable
  and elimination from educational
    research, 71, 151
  and positivism, 134

Verifiability, 127–142
  Alternate methods of, 128
  Analytic and arbitrary methods of, 132
  and certainty, 130
  and the concept of a mistake, 128–129
  in contextual isolation, 61, 134
  and contrived settings, 134
  and control of variables, 131–133
  crisis of, 135
  Critical reconceptualization of, 81, 133,
    135–138, 168–169
  and emancipatory system of meaning,
    141
  External validity, 135–136, 137, 138,
    140
  and fallibility, 129–131
  as historical struggle, 20
  Internal validity, 135–136, 137
  and measurability, 127, 158
  and operational definitions, 127
  and Piagetian schema theory, 140–141
  and positivism, 127–140, 141, 142
  and quality of inquiry, 135, 147
  Quantitative and qualitative
    perspectives on, 129–130, 135
  and reductionism, 133, 140
  and significance, 130–131, 133, 137
  and systems analysis, 75
  and transferability, 138
  and trustworthiness, 135–138, 174
Verification (see verifiability)
Verstehen, 147–148
Vietnam War, 175
Vocational education, 184, 189

Women
  Battered women, 33
  Exclusion from the curriculum, 36
  and history of suffering of, 183
  and illogical emotionalism, 195
  and liberal educational reform, 39
  Position in workplace, 10–11
  and rape, 193

Zeitgeist, 68